Sallie Morris has a diploma from the Edinburgh College of Domestic
Science. The author of several c
Oriental cookery, she worked on th
known women's magazines before
to Malaysia with her family. Wl
extensively throughout the region a
this book. She now lives in London.

By the same author

Cooking with Herbs and Spices
Oriental Cookery
Oriental Cooking
Salads & Vegetables
Winter Puddings

SALLIE MORRIS

South-East Asian Cookery

GRAFTON BOOKS
A Division of the Collins Publishing Group

LONDON GLASGOW
TORONTO SYDNEY AUCKLAND

Grafton Books
A Division of the Collins Publishing Group
8 Grafton Street, London W1X 3LA

A Grafton Paperback Original 1989

A CIP catalogue record for this book
is available from the British Library

ISBN 0-586-20423-7

Printed and bound in Great Britain by
Collins, Glasgow

Set in Janson

Contents

Acknowledgements

My oriental experience began in Kuala Lumpur over ten years ago. Being a compulsive cook I soon discovered that we were living in a gourmet's paradise where everyone, be they rich or poor, cares about what they eat.

Ah Moi Wong was my mentor, and I owe her and her lovely family an enormous debt. Anita Wong was another enthusiast who shared many hours with me in the kitchen and round the table.

In Bangkok, I would like to express my sincere thanks to Pornsri Luphaiboon at The Oriental and to Chalie Amatyukul, the Director of the Thai Cookery School, for his warm welcome and for his introduction to both Lemon Grass and Thanying restaurants.

Joanna Smith and Susie Thompson gave me some marvellous contacts in Burma. Each one invited us to their homes and not one dish was duplicated, so I left with a wealth of new recipes and many new friends. They were Mary and Richard San Lin, U Saw N Paw and his wife Rebecca, Monica Mya Maung and Professor U Than Nyun. I also had the good fortune to meet Mi Mi Khaing, the author of *The Burmese Family* and *Cook and Entertain the Burmese Way*, which was a great honour. We were courteously escorted by U Khin Myint over several days, and I thank him most warmly for making my trip to Burma such a memorable one. Fraser and Janet Wilson and Mrs Anna Allot were most generous to me. I also remember the five Burmese students here in London with whom I spent many happy, nostalgic hours. I thank them all.

To John and Janet Russell I owe an enormous debt for their unstinting generosity and hospitality in Jakarta and for the many kindnesses extended by their friends. It was my pleasure to meet Ibu Eri Sudewo, who not only gave much of her time to show me the markets of Jakarta but has also generously given me many recipes for this book.

Back home in England, Philip Tran has been a wealth of information on all aspects of Vietnam and has given me some recipes from his wide repertoire. Possim Moeng helped me on the Cambodian section and Michael Wong on the Malaysian section.

Finally there are a number of people without whom this book would not have happened. Beryl Castles typed most of it in her spare time, for which I would like to thank her most warmly. In the meantime Malcolm Welchman has been busy transforming my life. He persuaded me to change from writing longhand to using a word processor – a relatively painless process which I can still hardly believe. A thousand thanks for his patience and faith in one so untechnical. Anne de Gier Wintermans and I have cooked every single recipe in my kitchen. Each time we do a book together we enjoy the challenge and the widening of our knowledge on the cuisines of the Orient. Cooking is a pleasure to both of us and I value Anne's support and enthusiasm. Most of all I give my love and thanks to my husband Johnnie and my children Alexandra and James, for their wholehearted support over the past months as this book slowly took shape. So to my family and the friends and colleagues who came to partake of the food cooked for this book, thank you for sharing this with me.

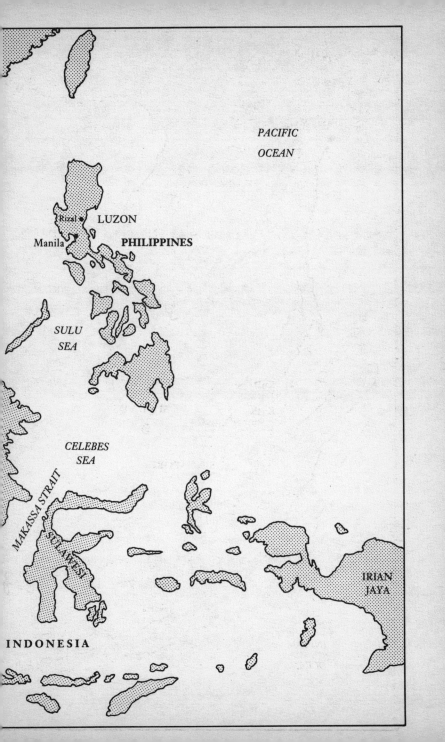

Food in South-East Asia

Food has been the most wonderful passport for me as a traveller. Through it I have met a wealth of fascinating people, many in chance encounters which have blossomed into lasting and valued friendships. When my family and I found ourselves bound for Malaysia little did I know what an impact this was to make on my future adventures in the kitchen.

If the kitchen is the heart of the home then surely the markets reflect the attitudes of people to their food. That being so, no one could ever doubt that the Orientals live to eat, not eat to live. To visit a market in any of the countries in South-East Asia is an unforgettable experience which sweeps you along with its bustle, activity, and the sheer enterprise of the ever-smiling people. Supermarkets and freezers have revolutionized our way of living; they have also made their mark in the cities of the East. Nevertheless, there are still vast numbers of housewives in these cities, and certainly in the towns and villages, who take pleasure in shopping daily, pitting their bargaining skills against the stall holders for top-quality produce. This excellence in quality is very noticeable, from glossy chillies to the rich green array of vegetables, jewel-coloured fruit and flowers, and mounds of wet spices which are scooped into a banana leaf parcel ready to take home to transform into an almost instant curry. Quality is the watchword. It would be a foolish man or woman who tried to sell anything of inferior quality to customers who return daily for their family needs.

Eating out is a way of life. For many people all over South-East Asia a cup of tea might suffice on waking, with breakfast taken later when it's cooler and some of the day's work has been done. This might be a bowl of rice porridge like *nasi lemak*, clear pork soup with noodles, chopped pork and a few green leaves, steamed buns from huge bamboo steaming baskets which are almost mahogany-col-oured from daily use, or the famous Burmese *mohinga*, a curried fish soup. These are eaten in completely unpretentious surroundings with groups of friends and colleagues while exchanging the news of the day. This same pattern is followed throughout the day in cities, towns and villages. The variety of snacks is amazing and impressive, from *dim sum* to *satay* to portions of carved fresh fruit or a bowl of simple rice with a *sambal*. At every stall, round the clock in many places, there will be a cluster of people enjoying not only the food but the gossip too. This is very noticeable in the country areas, where time never seems in short supply.

These market people and purveyors of food are, I think, the backbone of the countries of the East, and it is interesting to note that they represent the many migrant groups who have come to South-East Asian shores over the centuries. Food has no frontiers; the cuisine of each land is part of the country's culture and heritage and evolves further with each generation. No cooking style can claim to being pure. It merely reflects the ability of its cooks to adapt the best of their own with what they see as the best from another's cuisine, which might happen over decades or centuries. A Burmese friend says that food in his country has been much influenced by both India and China and has taken the best from each with the use of chillies and dried spices as well as a wealth of noodle-based dishes.

Indonesia, made up of thousands of islands, has been a focus for travellers since time immemorial. Indian and Arab merchants came to trade, and brought their religions as well as much-needed textiles, porcelains, medicines and precious stones in exchange for spices. The fortunes of the Spice Islands, as they were aptly named, boomed when the demand for spices in Europe became big business, bringing the Portuguese and Dutch as well as the Chinese, who are inveterate traders and entrepreneurs. The Indonesians love highly spiced food but from island to island there is a shift of emphasis in the food, from meat, chillies and turmeric in mainly Muslim Sumatra, to pork served in dozens of different ways in exotic Hindu Bali. Soy sauce was undoubtedly brought by the Chinese but the Indonesians, with their love of a hint of sweetness, added a rich, dark-brown sugar to the soy sauce which resulted in the renowned *kecap manis*, used throughout the islands. The many vegetable dishes cooked in the stir-fry style are another hallmark of Chinese cuisine.

As Indonesia became home to many over the centuries, so the Indonesians themselves spread into Cambodia, followed by tribes from Southern China who also moved south into Thailand and Vietnam. Like the Indonesians the Thais had a rich culture in the 13th and 14th centuries, and their elegant cuisine far outstripped comparable ones, not only in the excellence of the food but in the magnificent presentation which is still evident in Thailand today.

Although common ingredients are used throughout the countries of South-East Asia each country has its own way of preparing and serving them. *Satay* and curries are common throughout the region. In Malaysia *satay* is generally eaten with the famous spicy peanut sauce, cubes of cucumber, thin wedges of onion, and glutinous rice cooked in palm-leaf parcels which are cut into diamond shapes. The Indonesians are renowned for their *satay* and have lots of variations on the theme. A soy-based sauce is often used as the marinade (see page 174) and a spicy *kecap* sauce served as an accompaniment. In Thailand a spicy coconut cream is often used as a marinade and the charcoal-barbecued *satay* offered with a spicy peanut sauce plus a delightful cucumber salad with a sharp dressing, flecked with shredded chilli and a scattering of peanuts. In Vietnam the tiny strips of barbecued meat are served differently; they are enclosed in one of the dampened rice wrappers along with crisp lettuce leaves, cucumber, spring onion, a dash of lime juice and fish sauce. The whole parcel is then dipped into another sauce which might be soy bean and peanut, or the famous *nuoc cham*.

As with *satay*, so with curries. Generally speaking, in Malaysia and Indonesia you find that coconut milk is added after the meat has been fried in the spicy paste, as we would add a stock. In Thailand the meat, especially beef, might first be cooked in coconut milk, which has tenderizing properties. When almost tender some of the coconut milk is scooped off, reduced over a high heat, and then the spice paste fried in this to bring out the flavour before adding it to the meat in the remaining coconut milk to continue cooking. There are always exceptions, one such is Indonesian beef *rendang* which employs a similar technique. The cubes of meat are marinated with the pounded spices and turned into the coconut milk for cooking. Carrying Thai curry-making one stage further, rich coconut cream is carefully reduced in the wok and the spices fried in this before adding fish or chicken plus the remaining coconut milk and herbs or flavouring.

Herbs, spices and flavours of the region are becoming more and more widely available in the UK not only in the specialist oriental stores but also in high-street supermarkets, which are becoming increasingly aware of their customers' more varied tastes in food. When we first left the UK to go to Malaysia over ten years ago, parsley and garlic were about as exotic as you'd get. Three years later ginger and chillies had crept onto the shelves, and the trend towards the magnificent choice we enjoy today was under way. Now it gladdens my heart to go into my local supermarket and find fresh turmeric, ginger, coriander by the bunch, lemon grass, chillies and fresh coconuts. These, coupled with tamarind, fish sauce, lengkuas (a member of the ginger family), macadamia nuts, and *blachan* (fermented fish paste), are available from oriental stores and supermarkets, and form the backbone to the flavours of South-East Asia.

THE ORIENTAL KITCHEN

Simplicity is the watchword in the oriental kitchen, particularly in the relatively few pieces of equipment which the cook would consider essential to perform the daily task of providing nourishing food for her family, be it in Bali or Bangkok.

The kitchen might be housed in a separate building a few yards from the house where the cooking will be done over a charcoal or kerosene stove. For those who can afford it, bottled gas might be an option but for others a simple wood fire outdoors might have to suffice. I was taught the basics of Malay cooking by Ah Moi Wong, and I knew her kitchen as well as she knew mine. There wasn't a single piece of equipment which was superfluous and I marvelled at the way she would get up at 5.30 A.M. to cook the family meals for the day, which would then be placed into an old-fashioned safe so that her family could help themselves to food as and when they needed it. The European insistence on hot food and hot plates is lost on the Oriental. Certain foods, say *dim sum* straight from the steamer, or a soup, will be served hot, but most dishes are served warm so the spicy flavours are enhanced rather than masked by the hotness of the food. This fact should be of comfort to the cook when serving an oriental meal to guests!

Equipment

The wok. A wide, circular pan with a curved base which not only allows a large quantity of food to be cooked simultaneously over a large surface area but also allows for the evaporation of liquid essential in many recipes. It is the ideal shape for tossing food in stir fry recipes and a much more satisfactory shape for deep frying. In Malaysia it was called a *kuali*, in Indonesia a *wajan*. There are many different qualities of wok on sale these days and the best advice is to go for the heaviest quality you can find, as the very thin, lightweight woks are a waste of time and money. This type will burn food very easily, which is bound to destroy your confidence in cooking oriental food.

I like to serve food straight from the wok. I have three cast-iron woks which I bought in Malaysia and they have built up a dark, glossy, black surface which shows off food to great advantage. I am completely sold on the wok as an essential piece of kitchen equipment. It can be used not only for stir frying but for deep frying and steaming as well as for non-oriental cooking, which is why my woks have pride of place next to the cooker where they are always ready for action.

I have a gas cooker, so I use metal stands on which the woks sit firmly during cooking. These are usually sold at the same time as the wok. For those with electric cookers there are Teflon-coated models with a flat base, or plug-in electric woks which you might consider. I have no experience in using either, so it might be wise to watch a demonstration or even borrow one from a friend before you buy so that you choose the best for your needs.

Season your wok in the same way as a frying pan. Melt a little pure oil in the pan, swirl it round and leave over a very gentle heat for ten minutes. Cool it a little, empty out any excess, then rub vigorously with a pad of newspaper. This can be repeated regularly to build up a 'surface' on the wok, which over the years becomes truly 'non-stick'. Immediately after use, wash quickly in warm soapy water with a brush (do not use metal abrasive pads), then rinse, dry and brush over the cooking surface with oil.

A useful tip I learned from Ah Moi was to warm the wok over a gentle heat before adding the oil for cooking. The oil then floods over the surface more easily and prevents food sticking. The amount of oil needed when cooking in a wok is considerably less than the amount you would use in a conventional pan, which must be a plus point in these health-conscious times.

The slice. A wide-mouthed spatula which is a perfect shape for either stir frying or simply frying off a spice paste that must be kept on the move in the wok. A wooden spatula is usually recommended for the Teflon-surfaced woks.

Chopping board. The oriental version looks like a huge slice of tree trunk, which is precisely what it is. They can be several inches thick and are very heavy in order to withstand all the chopping and slicing which is so much a part of food preparation.

Cleaver. A multi-purpose, heavy, broad-bladed implement which is used with such skill by oriental cooks for chopping, slicing, mincing, or even crushing a peeled clove of garlic by simply pressing down on the broad side of the blade. Ginger and lemon grass can be bruised in the same way.

Pestle and mortar, food processor, blender, coffee grinder. The pestle and mortar and/or food processor feature a great deal in this book in the making of spice pastes and the pounding and blending of ingredients. These processes might seem long and laborious to us but to many oriental cooks they are a pleasurable activity. The traditional granite pestle and mortar is quite deep and is pitted, which makes it ideal for grinding and pounding wet spices. Chilli, garlic, laos, ginger, lemon grass are held by the rough surface and do not fly out all over the kitchen whilst being pounded. For grinding or pounding small quantities of either wet or dry spices this type of pestle and mortar is ideal. In some Malaysian markets the pounding of spices is done on a flat granite slab with a granite rolling pin, which is fun to watch as the different ingredients are turned into a smooth paste in no time. In Thailand deep, wooden pestles and mortars are used in the markets for making the famous salads.

The food processor makes everything possible for me and I really do recommend that you use one where appropriate in the recipes in this book. My Magimix is the next best thing to having a helper in the kitchen. The various blade attachments are invaluable where thin, even slices of onion, cucumber and similar are required. When preparing spice pastes I would suggest that the fibrous ingredients such as laos, ginger and lemon grass are sliced before processing and, if a particularly fine, smooth paste is required, they can be first bruised in the pestle and mortar. Some oil can be added to the spice paste ingredients to ease the blending but do remember to reduce the amount of oil for frying the paste to compensate for this.

A small coffee grinder can be a great help where small quantities of spices are to be ground but it is advisable that it is kept exclusively for this purpose.

Steamers. Bamboo, stacking-type steamers are available in a host of sizes from a wide range of stores. When not in use they look very attractive on a shelf in the kitchen, and I use my rather large versions as fruit baskets. Like all utensils in the oriental kitchen they are multi-purpose. Indeed the baskets can be used for serving as well as cooking the food. Where small items are being cooked, line the baskets with a piece of rinsed muslin. Several baskets can be stacked one on top of the other with the lid set on top. These are then set over the wok and the boiling water replenished as required. I have a metal trivet which sits in the wok over the water and enables me to cook, say, a whole fish in a large dish. Cover with a lid and keep an eye on the water level whilst steaming.

Barbecue. A friend in Indonesia sent me a special barbecue unit for cooking *satay* which is very lightweight and requires very little charcoal. A gas or electric grill can be used, of course, but I always feel that cooking over charcoal gives that extra flavour to *satay*. A fan made from woven palm fronds is used to keep the charcoal glowing. Again this looks very attractive hanging up in the kitchen when not in use.

Rice cooker. These are immensely popular and you can see why when up to three meals a day can be rice-based. The great advantage of the rice cooker is that it is foolproof and will happily keep the rice warm for up to five hours. Leftover rice can be reheated the following day and the cooker may also be used for steaming many dishes. (See p. 242 on cooking rice.)

Knives. Last but by no means least I would like to stress the importance of a good set of knives. In the right hands, the cleaver covers all the chopping and slicing functions but for those who do not have these skills then a well-balanced, stainless-steel knife is a must. Good knives are not cheap but are a marvellous investment for any cook.

Home cooking

Stir frying. No matter what is being cooked, all the ingredients must be ready before you start cooking, as the whole process is essentially fast in order to retain maximum flavour, colour and crispness, especially where vegetables are concerned. When all the ingredients are ready, warm the wok over a gentle flame then pour in the oil and swirl round before adding the first ingredients, be it spice paste or perhaps chopped onion, garlic and ginger. When stir frying you must keep everything on the move all the time to ensure even cooking.

Deep frying. The wok is ideal for deep frying, requiring less oil than conventional deep-frying pans yet providing a larger surface area for cooking. Use a thermometer to keep an eye on the temperature if possible.

Steaming. I have dealt with this style of cooking above. The beauty of bamboo baskets stacking neatly on top of each other is that they give great versatility. You can use just one basket or several over the same wok.

Barbecuing. Charcoal is used extensively for cooking throughout South-East Asia. Where this is not feasible in the UK then use the grill for *satay*, for example, or roast in the oven where portions of chicken, for instance, are being used in a recipe.

EATING OUT

The Malays in both Malaysia and Singapore are devout Muslims so there are some very important points of etiquette to remember should you be invited to a Muslim home. Before entering the house remove your shoes, even though your host may say it is not necessary. This gesture will be taken as a courtesy to your host and his family as well as showing that you are aware of Malay customs.

A Malay man may wear his *songkok*, the hat which is part of the Malay national costume, in the house and even when eating. If you take a gift to your host and hostess or even their children they may not open the present in front of you but wait until you have left.

Always accept whatever is offered with your right hand or both hands, never the left. Similarly, when food is eaten with the fingers the right hand only is used. In strictly traditional homes plates of food might be placed in the centre of the floor, which has a covering of mats. The family will then sit with their feet tucked in at the side so that no one sees the soles of the feet, which would be taken as an insult.

Modern urban homes now usually have a table and chairs for eating. Small bowls of food will be placed in the centre of the table and each person will use a spoon and fork. There is no necessity for a knife as the food is usually in pieces which can be eaten satisfactorily from a spoon. No alcohol will be offered in a Muslim home but fruit drinks or water will be available.

It is absolutely taboo for a Muslim to eat pork or even to eat any meat which has not been slaughtered by a Muslim without the ritual prayers having been said. In markets throughout the country the section selling pork, which is after all one of the favourite meats of the Chinese, is always tucked away at the back so as not to insult the Muslim community. They can pretend it's not there.

The Chinese eat at the table with the food served on small platters, as is common practice in Chinese restaurants. Round tables are usually favoured with a turntable called a *chun poon* (lazy Susan). Each person will have a pair of chopsticks, a bowl for soup, a bowl for rice, a dish for the main course, a tiny dish for soy sauce and a porcelain spoon for drinking the soup. Sometimes a small extra bowl is set to take any discarded bones. Napkins are often folded into exotic shapes. Before eating, the guests will be invited to drink, which is a form of greeting. This might be tea, beer or even brandy when a celebration is in order. Wait for the host to drink first and subsequently to raise his chopsticks which indicates that everyone can start eating. At the end of the meal, place your chopsticks at the side of your dish on the table to denote that you have had sufficient. Never place the chopsticks across the bowl or plate, as your host might interpret this as an insult meaning that he has not provided enough to eat. All the exchanges of conversation take place during the meal. Do not expect to linger after a meal as we do. The Chinese like to leave straight after the last morsel has been eaten.

Indian families, who make up part of Malaysian society, like to serve generous portions of food, allowing for two or three helpings each. The meal is usually served at a table with bowls of food placed in the centre. The rice is spooned into the centre of your plate and spoonfuls of the various curries placed around the edge of it. Beef is never served, as the cow is a sacred animal. Pork can be a problem too, as many Indians are Muslim. Meat is often not eaten on Fridays. Added to this, many are vegetarian, so if you are entertaining be sure to serve at least two suitable vegetarian or lentil curries to avoid embarrassment. Well-cooked food is the order of the day, and for this reason salads are not generally appreciated. Devout Hindus will set aside a morsel of food as a thanksgiving to God before beginning to eat. A spoon and fork are usually available for guests. Hands must always be washed before you eat and, like the Malays, if food is eaten by hand, only the right hand will be used. When giving a gift to an Indian person offer with your right hand supported by the left. Drinks will usually be non-alcoholic, a yogurt-based drink, lassi, being very popular.

Indonesians are also very generous hosts. As it is a mainly Muslim country many of the customs are similar to those of the Malays. Sitting on the floor for a meal is customary in rural communities. When a table is used the setting might be a wide-brimmed soup plate or a dinner plate with the napkin set on the plate. A fork and spoon are provided for guests, although often Indonesians eat with the fingers of the right hand like many other peoples of the region. A small finger bowl set at the right side of the plate is provided for rinsing the fingers and there may be a small bowl for bones on the left. Indonesians do not demand that the food be served piping hot, so usually food will have been placed in the centre of the table before you sit down. A helping of rice is taken first which is sometimes moistened with a little soup, or *sayur*, then spoonfuls of the other foods are placed round the edge of the rice, each flavour being savoured separately as the food is eaten. Everyone says, '*Selamat makan*', which means 'good eating'. It is perfectly acceptable to take another helping before finishing the first. Water is usually served with the meal. Desserts are not usually served, rather a bowl of fresh fruit concludes the meal together with a cup of sweet Indonesian coffee. Indonesian food is not for the fainthearted but for the enthusiasts!

Elegant Thai hospitality is a beautiful experience. Shoes are slipped off before entering the home. In traditional surroundings you should expect to recline on plump cushions set around a low table, though in some restaurants there is a well under the table which allows Westerners to look slightly more comfortable! Food will have been placed in the centre of the table so that guests help themselves. The table setting consists of a plate, spoon and fork. Chopsticks are given where a noodle dish is to be served. Knives are regarded as weapons and so would never be put on the table. Rice and food are synonymous in Thai culture, so a good helping of rice is central to the meal. From the other three, four or five dishes set in the middle of the table spoonfuls of hot, spicy, crisp, and generally delicious food are spooned around the rice. A bowl of soup and a salad are usually part of the meal, along with the famous *nam prik* sauce, which is an essential accompaniment to all Thai meals. The food will be attractively garnished, smell marvellous and taste out of this world. In Thai cuisine it is essential that the food appeal to the eye, nose and tastebuds. Thai beer is a popular beverage with food though fruit squashes and water are often served, or even a weak jasmine tea. Thais love sweet cakes and desserts, and the fruit-carving skills of both men and women produce breathtaking results, much too perfect to eat!

Burmese hospitality is boundless, as I experienced during my stay there. In her book *Cook and Entertain the Burmese Way* Mi Mi Khaing paints a wonderful picture of how to entertain in true Burmese style. 'Burmese food is for eating mainly just before morning's pleasantness is lost to the heat of the noon, and again as the cool of evening falls, and eating together is a buttress against dusk's approach.' Tables are low, about a foot from the ground, and usually round, so that everyone seated at the table can reach for the various dishes with ease. Eating is regarded as a real pleasure so excessive conversation is not encouraged. A plate, spoon and fork are set for each diner, the food, which again is not required to be hot, is set in the centre of the table. A bring-and-share meal is a frequent mode of getting friends and family together and there is always enough food for extra guests should they call as the food is served. The dishes are small and rather deep to accommodate the sauces, and no dish must be allowed to become empty. The meal will consist of rice, curries, vegetables and sauces for dipping, a soup, maybe some crisp fritters, and the famous *balachuang*, a relish that will be on the table as surely as our salt and pepper. Being devoutly Buddhist, alcohol will not be served. Usually fruit squashes or drinks are taken after the meal. Where beer is permitted there is a good locally brewed Mandalay beer, a legacy from the days of British colonialism. Desserts are not always served, although fresh fruit is popular. However, should you have a yen for something sweet at any time of day there are delightful young ladies selling sweet confections with names which make them irresistible – butterfly, heart cooler, confetti, moon, and many more. Lepet, the pressed tea leaf (see page 106), might bring the meal to a finale, though it can equally well be served to anyone who calls by at any time of day.

Vietnamese cooks are well known for their skilful presentation of food. They are wedded to the idea of serving tiny morsels of food wrapped into parcels which are then dipped into a sauce before eating. However, the three meals of the day start with a soup, usually pork with a few noodles and green leaves. Lunch and the evening meal are both rice-based with perhaps more soup to sup on the side, plus a meat or fish dish and vegetables, all served in bowls or plates in the centre of a round table. Food is normally eaten with chopsticks and the soup with a porcelain spoon. In addition to the soup bowl and a plate there is usually a little dish containing the famous *nuoc cham* sauce so essential to each meal. Tea and rice wine might be served alongside the meal, though for celebrations the Vietnamese like to drink wine or brandy. Pork, chicken and duck are very popular in Vietnam; beef is very expensive, yet one of the most famous soups, *pho*, is based on beef.

In Cambodia a soup is usually served as breakfast fare. Being a rural nation this meal is very important before people leave home for work. Lunch and the evening meal are again rice-based, served with a little meat or fish and vegetables. Again soup is drunk throughout the meal with a porcelain spoon and the food is eaten with chopsticks or even with the fingers. Chinese green tea or just warm water might be served, or occasionally a local beer.

Finally, remember that eating and sharing food, be it in the home or in a restaurant, gives pleasure to all Oriental people, so do relax and join in the spirit of the occasion. In doing this you will return untold pleasures to your host and hostess which in a small way can do much for international relations and understanding. Like music, food is an avenue we can explore and enjoy with people of many different cultures.

Malaysia and Singapore

MALAYSIA

Visitors to Malaysia cannot fail to be captivated by its gentle, elegant people, the diversity of the countryside and the delicious food, which played such an important part in my three-year stay. When I arrived in Malaysia I was not prepared for the onslaught on my tastebuds and the delights in store. Food is ever present, be it from wayside stalls, markets, or restaurants and coffee shops that serve food round the clock.

Malaysia is the long finger which shares a border in the north with Thailand down to Singapore Island in the south. Singapore broke away as an independent nation in 1965. Malaysia has eleven states on the mainland, and two, Sabah and Sarawak, in East Malaysia (or Borneo, formerly land of the White Rajas, as it used to be called). Each state has a Sultan who has great influence and lives in considerable style. We were in Kuala Lumpur for the first coronation recorded on television – a lavish and memorable affair with much pomp and ceremony, including gold umbrellas and bejewelled regalia. At this the Sultan of Pahang on the East Coast was proclaimed king for a five-year term. The present king is the Sultan of Johore.

Malaysia's long coastline has provided shelter to many a traveller from as long ago as 200 A.D. Indians, Arabs, Chinese, Portuguese, Dutch, British and a host of others have called. Some stayed and a few intermarried, like the Chinese traders and merchants who took Muslim wives, forming a new ethnic group called the Straits Chinese or Nonyas. These have their own particular cooking style, famous in Penang, Malacca and Singapore.

Intermarriage is unusual, however. The Malays are devout Muslims and in the main the Chinese are Buddhist and the Indians

Hindu. Indeed, each group retains its own identity even in its cuisine. As an introduction to the varied food of the East I can think of no better place to start than Malaysia.

Public holidays and festivals provide an opportunity for visitors to share some of the delights of the country's tables. I have never lived anywhere where there are quite so many public holidays. Each race honours the others' celebrations, and we joined in too.

Kong Hee Fat Choy is the greeting for Chinese New Year, the time the Chinese really let their hair down. The New Year takes place in late January/early February and the celebrations continue for up to two weeks. The Chinese are very superstitious and rules must be kept. It is a time of fresh beginnings – new clothes and shoes are worn, the entire house is cleaned from top to bottom, debts are cleared, the gods and the older generation revered, old scores forgotten, and peace and harmony restored between friends and family alike.

Michael Wong told me of the New Year celebrations held in his family home. They vary from family to family depending on which ethnic group the family belong to. His family are Hakka, and each New Year's Eve in the family home it is customary to eat a vegetarian dish made from bean-thread noodles, which are deep fried and 'sparkle like diamonds'. To the noodles (which ensure long life) are added bean curd, soy sauce and *fat choy*, a black, hairy seaweed, which is very difficult to come by. This gives an interesting crunchy texture to the dish and is believed to bring prosperity to all who eat it. In a Hokkien household a steamboat would more likely be served as the New Year meal, or even *popiah*, spring rolls wrapped in a thin pancake which are great fun for all the guests (see page 47 for recipes). No matter how many hundreds or thousands of miles away members of the family may live they will all endeavour to get home in time for this, the highlight of the year. The meal is followed by the giving of the *ang pow*. These are red envelopes (red being a lucky colour). Every effort is made to find brand new notes which are always given in even numbers, 2, 4, 6, or 100. Odd numbers are unlucky.

During Ramadan, Alot, a tiny person who lived with us at our first house, used to conform to the edict that no food must be taken after sunrise or before sundown. At 4.30 A.M. she would be in the kitchen clanking around with the pans in order to prepare and eat her food before sunrise. By 7 P.M. she was lethargic from lack of food. The very devout don't even drink during the day, and it's a small miracle that the country keeps ticking over. Alot had a wonderful saying: 'easy time' – when food from the previous day, like curry, could be served again. It's still one of our family expressions.

Hari Raya Puasa, the end of the fasting month, is a great relief all round. Devout Muslims celebrate it by first going to the mosque and then receiving friends and relations at home to share foods prepared over a period of several days: *ketupat* or *lontong* – rice cooked in small packets woven from coconut leaves – and *rendang* would almost always be served, as well as a myriad lurid-coloured cakes which I didn't find appealing. The Muslims do not drink alcohol, so fruit juices and soft drinks are served.

We were lucky enough to see a charming wedding procession whilst driving to Malacca once. The groom was resplendent in a gold-embroidered traditional *baju kurung* costume of trousers and a tunic with matching head covering and a *kris*, the Malay sword, in his belt. The bride's costume, a long elegant sarong with a tunic top, was in the same material as the groom's. Flowers hung in a garland round her neck and decorated her hair. Two little boys carried slim poles which looked like palm trees but the branches were made from brightly coloured papers with a spray of pink and red bougainvillaea nestling in the centre of the crown.

The happy couple returned to the bride's home for the wedding feast (if the groom is 'royal' the wedding takes place in his home), followed by a group of boys thumping out a welcome on their drums. The feast, an open-house affair, would feature mounds of turmeric – yellow rice decked with flower blossoms, and lots of curry. Guests are presented on leaving with a *bunga telor* – translated this means flower egg – the egg nestling in a gold basket, which is a lovely tradition. In this typically Malay setting close friends and relatives bring ingredients a few days before the feast to help with the preparation of the food for the wedding banquet. Uncooked rice, onions, oil, live chickens, and even firewood would be the usual offerings.

Although country traditions remain largely unaltered, the capital city, Kuala Lumpur, has gone through enormous changes recently, with skyscrapers going up at the expense of the delightful two-storey shophouses of yesteryear. However, no amount of progress will improve the climate, which is particularly oppressive in the city. In the country there is always a breeze but there is never a hint of it in Kuala Lumpur; it just seems to get hotter and wetter and steamier, following the almost daily thunderstorms. That said, everyone has to learn to cope with it, so we tended to get on with life and desperately tried to break the habit of living at the Westerner's pace.

To familiarize ourselves with the city, we would drive through Kuala Lumpur at night (we imagined it would be cooler) to see the minarets of the railway station, built in 1897, which looks like something out of the fabled Arabian Nights. Close by is the post office, a pretty, pink-and-white stone building just across the road from the Tudor-style Selangor Club, with its lush green cricket pitch and a reminder of colonial days. There are mosques galore, with frequent early-morning calls to prayer, and temples can be found all over the city, even in the urban sprawl called Petaling Jaya, always referred to as PJ.

There is an excellent restaurant in PJ called Gluttons Corner, on Gluttons Square. It is not a sophisticated establishment. Formica-topped tables and rather uncomfortable chairs are placed out on the pavement, and the whole area is lit by bare electric light bulbs nestling in the overhead trees. It is all very businesslike but the food is scrumptious: spare ribs, spring rolls, ginger chicken, crabmeat omelette, noodle dishes, *char kway teow* with squid and stir-fried vegetables. We usually drank either beer or soft drinks, though the Chinese frequently put away a fair quantity of brandy if they are really out to enjoy themselves. They toast each other '*Yam sing*' and drain their glasses, which abruptly curtails the pleasures of their evening!

The Klang food stalls are always popular, again a very unpreten-tious setting but the chilli crabs (similar recipe page 53) are out of this world – and hot to boot! Everyone helps themselves from a huge bowl in the centre of the table, occasionally taking a piece of cooling cucumber then mopping up the rich sauce with pieces of toast, or French bread in more sophisticated Singapore. In restaurants like these, puddings are a rarity – though a bowl of fresh fruit such as rambutan, bananas or lychees is sometimes offered.

Yazmins and the Bingtang are the best-known Malay restaurants, serving excellent *laksa rendang*, *satay*, *ikan lemak*, and sweet and sour fish, plus a wondrous array of other fish dishes.

Down in Brickfields, Devi's, a shophouse turned restaurant, is another gourmet's delight. Spicy Indian curries are served on a banana leaf, the original disposable plate!

Eating out is a way of life, as a visit to the stalls in Jalan Campbell and round by the Central Market in Jalan Benting will confirm. Car parks all over the city are transformed as the last office worker leaves and the *gerais* – mobile stalls – are wheeled into position for the evening's trade. These are often family affairs. A few simple tables and benches appear with the first customers who walk round the various stalls ordering a bowl of noodles (*mee*), *satay*, barbecued spicy chicken or prawns or, indeed, whatever takes their fancy. Miraculously the chosen dishes appear on the right tables and, even more amazingly, customers are presented with one bill at the end of the evening, not several as one would expect.

Though we tended to eat our evening meal around 8 o'clock, local people often eat anytime around 6 o'clock onwards, and invariably the whole family turns out – young and old. Breakfast is taken at 10.30 and might be a rice porridge or steamed buns from the numerous little restaurants, all of which are renowned for their particular speciality. There are lots of such establishments around the Central Market. This main market was a revelation which I discovered early in my stay in Kuala Lumpur, and I have never been able to pass by an oriental market since.

The covered market on the banks of the river at Kuching opposite the Istana (the Rajah's Palace) is a real joy with its beautifully arranged piles of morning-picked fresh vegetables and fruits. Young loofahs (the kind you use in the bath are the dried variety), cabbages, long beans, gourds, aubergines, pickled cabbage, lemon grass, curry leaves and glossy red chillies look irresistible, as do the piles of exquisitely arranged fresh fruits, pineapples, oranges, limes, bananas and starfruit. Nearby is a lady selling wet spices – pounded chilli, coriander, ginger, garlic, lemon grass, turmeric. A dollop of

whatever you like, or whatever is recommended, is wrapped in a
banana leaf then carried home to form the basis of a wonderful
curry without all the usual pounding. Bags of grated fresh coconut
are also available, to which you can add a little warm water before
squeezing out the rich coconut milk. These cut the corners on
curry-making and the results are superb.

Friendly stallholders beckon passers-by to their stalls, where jars
of soy sauce, tomato ketchup, pickled prawns, preserved bean curd
and evaporated milk stand to attention behind a display of preserved
eggs, pearl sago, *blachan* and betel leaves. From hooks above, clusters
of plastic bags containing lurid pink fish paste, dark brown liquid
(*nippah*) palm sugar, and pure, white, fresh coconut are a wonderful
contrast in colours.

Although a capital city reflects a society to some extent, it is also
important to get out into the countryside. Fortunately from Kuala
Lumpur (which sounds better than City of Muddy Waters, a literal
translation) this is quite easy to do. Travellers pass through extra-
ordinarily varied scenery: *kampongs*, or villages, shaded with coconut
palm trees, and simple, wood-built homes on stilts with bougainvillaea threading its colourful way along the balconies; the mountains,
the steamy jungle, and cool highland regions with names like Frasers
Hill and Cameron Highlands; the plantations of rubber, palm oil,
coconut palms with cocoa nestling underneath as a profitable second
crop, coffee, and tea bushes, pepper gardens and, of course, the
acres and acres of paddi which stretch in a patchwork all over the
lowland areas of Malaysia. This is not to forget the market gardens
and smallholdings, which produce an abundance of chillies, ginger,
and every conceivable vegetable, spice and fruit for the innumerable
markets, large and small, throughout the country.

Once we undertook an eight-hour train journey through the
jungle, from Kuala Lipis, slap in the middle of the country going
north, to Kuala Krai, a distance of about 100 miles, and skirting the
edge of Taman Negara, the National Park. There is no road, so
literally everyone travelling in the area uses the 'Golden Blowpipe'
train. The restaurant car menu on that journey was simple. It
provided thick, black, local coffee with lashings of condensed milk
and toast made over charcoal. We have had more exotic fare on
trains – fried rice wrapped in a parcel of banana leaf was quite a

feature on the train to Singapore, with the option of *satay* and *longtong* from vendors who ran up and down the platform as the train pulled in at stations on the way.

On the journey to Kuala Krai we stopped off at Trengganu where the market buzzed with activity, and marvellous basketware of every shape and size spilled onto the pavement. I still use some of my purchases from that visit even now. The time to be there is early in the morning when the fishermen come back in their boats, which have beautifully carved mastheads called *bongau*. The whole place takes on a curious excitement as the catch is brought into the market. Fresh-water river fish, *ikan jelawat*, *kerai* and the fine-flavoured *kelah*, are much sought after as well as *ikan bawal hitam*, black pomfret, *ikan merah*, snapper, *jenetak*, *tengirri* (mackerel), and shellfish galore.

Brightly coloured souvenir kites feature at the market too, along with brassware, batik as fine as cotton lawn, bags, mats and figures for the shadow play, *wayang kulit*, the Eastern answer to Punch and Judy.

On my way out of the market I spotted some pingpong balls on the egg stall, which turned out to be turtle eggs. This eastern coastline is renowned for its beaches, which are used by the giant leatherback turtles year after year to lay their eggs. Certainly while we were there, there was a great deal of concern about the number of eggs which found their way on to the market. They are highly nutritious. The egg-laying process is extremely laborious. Some of these huge turtles are said to be several hundred years old. I once watched one slowly make her way up the beach to a spot above the tide line, manoeuvre herself into position and dig a hole with her rear flippers till it was deep enough for her eggs, which numbered over a hundred. The effort looked almost too much as she flipped the sand back over the eggs and, in a state of absolute exhaustion, returned to the sea never knowing whether her young would survive. Some people even claim to have seen the turtle shed tears after laying her eggs, and personally, having witnessed the exhausting process these poor creatures go through, I can never bring myself to buy their eggs.

I learned the basics of Malay cooking from Ah Moi Wong, who was one of life's blessings. She was Chinese, a Hokkien, born in

Malaysia with an amazing knowledge of Chinese, Malay and Indian cuisine. I can still see her sitting on the doorstep pounding the wet or dry spices in the granite pestle and mortar, making the finest spice paste imaginable. We could have done it in the food processor, as I have indicated in the following recipes, but Ah Moi felt her way was best. She taught me the preparation and use of coconut milk, *blachan*, tamarind, chillies, ginger, and *lengkuas*. These first steps were to become second nature to me, as were *satays*, *rendang*, *laksa*, *acar*, and *gula melaka*, to name a few.

Food is eternally fascinating – you never stop learning and for me Malaysia was to open the doors to a new world of cooking and eating.

SINGAPORE – crossroads of the East

Thomas Stamford Raffles (1781–1826) was a man with vision, yet the Singapore of today would be beyond his wildest expectations. Singa pura Island (Lion City), as it was known, was his choice as a trading post between East and West. The island, similar in size to the Isle of Wight, was at that time a pretty unsavoury and unhealthy place to choose. Either the sea gypsies (*orang luat*), the mosquitoes, the rats, or all three saw off potential invaders.

In 1805 Raffles went to Penang as a clerk, aged twenty-four. He was an Empire builder, workaholic, linguist (he learned Malay on the long voyage out from England), and employee of the British East India Company. Later, in 1819, he proceeded with his grand plan for Singapore, which was not without its critics. He allotted land and planned the city on a grid system, he implemented a legal system, designed the Botanical Gardens, and built a college to promote the study and teaching of Malay, Chinese and Siamese.

Soon migrants came flocking to this burgeoning town, not only from Malaya but from China and Indonesia too. News of the tin mining and rubber industries was like a magnet to the poor, downtrodden Chinese from the mainland, who came by the ship-load. For them the streets of Singapore were truly paved with gold and, sadly, for some the smoking of opium was to be their downfall.

It was in Singapore that the first batch of rubber seedlings from Kew Gardens was nurtured. The director of the Botanical Gardens in Singapore – Rubber Ridley, as he was affectionately known –

was convinced that rubber was a perfect crop in this hot, humid climate. He was right. The rubber industry owes him an enormous debt today, as we acknowledge another of Singapore's men of vision. Rubber tapping is very labour-intensive. As ever, many Chinese were ready to accept the challenge of work, mostly in the tin mines, but some on the plantations. However, their numbers were boosted and eventually overtaken by the Tamil Indians – further increasing the migrant population which has today developed into the multi-ethnic societies of Malaysia and Singapore. In today's Singapore the population is principally Chinese. Very few of the original migrants were women and so marriages between wealthy Chinese merchants and Muslim women formed the basis of a new ethnic group called the Nonyas. The Nonya style of cooking takes its name from these women. It is a fascinating mixture of Chinese and Malay, with a hint of Indonesian and Thai cooking. Some would say it combines the best aspects of each, resulting in this unique cuisine famed throughout Singapore, Malacca and Penang. Its faithful and growing following of enthusiasts worldwide appreciate the subtle blend of textures and spicy flavours and the use of pork and coconut milk in true Nonya food. Without doubt the traditional preparation of Nonya food can be a time-consuming operation, but with food processors in today's kitchen the time can be dramatically reduced. Chopping, pounding and grinding of garlic, chillies, onions, *lengkuas*, lemon grass and *blachan* become the work of a moment.

Perhaps the best-known Nonya family in Singapore is that of the Prime Minister, Lee Kuan Yew. He has led the country for thirty years, twenty-four of those as an independent nation.

Everything in Singapore works, from telephones and electricity to taxis. Streets are ultra-clean and you can drink the water. New hotels are mushrooming but thankfully Raffles Hotel is still standing, though even its future had a big question mark over it in the drive to modernize or pull down any building which smacked of the past. Reprieved, Raffles is now a hundred years old and a major tourist attraction. Nowhere in Singapore do people rest on their laurels – the hotel follows a modern trend and now sells Raffles merchandise. The famous Singapore sling, made from gin, cherry brandy, Cointreau, bitters, orange, lime and pineapple juice, is still available in the long bar, where you can take a breather and soak up the old colonial past enjoyed by Kipling, Conrad and Somerset Maugham. Close by is the area called Little India, famous for its fabrics and fish-head curry, and the Arab quarter where you can buy marvellous baskets, batik and rattan.

At the end of the day just watch where the Singaporeans go to eat. They are very discerning and always happy to 'talk food' or suggest places for you to try. There are lots of open-air plazas with food from dozens of stalls, as there are in Kuala Lumpur – try the Telok Ayer market near Raffles Quay, the Satay Club in Queen Elizabeth Walk, Rasa Singapura, Tanglin Road, Cuppage Road centre near Orchard Road, or the Ellenborough Market complex: you won't have to travel far – just follow your nose or take some advice and a taxi!

There are markets in virtually every street in the city. Walk down streets in Chinatown where past and present live side by side, temples with the fragrance of incense, coffee shops selling wine cakes and traditional medicines, food stalls in China Square. Watch the skill of the man making *popiah* skins (wrappers for spring rolls); search out kitchen utensils in Temple Street or settle for *dim sum* at Tai Tong in Mosque Street; see the Chinese housewives in their *samfoo* (a cotton, printed trouser suit), the Indians in their jewel-coloured saris, and the Malays and Nonyas in their batik sarongs, as they pass the calligraphers, fortune tellers and street doctors on their daily walk to the market. Watch how they bargain in the vibrant atmosphere of the markets all over town.

This is Singapore – a truly cosmopolitan city full of change and challenge, a meeting place for peoples from all over the world, which is perhaps Raffles' dream come true.

LAKSA LEMAK
Spicy coconut milk soup

This is marvellous party food, requiring everyone to help themselves to all on offer. It was one of Ah Moi's favourite recipes, and I was thrilled to find that I could get all the necessary ingredients to make it when I came back to England. I have to be honest, it does take time to prepare, but it can be done ahead of time which is a real bonus for the cook.

Laksa means soup and lemak is coconut milk. This recipe has Nonya origins and is very popular in Singapore as a result.

50 g/2 oz ikan bilis (see page 236) and 900 ml/1½ pints water to make stock

3 aubergines, ends trimmed

675 g/1½ lb shelled prawns sprinkled with 2 teaspoons sugar, or use frozen prawns

1–2 lettuces, shredded

100 g/4 oz beansprouts

2 spring onions, finely chopped

50 g/2 oz crispy fried onions (see page 200)

100g/4 oz shallots, peeled

4 cloves garlic, peeled

2 macadamia nuts or shelled blanched almonds

3 stems lemon grass, bruised

6 tablespoons coconut or groundnut oil

1 cm/½ in prepared blachan (see page 228)

25 g/1 oz mild curry powder

1 litre/1¾ pints coconut milk and 120 ml/4 fl oz coconut cream (see page 231)

a few curry leaves (optional)

salt to taste

2 packets fried bean curd (see page 227)

SELECTION OF NOODLES

laksa noodles, mee, beehoon – allow approximately 100 g/4 oz per person, of the three noodles combined, not 100 g/4 oz of each one!

½ 225 g/8 oz packet prawn crackers, fried in oil (see page 236)

1. To make the stock: first cook the ikan bilis in the water for 15 minutes. Strain and discard the fish, then add the aubergines to the stock and cook for 5 minutes until they are tender and the skins can be peeled off easily. Cut into quarters and then into pieces about 7.5 cm/3 in long.
2. Next cook the prawns in the stock for 4 minutes until just tender.

If using frozen prawns omit the sugar and when thawed pop them into the stock briefly.

3. Arrange the aubergines and prawns on a platter with the shredded lettuce, beansprouts, spring onions and crispy fried onions.

4. Pound the shallots with the garlic, nuts and one sliced stem of lemon grass. Fry this in the oil, turning all the time. Do not allow to brown.

5. Add the two remaining bruised lemon grass stems, and the blachan and the curry powder mixed to a paste with a little of the coconut milk. Fry to bring out the full flavour.

6. Stir all the time to prevent the soup curdling as you add half the coconut cream and all the coconut milk. Add the curry leaves if using, and simmer for 10 minutes without cover. Taste for seasoning.

7. Add the prepared ikan bilis stock and stir in the remaining coconut cream as it comes to the boil. Rinse the fried bean curd in boiling water and squeeze to remove excess oil. Add to the soup.

8. Finally prepare the noodles (see page 239), drain and arrange on a platter.

9. Serve the soup in a large tureen. Guests spoon noodles and a selection of the other accompaniments into their bowls and top up with the soup. Eat with chopsticks and soup spoons, and hand round a bowl of prawn crackers.

Serves 6–8

HAM CHOY TONG
Kuching fish soup

FISH STOCK

1 fish head, plus bones from the mackerel, bawal hitam or tengirri (see below)	1 small onion, peeled and sliced
	1 stick celery
	1 cm/½ in piece ginger peeled and sliced
1½ litres/2½ pints water	seasoning to taste

SOUP

50 g/2 oz pickled cabbage

500 g/1 lb firm-fleshed fish such as mackerel, bawal hitam, black pomfret or tengirri – skinned and boned.

2 tablespoons cooking oil

2.5 cm/1 in piece fresh ginger, finely chopped

1 onion, peeled and diced

1 red chilli, deseeded and shredded

1 large tomato, skinned, deseeded and diced

4 salted Chinese plums, coarsely chopped, plus 1 tablespoon of juice

TO GARNISH

chopped spring onion and coriander

1. Wash the fish head and bones then cut into chunks if necessary.
2. Bring the water to the boil in a large pan, add the fish head, bones, onion, celery, ginger and seasoning. Half cover and cook over a gentle heat for 20 minutes, then strain and reserve the stock.
3. Wash the pickled cabbage to remove saltiness. Soak for 10 minutes in water then drain and shred finely.
4. Cut the fish fillets into neat cubes. Heat the oil, and fry the ginger, onion and chilli for 1–2 minutes. Add the fish, stir gently then add the tomato.
5. Stir in the reserved stock, pickled cabbage, Chinese plums and juice. Bring to the boil, and simmer for five minutes. Skim if necessary. Taste for seasoning and serve sprinkled with chopped spring onion and coriander.

Serves 6–8

TA PIN LO
Steamboat

A few days after we arrived in Kuala Lumpur friends took us out for a steamboat – my first encounter with this style of cooking, which is not only nutritious but also the most enormous fun. I have heard it said that the Chinese measure the success of the party by the state of the tablecloth! My brass firepot or steamboat came from Peking, but aluminium ones can be bought here from Chinese emporiums. You can alternatively use a fondue set, filling the pot with the stock, which I almost had to resort to when testing this recipe as my firepot developed a leak. The problem was resolved in no time by a practical friend and the soldering iron! Glowing charcoal is dropped into the central funnel which keeps the stock in the moat bubbling throughout. I make the chicken stock for this over a week or two and store it in the freezer – or you can use stock cubes and water if you must. My butcher is very obliging and cuts the meat into fine slices on the slicing machine, having left it in the freezer for a while. He then layers it up with waxed paper between the slices so that it is easy to transfer to a serving platter.

I have a *chun poon* (lazy Susan) which is placed in the centre of the table. The steamboat takes pride of place with the meat, fish and vegetables on platters and the sauces in bowls around it.

STOCK

2½ litres/4½ pints seasoned chicken stock

4 tablespoons Chinese rice wine or dry sherry

MEATS AND FISH

225 g/8 oz beef fillet, sliced paper thin, and/or 225 g/8 oz pork fillet, sliced paper thin

1–2 chicken breasts, thinly sliced

225 g/8 oz chicken livers

225 g/8 oz large peeled prawns and/or large New Zealand mussels

FISH BALLS

450 g/1 lb any white fish fillets, skinned

1 egg white, lightly whisked with a fork

1 tablespoon cornflour

seasoning

2 spring onions, finely chopped, or use chives

VEGETABLES AND EGGS

4 spring onions made into curls (see page 240)

8 Chinese mushrooms

100 g/4 oz green leaves – spinach, Chinese leaves and watercress – washed and dried

coriander, finely chopped

8 quail's eggs, hard-boiled for 3 minutes and shelled

225 g/8 oz beeboon (rice vermicelli)

Dipping sauces

bottled tomato sauce mixed with a little
  chilli sauce

thin soy sauce with sesame seeds

thin soy sauce with finely grated fresh
  ginger

rice wine vinegar

tahini (sesame seed paste)

1. Prepare the stock, add the rice wine or sherry and set aside to reheat when all the other ingredients are ready.
2. Arrange the beef, pork, and chicken breast slices on a platter. Snip the threads from the chicken livers and rinse and dry on kitchen paper. Place on the platter or divide the meats between two platters if liked. Garnish with the spring onion curls.
3. Arrange the prawns and/or mussels on another platter, leaving space for the fish balls.
4. Make the fish balls by blending the fish, with sufficient egg white to bind, cornflour, seasoning and spring onions or chives into a paste in a food processor. You may not need all the egg white, depending on the fish used.
5. Form into 16 small, even-sized balls with wetted hands and arrange with the shellfish on the platter. Cover all meats and fish with cling film and leave in the refrigerator till required.
6. Soak the mushrooms for half an hour in warm water to cover. Drain, adding the soaking juices to the chicken stock. Cut each mushroom into four slices and arrange in a pile on a plate with the green leaves. Add the quail's eggs.
7. Soak the rice vermicelli in warm water for 30 minutes, then drain and turn into a large bowl. Arrange the dipping sauces in small bowls.
8. Pour some of the stock into the moat of the firepot before placing pieces of hot charcoal in the central funnel. Bring the remaining stock to the boil in a saucepan and pour as much as necessary into the moat. Keep the rest aside for topping up as necessary.
9. Each guest should have a fondue fork onto which they spear morsels of the meat and fish, cooking them to taste in the hot stock. The fish balls should be lowered into the stock on a spoon rather than on a fondue fork. Use chopsticks (or forks)

for eating, dipping morsels of cooked food in the sauces. Do not eat from the fondue forks, which will be very hot.

10. Replenish the stock and charcoal as necessary, and at the end of the meal, when the stock in the firepot is brimming with goodness, add the mushrooms then, after a few minutes, the green leaves and coriander.

11. Meanwhile divide the drained vermicelli between bowls with a quail's egg per person. Ladle the soup over the noodles to bring the meal to a delicious finale!

Serves 8

DIM SUM

DOUGH

225 g/8 oz plain flour
1 teaspoon salt
15 g/½ oz lard or butter

150 ml/5 fl oz warm water
1 teaspoon dried yeast

FILLING

2 Chinese mushrooms, soaked for 15 minutes in warm water
75 g/3 oz pork meat with some fat
50 g/2 oz cooked prawns
2 spring onions, finely chopped
½ teaspoon sesame oil

1 tablespoon Chinese rice wine or dry sherry
a little peanut or vegetable oil
2 teaspoons cornflour
salt to taste

1. Sift the flour with the salt into a bowl. Rub in the fat. Dissolve the sugar in 75 ml/3 fl oz of the warm water, stir in the yeast and leave on one side for 10 minutes until frothy.

2. Add the remaining warm water to the yeast and mix into the dry ingredients. Mix to a dough, and knead for 8–10 minutes by hand or in a food processor for one minute.

3. Put a few drops of oil in a large polythene bag and rub well to distribute the oil round the sides of the bag. Place the dough in the bag, seal with a tie and leave in a warm, not hot, place for about 1 hour or until the dough has doubled in size.

4. Meanwhile prepare the filling: cut away the stalks from the

mushroom caps and discard. Process the mushrooms and pork fairly finely in a food processor. Add the prawns, spring onions, sesame oil, rice wine or sherry, oil, cornflour, and salt. Process briefly.

5. Turn the risen dough onto a lightly floured board and form into a long sausage, then cut into 32 even-sized pieces. Roll into rounds approx 7.5–9 cm/3–3½ in and place a teaspoonful of the filling into the centre of each. Damp the edges and gather up into little pouch shapes.

6. Stand the dim sum on a round of kitchen parchment (Bakewell paper) and leave to rise in a warm place for 30 minutes, then steam for 20 minutes.

7. Serve with one or other of the following dips: add a few dry-fried sesame seeds to 2 tablespoons soy sauce and drizzle 1 teaspoon warmed sesame oil on top; or add 1 tablespoon rice wine vinegar to the soy sauce with a crushed clove of garlic.

● The dim sum can be frozen after cooking. Steam for a further 15 minutes straight from the freezer.

Makes 32

NONYA SATAY BABI
Pork satay

675 g/1½ lb pork tenderloin, trimmed and cut into even-sized cubes

350 g/12 oz belly of pork, derinded and cut into cubes

2–3 tablespoons soft brown sugar

2 tablespoons coriander seeds, dry fried (see page 233) and pounded

2 tablespoons ground turmeric

½ teaspoon salt

coconut or peanut oil for basting

SATAY SAUCE

1 cm/½ in square prepared blachan (see
  page 228)
100 g/4 oz shallots or small onions,
  peeled
½–1 tablespoon chilli powder
1 tablespoon coriander seeds, dry fried
  (see page 233) and pounded

2 stems lemon grass
4–6 tablespoons coconut or peanut oil
450 ml/¾ pint coconut milk (see page
  231)
4–6 tablespoons (i.e. one-third 350 g/
  12 oz jar) crunchy peanut butter
2 tablespoons soft brown sugar
salt to taste

TO SERVE

chunks of fresh pineapple

slices of raw onion

1. Sprinkle the tenderloin and belly of pork with the sugar and mix well. This will release the juices in the meat. Spoon over the coriander, turmeric and salt. Toss well to coat the meat cubes thoroughly and leave for 1½–2 hours.
2. At the same time soak satay skewers in water to prevent scorching when cooking, and prepare the sauce: pound the blachan with the onions, chilli and coriander and the sliced lower part of the lemon grass stems. Reserve the remainder of the stems.
3. Fry this spice paste in the oil for several minutes, stirring all the time to bring out the flavour. Add half the coconut milk and the peanut butter and sugar. Taste for salt; slowly bring to the boil, stirring, then add the remaining coconut milk to make a coating sauce.
4. Thread approximately 2 pieces each of tenderloin and the belly of pork alternately on the soaked skewers. Bruise the ends of the 2 lemon grass stems so that they look like brushes, and use them to anoint the satay with a little oil. This gives an added dimension to the flavour.
5. Place the satay sticks under the grill or over charcoal to cook for 10–12 minutes, depending on the thickness of the pork pieces. Keep turning throughout.
6. Serve the satay sticks on a platter with a pile of chopped onion and fresh pineapple at the side. Reheat the sauce and serve

separately. Guests put a spoonful of sauce onto their plate and dip the meat into this before eating.

Makes 24 sticks

MUNG BEAN FRITTERS

175 g/6 oz skinned whole or split mung
  beans, soaked in water overnight
1–2 red chillies, deseeded and sliced
1 medium onion, peeled and sliced
1 teaspoon coriander seeds, dry fried (see
  page 233) and pounded

½ teaspoon cumin seeds, dry fried (see
  page 233) and pounded
salt to taste
oil for deep frying

1. Wash and drain the mung beans.
2. Place the chillies and onion in a food processor and chop finely, then add the mung beans and process till the mixture is almost smooth.
3. Add the coriander, cumin and salt and process briefly once more.
4. When required, drop the mixture from a dessertspoon into hot oil (375°F) in a wok and cook for about 4–5 minutes until the fritters are quite cooked through.
5. Drain on absorbent kitchen paper and serve warm.

Makes 25 approximately

POPIAH
Homemade wrappers

These Nonya-style popiah are more closely related to the lumpia of the Philippines than the ubiquitous deep-fried spring roll of Chinese restaurants. They are a marvellous party idea, as the pancakes, fillings and bits and pieces can all be made ahead. This is another chance to use the *chun poon* (lazy Susan). Place all the ingredients attractively on platters or in bowls and set these in the centre of the table. For guests who may be unfamiliar with the popiah I demonstrate how to make up the first one then let everyone take a turn.

50 g/2 oz cornflour, sifted
200 g/7 oz plain flour, sifted
450 ml/¾ pint water approx

6 size 2 eggs, beaten
salt

COOKED FILLING

1 onion, peeled and finely chopped
2 cloves garlic, crushed
2 tablespoons oil
100 g/4 oz cooked pork, chopped
100 g/4 oz crabmeat or prawns, thawed
*   if frozen*
100 g/4 oz canned bamboo shoot, cut
*   into shreds*

1 yambean (bangkuang), peeled and
*   grated, or 8–10 water chestnuts,*
*   finely chopped*
1–2 tablespoons yellow salted beans
*   (from a can or jar)*
1 tablespoon light soy sauce
freshly ground black pepper

FRESH FILLINGS

2 eggs, hard-boiled, shelled and chopped
2 Chinese sausages, steamed and sliced
100 g/4 oz packet fried bean curd, sliced
225 g/8 oz beansprouts, blanched in
*   boiling water for 30 seconds then*
*   rinsed in cold water*

100 g/4 oz crabmeat or prawns
½ cucumber, coarsely grated
small bunch spring onions, chopped
20 lettuce leaves, rinsed and dried
sprigs of fresh coriander

SAUCES

1. 6–8 red chillies, deseeded and
*   pounded to a paste*
2. 6–8 cloves garlic, pounded to a paste

3. 4–6 tablespoons hosein sauce (see
*   page 235)*

1. Blend the sifted cornflour and flour with the water, eggs and salt to make a smooth batter.
2. Grease an omelette pan with lard and use to cook 20–24 pancakes, stirring the batter between each one. They should not be thick, so note how much batter you use for the first one or two. It is a good idea to use a measuring jug for pouring the batter into the pan.
3. Pile the pancakes (wrappers) on top of each other, interleaved with Bakewell paper to prevent sticking.
4. Make the cooked filling by frying the onion and garlic in the oil without browning. Add the pork, crabmeat or prawns, bamboo

shoot and grated yambean. Stir gently and cook for 2–3 minutes. Now add the salted beans, soy sauce and pepper to taste.

5. Cover and cook gently for 20 minutes, checking from time to time that the mixture has not dried out. Add a little water if necessary to prevent this. Turn into a serving bowl and allow to cool whilst preparing the other fillings.

6. Arrange the hard-boiled eggs, sausages, beancurd, beansprouts, crabmeat or prawns, cucumber, spring onions, lettuce leaves and coriander either in piles on a large platter or in separate bowls.

7. Similarly spoon the chilli, the garlic and the hosein sauce into small bowls.

8. Guests make up their own popiahs by spreading the minutest amount of chilli or garlic or both, and/or the hosein sauce, on the wrapper followed by a lettuce leaf, some cooked filling and a selection of the fresh ingredients. Do not overfill the wrapper. Roll up, tucking in the ends and eat at once.

Makes 20–24

GULAI IKAN
Aubergine and fish curry

2 aubergines (350 g/12 oz), cut into chunky cubes
salt
450 g/1 lb skinned fish fillet, use cod or haddock
1 medium onion, peeled
2.5 cm/1 in piece lengkuas, peeled and sliced
1 cm/½ in prepared blachan (see page 228)
2 stems lemon grass, slice lower 5 cm/2 in – reserve top

1 teaspoon ground turmeric
4 tablespoons coconut or vegetable oil
450 ml/¾ pint coconut milk (see page 231)
450 ml/¾ pint tamarind juice prepared by soaking 3 tablespoons tamarind pulp in 450 ml/¾ pint water; leave for 15 minutes then strain and reserve juice
salt to taste

1. Sprinkle the aubergine cubes with salt and set aside for at least half an hour then rinse, drain and dry.

2. Cut the fish into cubes. Keep covered in the refrigerator till required.
3. Prepare the spice paste by pounding the onion, lengkuas, blachan, sliced lower stems of lemon grass and turmeric to make a smooth paste.
4. Fry the spice paste in the oil to bring out the flavour, stirring all the time. Add half the tamarind juice, cook for 2 minutes, then stir in the remainder plus the coconut milk.
5. Add the aubergine pieces and leave to cook till tender – about 20 minutes. Now add the fish and cook for only 3–4 minutes. Taste for seasoning and serve.

Serves 3–4

ACAR IKAN
Malay fish pickle

450 g/1 lb mackerel fillets, cubed or left whole
salt
6 tablespoons oil
4 tablespoons vinegar made up to 300 ml/½ pint with water
2 tablespoons soft brown muscovado sugar

3 red, 3 green chillies, deseeded
5 cm/2 in piece fresh ginger
2 small onions, peeled and quartered
2 cloves garlic, peeled and crushed
3 macadamia nuts or 6 blanched almonds
1 teaspoon ground turmeric

1. Sprinkle the fish with the salt. Fry in 3 tablespoons of the oil to brown on both sides. Lift out into a glass or non-corrosive dish.
2. Bring the vinegar and water to the boil. Add the sugar and boil for 3 minutes, then set aside.
3. Cut 1 red and the 3 green chillies into fine strips. Finely shred half the ginger and slice 1 quartered onion thinly from top to root, which results in attractive slices. Set these aside.
4. Prepare the spice paste by placing the 2 remaining chillies, the remaining onion, the garlic, macadamia nuts or almonds, the remaining ginger and the turmeric in a food processor and blending to a paste. Fry this in the remaining oil to bring out the flavour fully.
5. Add the vinegar and water mixture, cook for 2–3 minutes then

add the reserved ginger, onion and chilli strips. Pour over the fish. Cover and leave for 12–24 hours before serving.

Serves 8 as part of a buffet

SOTONG SAMBAL
Stuffed squid in sauce

8 squid weighing 350 g/12 oz altogether and approx. 10 cm/4 in long

STUFFING

175 g/6 oz white fish, skinned and boned
2.5 cm/1 in piece fresh ginger, peeled and finely sliced

2 spring onions, finely chopped
salt
50 g/2 oz cooked prawns, roughly chopped

SAMBAL SAUCE

4 macadamia nuts or blanched almonds
1 cm/½ in piece lengkuas, peeled
2 stems lemon grass
1 cm/½ in prepared blachan (see page 228)
4 red chillies, deseeded

175 g/6 oz small onions, peeled
4–6 tablespoons oil
450 ml/¾ pint coconut milk (see page 231)
salt to taste
lime juice (optional)

1. Clean the squid as shown overleaf, but leave whole.
2. Pound the white fish, ginger, spring onions and salt to a paste. Turn into a bowl and stir in the roughly chopped prawns.
3. Divide this mixture between the squid. I use a forcing bag fitted with a large plain pipe. Put the heads back into position and secure with a toothpick.
4. Pound the nuts, lengkuas, lower stems of lemon grass (bruise the rest of the lemon grass stems to use later), blachan, chillies and onions to a paste. Fry in the oil to bring out the full flavours.
5. Add the coconut milk, and the remaining lemon grass stems and stir till the sauce comes to the boil. Simmer for 5 minutes, then add the sotong or squid with salt to taste and cook for a further 15–20 minutes. Taste again and add lime juice if liked. Serve with freshly boiled rice.

Serves 2 hungry people, or 8 as part of a large buffet

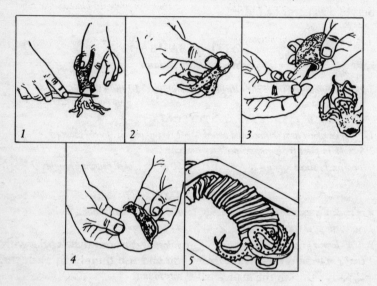

PREPARING SQUID

1 Cut the tentacles from the head and discard.

2 Squeeze the tentacle gently to remove the central bone.

3 Using your fingers, pull the quill and innards from the body cavity and discard.

4 Pull off and discard the body's mottled skin, which should come off easily.

5 Wash the squid well. Either leave whole for stuffing or cut into rings.

CHILLI KEPETING
Singapore-style chilli crabs

2 cooked crabs, weighing 1kg/2¼ lb
  each
175 g/6 oz shallots or onions, peeled
2 cloves garlic, peeled
2.5 cm/1 in ginger, peeled
6 red chillies, deseeded, or 1½ teaspoons
  chilli powder

1 cm/½ in prepared blachan (see page
  228)
1 stem lemon grass
6 tablespoons oil
150 ml/5 fl oz tomato ketchup
1 tablespoon brown sugar
450 ml/¾ pint boiling water
salt

To garnish

50 g/2 oz crushed peanuts

To serve

hot French bread

1. Twist off the large claws. Turn the crabs onto their backs with the head furthest away from you and use thumbs to push the body up from the main shell.
2. Remove the stomach and dead men's fingers (lungs), which are easily recognizable. Use a large cleaver to cut the body shell in half and then the body.
3. Crack the claws with the blade of the cleaver or a hammer. Use a short, sharp tap to crack, not splinter, the shells.
4. Make the spice paste: pound the shallots or onions with the garlic, ginger, chillies or chilli powder, blachan and the lower part of the lemon grass stem. Fry this paste in the oil in a large wok, stirring all the time to bring out the flavour.
5. Add the ketchup, brown sugar and boiling water to make a coating sauce, then taste for seasoning. Add the crabs and cook over a high heat until thoroughly heated through.
6. Turn into a serving dish (or leave in the wok) and scatter with the peanuts. Serve with French bread to soak up the sauce, and give your guests a damp cloth for wiping their hands during and after eating.

Serves 4

IKAN LEMAK
Sweet and sour fish

*1 whole snapper (675 g/1½ lb),
   head on, cleaned and scaled*
seasoning
5 shallots, chopped
2 cloves garlic
2 red chillies, deseeded and sliced
*2.5 cm/1 in piece ginger, peeled and
   sliced*
200 ml/⅓ pint oil for frying

*1 medium onion, peeled and cut into
   rings*
salt
1–2 teaspoons sugar
*1 teaspoon tamarind pulp soaked in 2
   tablespoons warm water and strained*
*300 ml/½ pint coconut milk (see page
   231)*

To garnish

shredded spring onion

1. Wipe the fish and make 3 slashes on each side. Rub with salt and pepper.
2. Roughly pound together the shallots, garlic, chillies and ginger.
3. Heat the oil in a wok or deep frying pan and cook the fish for 8–10 minutes or until cooked through, turning once. Lift out into an ovenproof dish and keep warm.
4. Pour away all except 4 tablespoons of the oil; the remainder can be kept if liked. Add the spice paste and cook to bring out the flavour of the chilli. Add the onion rings, salt and sugar to taste.
5. Mix the tamarind juice with 2–3 tablespoons of coconut cream from the top of the coconut milk. Strain into the pan, stir well, then add the remaining coconut milk to make a sauce of a light, coating consistency. Cook for 2–3 minutes over low heat.
6. Pour the sauce over the fish and serve garnished with shredded spring onion. Eat with rice and stir-fry mixed vegetables.

Serves 2, or 6 as part of a buffet

IKAN MOOLIE
Mild fish curry

This fish curry is one of my favourites with its delicate flavour and pretty, pale-yellow curry sauce. All the ingredients can be prepared well ahead then the cooking can be done at the last minute.

450 g/1 lb fish fillet, such as cod or
    haddock
salt
50 g/2 oz desiccated coconut, dry fried
    and pounded (see page 232)
3 small onions, peeled
2 cloves garlic, peeled
2.5 cm/1 in piece ginger, peeled and
    sliced

2 stems lemon grass
2 teaspoons turmeric powder
3 tablespoons groundnut oil
600 ml/1 pint coconut milk (see page
    231)

TO GARNISH
2 fresh chillies, deseeded and shredded

1. Skin the fish and cut into cubes, then sprinkle with salt.
2. Pound the onions, garlic, ginger and lower stems of the lemon grass with the turmeric. Fry this paste in the oil in a wok to bring out the flavour. Do not allow to brown.
3. Spoon off 3 tablespoons of cream from the top of the coconut milk then add the milk to the spice paste, stirring all the time till it comes to the boil. Reduce the heat and simmer for two minutes.
4. Add the cubes of fish and cook for 3–4 minutes only before stirring in the pounded coconut and the coconut cream. Turn into a serving bowl and top with the shredded chilli. Serve hot with freshly cooked rice.

Serves 3

TSUI CHI
Anita's crystal chicken

1.4 kg/3 lb chicken, fresh, not frozen   *1–2 tablespoons soy sauce*
2.5 cm/1 in piece fresh ginger, bruised   *1 teaspoon sesame oil*
6 spring onions   *sesame seeds*
salt

1. Rinse and dry the chicken. Place the bruised ginger and two of the spring onions in the body cavity. Place the chicken in a large pan and cover with cold water. Add salt, then bring to the boil, and cook for 20 minutes. Turn off the heat and leave for at least 3 hours.
2. Lift the chicken out of the water (this can be used as a stock to make soup) and allow to drain, then rub all over with soy sauce to make it look golden. Drizzle over the sesame oil and rub into the breast and legs.
3. Just before the chicken is to be served, cut into manageable-sized portions: cut off the legs first and divide into two at the joint. Then cut the wings with some of the breast and the remaining breast portions.
4. Assemble on a serving platter and garnish with sesame seeds and the remaining spring onions, made into curls (see page 240).

Serves 4, or 8 as part of a buffet

AH MOI'S RENDANG
Chicken curry

This rendang is frequently served at Sunday lunch tiffin at many of the clubs in Malaysia and Singapore. Traditionally a rendang should be cooked till almost all the liquid is absorbed. This recipe is for a moister curry, which I prefer.

*1 fresh 1.6 kg/3½ lb chicken, jointed
into 8 pieces (see page 59)
1 tablespoon sugar
4 small red or white onions, peeled and
roughly chopped
2 cloves garlic, peeled and roughly
chopped
2.5 cm/1 in piece fresh ginger, peeled
and roughly chopped
5 cm/2 in piece fresh lengkuas
2 stems lemon grass*

*5 tablespoons coconut oil or vegetable oil
1–1½ tablespoons chilli powder, or to
taste
600 ml/1 pint coconut milk (see page
231)
salt to taste
75 g/3 oz unsweetened desiccated
coconut, dry fried and pounded (see
page 232)
2 pandan leaves, scraped with a fork
and tied in a knot*

1. Rinse the chicken pieces and dry on kitchen paper. Place in a bowl, sprinkle with the sugar and toss to release the juices.
2. Pound the onions, garlic, ginger and lengkuas with the lower stems of the lemon grass until fine. Fry for several minutes in the oil in a wok to bring out the flavour.
3. Lower the heat, add the chilli powder and cook for 3–4 minutes stirring all the time as the mixture comes to the boil to prevent curdling, then add salt and 4 tablespoons of thick coconut cream, spooned off the top of the coconut milk.
4. Add the chicken pieces, turning frequently so that the rendang mixture coats each piece. Reduce heat and stir in the remaining coconut milk. Bruise the tops of the lemon grass and add to the wok with the pandan leaves. Cook over a gentle heat for 45–50 minutes or till the chicken is tender.
5. Just before serving spoon some of the sauce into the pounded coconut. Mix well, then return this to the pan. Stir without breaking up the chicken and cook for a further 5 minutes. Remove the pandan leaves if preferred.
6. Serve with white rice and accompaniments such as pineapple and cucumber sambal (see page 62).

Serves 4, or 8 as part of a buffet

GINGER CHICKEN OR DUCK

Duck breasts, which are available from supermarkets, are an interesting alternative to the chicken normally used in this recipe.

2 boned chicken or duck breasts,
    weighing 350 g/12 oz
salt, pepper and a little sugar
5 cm/2 in piece ginger, peeled and sliced
2 tablespoons sesame or groundnut oil

150 ml/5 fl oz water
1 tablespoon brandy
1 teaspoon cornflour mixed to a paste
    with 2 tablespoons water
1 teaspoon thin soy sauce

To garnish

coriander sprigs

1. Cut the chicken breasts into 6 pieces each. If using duck, remove the fat and slice the meat very thinly. Season, and sprinkle the slices with sugar to release the juices.
2. Fry the ginger slices in the sesame or groundnut oil. Do not allow to brown. Add the chicken or duck pieces and fry for 3–4 minutes.
3. Pour in the water, cover and cook till tender, then add the brandy. Thicken the sauce with the cornflour paste, and stir in the soy sauce.
4. Taste, and serve garnished with the coriander. Eat with rice or noodles.

Serves 2

ENCIK KEBIN
Spicy deep-fried chicken

1.4 kg/3 lb chicken

Marinade

1 tablespoon coriander seeds
1 teaspoon fennel seeds
½ teaspoon cumin seeds
1 teaspoon ground turmeric
1 tablespoon chilli powder

2.5 cm/1 in piece fresh ginger, peeled
120 ml/4 fl oz coconut milk (see page
    231)
salt to taste
oil for deep frying

To garnish

wedges of cucumber

1. Wipe the chicken. Remove the legs and cut each into 4 pieces. Cut away the wing and breast portions and cut each into two, making 16 pieces in all (see below).
2. Dry fry the coriander, fennel and cumin seeds, then pound in a pestle and mortar. Add the turmeric and chilli powder.
3. Finely grate the ginger onto a plate so that you collect any juices too. Add to the spice mixture with the coconut milk and salt. Pour it over the sixteen chicken pieces in a bowl. Leave to marinate for about one hour.
4. Lift the chicken pieces out of the marinade, drain and fry in hot oil for 2 minutes then reduce the heat and fry for a further 8–10 minutes or until the chicken pieces are cooked through. Pile on a serving plate and garnish with the cucumber.

Makes 16 pieces

DIVIDING A CHICKEN
INTO 16 PORTIONS

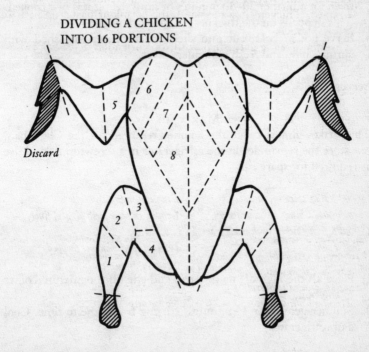

Discard

CHA SHAO
Barbecued roast pork

900 g/2 lb pork fillets, trimmed   1 tablespoon honey
250 ml/9 fl oz marinade (see below)   3 tablespoons Chinese wine or sherry

TO GARNISH
chopped spring onion   coriander leaves

1. Marinate the fillets overnight or for at least 8 hours, spooning over the marinade occasionally.
2. Drain and reserve the sauce. Place the meat on a metal grid over a roasting tin containing water to a 1 cm/½ in depth. Set in a hot oven (200°C, 400°F, Gas Mark 6) and roast for 20 minutes.
3. Add the honey and Chinese wine or sherry to the reserved marinade and turn the pieces of meat in this, then return to the oven for a further 20–30 minutes or until the meat is just cooked. This depends on the thickness of the pork fillets.
4. Serve hot or cold, cut into slices, on a platter garnished with spring onion and fresh coriander leaves.

Serves 6–8

MARINADE
This makes almost twice the amount required for the Cha Shao, but store the remainder in the refrigerator in a screwtop jar and use as required for spare ribs.

150 ml/5 fl oz thick soy sauce   1 tablespoon brown sugar
6 tablespoons Chinese wine or sherry   1 cm/½ in piece fresh ginger, finely
150 ml/5 fl oz chicken stock made from   sliced
     half a cube   1½ tablespoons onion, chopped

1. Place all the ingredients in a pan and stir till the mixture comes to the boil.
2. Simmer gently for 15 minutes, stirring from time to time. Cool and refrigerate.

DAGING ASSAM
Beef with tamarind

2 tablespoons tamarind puree in 750 ml/1¼ pints warm water
900 g/2 lb good-quality stewing beef, trimmed and cut into even-sized pieces
1 cm/½ in prepared blachan (see page 228)
4 macadamia nuts or blanched almonds

2 medium onions, peeled
2.5 cm/1 in piece lengkuas, peeled
½–1 tablespoon chilli powder
1 teaspoon ground turmeric
4 tablespoons vegetable oil
salt
2 teaspoons muscovado sugar (optional)

To garnish
thin slivers of red or green chillies, or crispy fried onions (see page 200)

1. Leave the tamarind to soak in the water for 20 minutes. Strain and reserve the liquid.
2. Make the spice paste by pounding the blachan, macadamia or almonds, onions and lengkuas to a fine paste. Add the chilli and turmeric.
3. Fry the spice paste in the oil to bring out the flavour, stirring all the time. Add the meat and stir so that it is coated with the paste. Reduce the heat and cook for 5–8 minutes till the meat is nicely browned.
4. Add the tamarind juice and bring to the boil. Taste for salt and add sugar if liked. Simmer for 1½–2 hours or until the meat is tender. Serve garnished with strips of chilli or fried onions.

Serves 6–8

ANITA WONG'S VEGI
Chinese-style vegetables

1–1½ tablespoons oil
pinch of sugar
450 g/1 lb spinach, chard, kale, Chinese leaves or kai lan, washed
1–2 tablespoons oyster sauce, mixed with 1 tablespoon boiling water

1–2 cloves garlic, peeled and finely sliced
a little sesame oil
a few sesame seeds (optional)

1. Bring a large pan of salted water to the boil. Add ½ teaspoon of the oil, and the sugar.
2. Plunge the vegetable into the pan for less than a minute. Use a collapsible vegetable strainer if you have one so that the vegetable does not have a chance to overcook.
3. Lift out and immediately plunge the vegetable into cold or iced water to halt the cooking, then pour boiling water from the pan over the vegetable and drain well. Arrange on a serving dish and drizzle over the oyster sauce.
4. Heat the remaining oil in a small frying pan or wok. Add the garlic slices and fry till just turning golden. Scatter this over the vegetable then finish off with a little sesame oil which has been warmed in the same pan, and sesame seeds if liked.

Serves 4–6

SAMBAL NANAS
Pineapple and cucumber sambal

½ fresh ripe pineapple	*1 cm/½ in prepared blachan (see page*
½ cucumber	*228)*
50 g/2 oz dried shrimps	*juice of 1 large lemon or lime*
1 large red chilli, deseeded	*brown sugar to taste (optional)*

1. Trim the base of the pineapple and cut away the pines in slices from top to bottom, then discard. Cut the pineapple into slices, removing the central core. Cut into neat, even-sized pieces and set aside.
2. Trim the ends from the cucumber and cut into similar-sized pieces. Sprinkle with salt and set aside.
3. Place the dried shrimps in a food processor and chop fairly finely. Add the chilli, prepared blachan and lemon or lime juice and mix again.
4. Rinse the cucumber and dry on kitchen paper. Turn the cucumber and pineapple into a bowl and chill. Just before serving, spoon in the spice mixture with sugar to taste. Mix very well and serve with rendang (see page 56).

Serves 8–10 as an accompaniment

SAMBAL KELAPA
Coconut sambal

50 g/2 oz dried prawns
175 g/6 oz desiccated coconut
2 red chillies, deseeded
1 medium onion, peeled and sliced

1 clove garlic, peeled
1 stem lemon grass
3–4 tablespoons oil

1. Pound the dried prawns until fairly fine, then add to the coconut.
2. Pound the chillies, onion, garlic and the lower 6 cm/2½ in of the lemon grass stem, then heat the oil and fry this spice paste, turning all the time to bring out the flavour.
3. Add the coconut and prawns and keep stirring till the coconut is golden and crisp. Taste for seasoning then allow to go cold. Use with curries as an accompaniment and store any leftover in a screwtop jar in the refrigerator. It will keep for several weeks.

Serves 8 as an accompaniment

SAMBAL BLACHAN
Chilli and shrimp paste sambal

2–3 fresh red chillies, deseeded and sliced
salt

1 cm/½ in square prepared blachan (see page 228)
juice of ½ lemon or lime

1. Pound the chillies with a little salt in a pestle and mortar rather than the food processor, as it is a very small quantity.
2. Add the prepared blachan and lemon or lime juice to taste. Serve as an accompaniment to any rice-based meal. It is best made in small quantities. Vary the amount of chilli and blachan to your taste but remember a little goes a long way, especially for the uninitiated.

CHAR KWAY TEOW
Stir fry noodles with pork

This is a favourite food which is likely to be available round the clock from a number of stalls throughout Kuala Lumpur. Follow the hawkers' speedy cooking and serving by always preparing all the ingredients for a stir fry *before* you start cooking.

225 g/8 oz packet frozen cockles or prawns
3–4 Chinese sausages (see page 230)
675 g/1½ lb flat rice noodles (kway teow), frozen
2 chillies, deseeded
3 cloves garlic, crushed

bacon or pork fat, or 3–4 tablespoons oil for frying
50 ml/2 fl oz warm water
2 eggs, beaten
1 tablespoon thick soy sauce
2 tablespoons thin soy sauce
225 g/8 oz packet fresh beansprouts

To garnish
chopped spring onion tops

To serve
bottled chilli sauce

1. Thaw the cockles or prawns and place in bowl.
2. Steam the Chinese sausages for about 20 minutes. Cool for a few minutes then slice thinly at an angle.
3. Place the noodles in a large colander and set the kettle to boil. Pour boiling water over the noodles just before needed and drain well. Cut into thin strips.
4. Pound the chillies and garlic together finely in a pestle and mortar. Fry these in the hot fat or oil without browning.
5. Add the drained noodles and toss well, sprinkling with the warm water as you cook. Push to one side then add the beaten eggs and quickly stir in with the noodles so that you now have little flecks of egg here and there.
6. Stir in the cockles or prawns, and sausages then the soy sauces and beansprouts. Do not overcook. Taste for seasoning.

7. Serve immediately, garnished with chopped spring onion tops and chilli sauce for the enthusiasts!

Serves 6–8

HOKKIEN MEE
Fried Hokkien noodles

350 g/12 oz squid, cleaned (see page 52)
225 g/8 oz pork fillet, thinly sliced
2–3 tablespoons oil
4 cloves garlic, crushed
100 g/4 oz cooked prawns
2 stems Chinese leaves or mustard
   greens, torn

675 g/1½ lb fresh yellow noodles or
   350 g/12 oz dried noodles, cooked (see
   page 239)
150 ml/5 fl oz hot stock or water
1 tablespoon thick soy sauce
salt to taste

To garnish

chopped spring onion tops
shredded lettuce leaves

1 lime, cut into wedges

1. Cut the body sacs of the squid into rings and leave the heads intact.
2. Fry the pork in 1 tablespoon of the oil in a wok, turning frequently so that the pork is cooked all over. Remove from the pan. Add the extra oil to the wok and stir in the garlic. Do not allow to brown.
3. Add the squid to the wok first, stirring for 2–3 minutes, then add the prawns and the torn leaves or mustard greens. Toss well.
4. Add the noodles, turn up the heat and keep moving all the ingredients so that they are hot. Add the pork, stock or water, soy sauce and salt to taste. Reduce heat, cover and leave for 1–2 minutes.
5. Serve in individual bowls garnished with chopped spring onion tops, a fringe of shredded lettuce and a wedge of lime which can be squeezed over the top.

Serves 6

NASI LEMAK
Breakfast coconut rice

If there is a universally popular breakfast dish in Malaysia and Singapore this is it. The really hungry, such as the rubber tappers who have been working since dawn, may eat their nasi lemak with a chicken or fish curry. Others might settle for deep-fried ikan bilis (page 236), a hard-boiled egg, chunks of cucumber and a chilli sambal.

600 ml/1 pint coconut milk (see page 231)

1 stem lemon grass, bruised

225 g/8 oz long grain rice, washed several times

salt to taste

To garnish

fresh coriander sprigs

1. Rinse a heavy-based pan with water then pour in the coconut milk. Add the bruised lemon grass stem and bring to the boil, then lift off the heat and stir in the rice and salt.
2. Return to the heat and bring to the boil, stirring occasionally, then cover and cook over the lowest possible heat for 12 minutes or until the rice is tender.
3. Stir with a chopstick or a fork. Leave, covered, in a warm place till required.
4. Remove the lemon grass before serving. Garnish with chilli and coriander and/or some of the suggested accompaniments.

Serves 4

SAYUR CAMPUR
Stir fry vegetables

4 Chinese mushrooms, soaked in warm water for 10 minutes

2 teaspoons cornflour

2 cloves garlic, crushed

1 cm/1/2 in fresh ginger, peeled and finely shredded

1 small onion, peeled and finely sliced

6 tablespoons oil

soy sauce to taste

A selection of the following vegetables:

225 g/8 oz carrots, peeled and diagonally sliced

½ each green and red pepper, deseeded and sliced

½ cauliflower in tiny florets

50 g/2 oz mangetout

1 small bangkuang (Chinese turnip) peeled and cut into matchstick pieces

225 g/8 oz Chinese leaves, shredded

100 g/4 oz beansprouts

To garnish

finely shredded spring onions

1. Drain the mushrooms and use some of the water to make a thickening paste with the cornflour. Reserve the remainder. Slice the mushrooms finely, discarding the stalks.
2. Fry the garlic, ginger, and onion in the oil in a wok to bring out the flavour but do not allow to brown.
3. Now add the longest-cooking vegetables, such as the carrot and cauliflower, followed after a few minutes by the other vegetables, stirring all the time with a slice so that they are evenly cooked.
4. Add the mushroom slices and then a little of the reserved soaking liquid. Cover and cook for 1 minute.
5. Add the cornflour paste, stirring all the time. This will give the vegetables a glossy appearance. Add a dash of soy sauce then taste for seasoning.
6. Serve from the wok or transfer to a serving platter, and garnish with the spring onions.

Serves 6

AH MOI'S MEE
Stir fry noodles

350 g/12 oz fresh mee noodles

4–6 Chinese mushrooms, soaked in warm water for 15 minutes

100 g/4 oz prawns

100 g/4 oz cooked chicken, finely sliced

100 g/4 oz kai lan, mustard greens or choi sum, torn into shreds

1 egg, beaten

seasoning

4–5 tablespoons oil

3 cloves garlic, crushed

1 onion, peeled and sliced

1 cm/½ in piece ginger, peeled and finely shredded

oyster or soy sauce

To garnish

omelette made from egg (above)

1 spring onion, sliced

100 g/4 oz crabmeat (optional)

1. Cook the mee noodles in a large pan of boiling water for about 3 minutes, rinse, drain and set aside. Slice the mushrooms, discard stalks, and keep the soaking liquid. Place prawns, chicken slices and torn greens into separate bowls.
2. Beat the egg with 1 tablespoon of water and add seasoning. Heat 1 tablespoon of the oil in a wok or frying pan, pour in the beaten egg and swirl round to make a thin omelette which will only be cooked on one side. If a very small pan is used make two.
3. Flick the omelette over at one end and roll up into a sausage shape. When cool slice across into rings and keep for garnish.
4. Add the remaining oil to the pan and fry the garlic, onion and ginger without browning. Add the chicken slices and prawns, followed quickly by the green vegetables. Stir all the time.
5. Add the mushrooms then the noodles, plus enough mushroom soaking liquid to keep the dish moist. Finally add the oyster or soy sauce and taste for seasoning. Arrange on a warmed serving platter with a garnish of crab, if using, omelette strips and spring onion.

Serves 3–4

ACAR TIMUN
Cucumber and vegetable pickle

1 cucumber
2 carrots, peeled
2 medium onions, peeled
salt
4 tablespoons oil
2 cloves garlic, crushed
1 teaspoon chilli powder
1 teaspoon turmeric

150 ml/5 fl oz rice wine vinegar
75 ml/3 fl oz water
25 g/1 oz brown sugar, or to taste
2 tablespoons tomato ketchup
1 red and 1 green chilli, deseeded and
finely sliced
5 cm/2 in piece ginger, peeled and finely
sliced

1. Cut the cucumber, carrot and onion into neat, bite-sized pieces. Sprinkle with salt and leave for several hours, then wash thoroughly and dry on absorbent kitchen paper or a cloth.
2. Heat the oil and fry the garlic, chilli powder and turmeric. Stir in the vinegar, water, sugar and tomato ketchup.
3. Add the vegetables, sliced chillies and ginger and toss over a gentle heat for a few minutes.
4. Serve when cold with a variety of curry dishes.

Serves 6–8 as accompaniment

GULA MELAKA
Three-palm pudding

This is one of the best-known puddings ·throughout South-East Asia. For most people sago immediately transports them back to school days where it was appropriately known as 'frog spawn'. That said, one taste of this pudding will dispel all those unkind memories.

Gula melaka is known as the 'three-palm pudding': sago from the sago palm, dark sugar from the nippah palm and coconut milk from the coconut palm. Originally sago came exclusively from the sago palm but a lot of our sago comes from the root of the cassava these days. The sago palm usually grows in a swampy spot, several in a clump, and takes up to fifteen years to mature. It flowers, then promptly dies. The fallen tree is then split open and the fleshy starch scooped out of it. This is washed and passed through fine sieves to make the little grains, or pearls as they are known, which are processed and dried. Huge quantities of sago originally came from Borneo where the palm grows profusely. Now it is cultivated in Indonesia.

Similarly the nippah palm, which produces the sugar for this pudding, grows in a swampy place. The crown of the palm is tapped, giving the rich, dark-brown sugar, which is formed into wheel-like cakes and wrapped in strips of palm fronds.

225 g/8 oz sago, washed several times   *1 egg white, stiffly whisked*
2 tablespoons coconut cream (see page 231)

Syrup

150 g/5 oz palm sugar or dark brown   *slice fresh ginger*
  sugar such as muscovado   *1 pandan leaf (if available)*
150 ml/5 fl oz water

To serve

300 ml/½ pint thick coconut milk (see page 231)

1. Bring a large pan of water to the boil, add the sago and cook till the granules become clear, stirring frequently. This will take 12–15 minutes. Strain through a sieve, washing well with cold running water until all the starch is removed.
2. Turn into a bowl, add the coconut cream, then fold in the stiffly whisked egg white and pour into a 1 litre/1¾ pint dish or individual serving dishes. Leave for at least 6 hours in the refrigerator to set.
3. Prepare the syrup by dissolving the palm sugar with the water in a pan. Add the slice of ginger and pandan leaf, if using. Cook for several minutes until the syrup thickens, then remove the pandan leaf and ginger and leave to cool.
4. Each guest pours the sugar syrup and coconut milk over their helping at the table. Stir the coconut milk before serving as the cream will have floated to the top.

Serves 8

SERIKAYA
Malay coconut custard

*600 ml/1 pint coconut milk (see page
  231)*
1 pandan leaf

*4 eggs and 2 extra yolks
75 g/3 oz caster sugar*

To garnish
toasted or dry-fried coconut

1. Warm the coconut milk without letting it boil. Use a fork to run through the pandan leaf, which will release the flavour. Tie in a knot and pop into the milk. Set aside for 15 minutes.
2. Whisk the eggs and egg yolks with the caster sugar. Stir in the coconut milk and remove the leaf.
3. Pour into a 1 litre/1¾ pint buttered ovenproof soufflé or baking dish and cover with foil. Cook in a steamer for 1¼ hours or until set when tested with a knife. Alternatively bake in a moderate oven (160°C, 325°F, Gas Mark 3) for the same time, but set the dish into a roasting tin of warm water to prevent the mixture overheating.
4. Chill in the refrigerator before serving. The top could be decorated with some dry-fried or toasted coconut if you like.

Serves 6–8

Burma

'This is Burma and it will be quite unlike any land you know about.' Rudyard Kipling's words, written early this century, convey the mystery and fascination of this, the Golden Land.

The Irrawaddy, the famous river immortalized by Kipling as the 'Road to Mandalay', rises high in the Himalayas almost 1000 miles from its mouth. North of Rangoon the river fans out into a delta flowing into the Bay of Bengal. Shaped like a kite, Burma shares common borders with Bangladesh, India, China and Thailand. Over the centuries the comings and goings between Burma and these countries either in peace or in war have left their mark.

Marco Polo was an early visitor to Pagan in 1298, followed in the early 16th century by the Portuguese and a century later by the British, French and Dutch, who set up trading posts. The British 'stayed on' after the third Anglo-Burmese war in 1885–86 at which time Burma became a colony. The Indian army and civil servants came in substantial numbers then, but most have now left. The country was overrun by the Japanese in 1941 and recaptured by the allies in 1945. Independence was granted in 1948, and in 1962 the country's future was decided with its own brand of socialism, a path which it still follows today.

The Burmese people are made up of an amazing number of ethnic groups – well over fifty. The largest are the Chins, the Shans (hill farmers), the Karen, the Kachin, the Arakanese, the Mon, and the Burmans. A good eighty per cent of Burma's people work in the rural areas, which is a great blessing – there has not been the drift to the towns with its inevitable problems. Another of Burma's blessings is that it has not had the population explosion which happens in so many Third World countries. Though poor by any standards, no one goes hungry.

Burma is off the tourist trail and clearly intends to stay that way. From this you might imagine that the people would be unwelcoming. Not a bit of it. I enjoyed generous hospitality from complete strangers, which I still remember with deep affection.

The serenity of the Burmese comes from an inner peace brought about by their deep Buddhist faith – it is truly a way of life, followed by the whole family on a daily basis and embracing rich and poor alike. The five great precepts of Buddhism forbid stealing, adultery, lying, drinking alcohol and the taking of life. You might wonder how they square the latter with the eating of fish, poultry and meat. They have the simplest of answers: the fishermen claim that they are saving the fish from drowning, whilst meat and poultry can be purchased with equanimity as long as the animal has not been ordered to be killed by the eventual purchaser. As it happens, the butchers are in the main Chinese or Muslim.

I am indebted to Mary San Lin, who has lived in Rangoon for over thirty years, for showing me round the city. The capital of Burma has certainly seen better days, but it was built to impress all those years ago. The tall, handsome, Victorian buildings with beautiful balconies and solid portals show decades of neglect; the pavements, where they exist, are broken with slabs missing. Cars, lorries and buses are all very dated, and there is a good number of World War II jeeps around.

From first thing in the morning till about 9 P.M. when everything shuts down you can buy Burma's favourite food, *mohinga*, a curry-flavoured fish soup, from the hawkers and stallholders in the market or on the pavements. Noodles are piled high in banana-leaf-lined bowls, a huge pot of the *mohinga* bubbles away, little extras – finely chopped shallots, extra chillies, lemon or lime wedges, and crispy fritters – are ready to be crumbled on top of the noodles and soup in the bowl. Customers sit down on simple stools and tuck in to this fiery fare with enormous relish (recipe page 83). Another popular dish, which emphasizes the strong links with Chinese food, is fried Shan noodles. Pork, spices, onion and tomato are cooked first, then the noodles, all cooked 'stir fry' style. Omelette strips are added next, and each serving is topped with a few chopped chives and a squeeze of lime. A clear soup made from the pork bones is eaten at the same time. Extra accompaniments might be a drizzling of dried chilli which has been powdered and fried in oil, and crisp-fried garlic or shallots, with maybe a few coriander leaves.

Those with a sweet tooth can also buy one *kyat*'s (pronounced 'chat') worth of *san win ma kin* (recipe page 104). It is a semolina-based pudding, made with coconut milk and baked in a large, shallow, stainless steel dish till the top is a rich golden brown. A portion is spooned onto a glossy banana leaf and deftly folded into a parcel.

A heady aroma of spices pervades Bogyoke market, still called Scott market by anyone over twenty. Fresh and ground chillies, turmeric, coriander and cumin are all for sale in pyramid-like mounds. Dried octopus, squid and prawns are very popular, and turtle eggs are available too. Ice is bought by the sack and peanut oil for cooking is sold in four-gallon tins. Shiny cooking containers with a lid but no handles (*degshee*) and large Chinese woks caught my eye on my visit there. The biggest wok I have ever seen was on my way up to Schwedagon Pagoda a few days later – it must have been 60 cm/24 inches in diameter.

One stall in the market sells nothing but cheroots, tied into neat bundles and stacked high to the roof. The outer wrapping leaf is picked from a tree in the Shan states. Tobacco is shredded with tamarind juice and some nuts and left to dry for two days before wrapping the cheroot. A filter is made from the dried outer skin of the maize cob. You buy four for one *kyat* – ten pence. At that price no wonder they are so popular.

The next part of the market is a shock to the system. When I was there 225 g/8 oz tins of Sainsbury's drinking chocolate were selling at £18, there were bars of chocolate, Maxwell House coffee, HP sauce, and Crawford's cream crackers at £5. This is the 'black market', stuffed with goodies openly on display and brought in by seamen or smugglers over the Thai/Burmese border. With the minimum wage of 6.5 *kyats* per day I wondered who could afford the astronomically priced luxuries. Indeed most government employees have such a struggle to make ends meet that many have a second job. Wives and children make their contribution too – the latter selling cheroots or even bottles of water in the streets.

Burma is truly a land of surprises. Strawberries were so unex-pected, along with exquisitely formed pink rosebuds which graced the dinner table on my first night in Rangoon. One of the most spectacular sights in Rangoon is the majestic Schwedagon Pagoda which is said to have been built 2,400 years ago and is entirely covered in gold leaf. It is believed that inside the massive gold stupa are eight hairs of the last Buddha as well as relics of the three previous Buddhas. The top of the pagoda, the *hti*, is set with diamonds, rubies, sapphires and topaz which glisten in the sun. There are dozens of other temples set around the Schwedagon complex, some white, some beautifully carved in teak. It is a breathtaking place to which I vowed to return. Thousands of visitors a year make the same pledge by ringing the massive Singu Min bell three times, which it is said ensures you will come back.

In the countryside acres and acres of *padi* stretch as far as the eye can see. Pagodas, some lovely and some neglected, punctuate the view. Tall palm trees (*palmyra*) grow freely and are tapped twice a day for their jaggery into little earthenware pots tied to the crown. This liquid is boiled to drive off the moisture, then cooled on trays or on bamboo mats to dry further, resulting in a delightful flavoured sugar broken into lumps and wrapped in a woven palm leaf box.

I visited Burma in late January when the rice harvest, a good one, was almost over. We passed huge 'rice mountains' in perfectly symmetrical shapes and watched men winnow the rice (in Africa it would have been the women!) with huge bamboo trays, while muzzled oxen trod the grain from the stems. A few miles further on we saw sacks of rice loaded into the Mandalay-Rangoon train (steam driven) and learned that the farmer can keep a quarter of his crop and sells the rest to the government for distribution.

Burma, once called the rice bowl of the world, has lost that crown to Thailand, its neighbour. In spite of this the country is self-sufficient and the farmer who harvests only one crop (in Malaysia it is two or even three crops a year) plants a cash crop of sunflower or beans to follow on. It cannot be an easy existence. Oxen are used for ploughing and for much of the transport, which accounts for the leisurely pace of life. There is no public transport in these areas, people wait for a lorry or a pick-up to pass by. If there isn't room they cling on somewhere – it is not unusual to see a lorry loaded with sacks of rice and about fifty passengers. Climbing up from the rich *padi* plains the land gradually becomes very arid, and new crops appear, such as groundnuts. Groundnut oil is popular for cooking in Burma, sesame oil too, which is another crop in this area. I asked about coconut oil, which is very popular for cooking in Malaysia, but was told that it is only used on the hair in Burma.

All over Burma the women wear thanaka bark powder on their faces. Sometimes it is applied in a circle or square shapes over the cheeks, with more on the forehead, frequently it is smoothed thinly all over the face. Its purpose is as a protection against the sun as well as softening and cooling the skin and enhancing the beauty. The thanaka tree (*linnoria acidissiura*) is a hardwood tree from upper Burma. A 20 cm/8 in length of this might cost forty *kyats*. The powder is made from the bark by rubbing on a flat stone, a *kyankpyin*, with a little water which results in a pale yellow paste. This collects in a groove round the edge of the stone. Nowadays it can be bought in powder or cake form.

On my visit to Magwe the market was crowded with people. Piles of glossy red onions, aubergines, tomatoes, chillies and green leaves were laid out on banana leaves or baskets, alongside dried fish, wet fish, and chickens squawking while the ox carts, bicycles and tongas trundled by. Magwe also has a massive market garden close by, in the middle of the mighty Irrawaddy. Islands are thrown up in the river as the water subsides after the rainy season. The rich fertile soil, enriched by the silt deposits, provides work for hundreds of local people and results in a wonderful array of fruit, vegetables and flowers. There is one difficulty though – after the floods the islands pop up in different places, which causes many a problem as several people may have a claim to the same piece of land. Magwe is 300 miles up country from Rangoon. When in flood the Irrawaddy is at this point a magnificent one and a half miles wide.

Pagan, with its pagoda-studded plain on the banks of the Irra-waddy, is unforgettable. Two thousand of the original pagodas still stand as a monument to Pagan's illustrious past – it was once the capital of Burma. Were this in any other country in the world its name would be as much on everyone's lips as the Taj Mahal or the Pyramids. Watching the sun set over the Irrawaddy here is a magical experience. The deep-orange sun slowly sinks behind the hills, almost illuminating the red bricks of the many temples near and far. The stillness of the evening is most poignant.

Modern Pagan is little more than a village, with only a handful of restaurants to choose from for the evening meal after a day spent visiting pagodas. Surprisingly every restaurant displays a huge menu board itemizing Chinese dishes with only a postscript for 'Burmese Curries'. It is true that the Burmese invariably eat Chinese food when they go out (just as we perhaps eat French and Italian), reserving their own dishes for home consumption.

However, we were lucky enough to eat several meals at a restaurant whose owner's name translates as 'Sharer of Paradise' and which served authentic Burmese fare. As is the custom all over Burma a pot of weak black tea was placed on the table with little cups. This is drunk throughout the meal, the pot replenished frequently without even asking. We ordered three curries – fish, pork and beef. These were served in small, deep bowls which is very traditional and logical – they accommodate the thin sauce and ensure that a substantial number of dishes can be fitted on the table at the same time. We had mixed vegetables – okra, cauliflower and beans with onion-flavoured oil as a dressing (see page 212) and scattered with sesame seeds; bitter gourd relish to which some *ngapi*, the Burmese fermented shrimp paste had been added, along with powdered prawn (page 242), pickled mango, shredded and left for three to five days in brine then drained, plus a fiery chilli accompaniment – dried pounded chillies fried in groundnut oil with powdered prawn. We finished our meal with slices of ripe papaya with a squeeze of lime and a dish of jaggery, the brown sugar lumps I have already described.

On another occasion we ate Irrawaddy fish with chilli and tomato, chicken curry, rice, snow peas (mangetout) and accompaniments as before. A dish of *lepet* followed, which was a new experience. The fermented green tea leaves had some shredded fresh ginger mixed into them and were served in a pile on a plate with peanuts and deep-fried dried beans. A multitude of other ingredients can be served with *lepet*: deep-fried crisp onions, slivers of garlic, toasted sesame seeds, and dried shrimp (see page 106). Later I bought a fat, sausage-shaped pack of *lepet* from the market wrapped up in banana leaf and tied with bamboo. I have not been able to locate a supplier in Britain, but some Burmese student friends came to my rescue with dried *lepet* which can be reconstituted with water. It is such a unique taste sensation. If the Burmese nation hold it in such high esteem, perhaps we are missing out. I leave it for you to decide!

Our farewell to Pagan had to end with a quick meal at a restaurant run by a lady whose name was Precious Diamond. With the customary tea on the table we asked for Burmese food. Soon a delicious chicken curry arrived with rice and a green tomato, onion and coriander salad with a dressing of crushed peanuts and peanut oil (see page 99). We drank lentil soup which seemed a strange choice but it is very traditional. Finally she brought us peanut brittle (page 105) and presented us with two more little packages for the journey. Little touches like that are so endearing and serve to underline the spontaneous generosity we enjoyed from day to day.

By this time I had begun seriously to question the bad press given to Burmese food – when I said that I was researching for a cookbook people made remarks like, 'It will be a slim volume then.' I think British food is burdened with the same view, yet if in either country you are lucky enough to be invited into someone's home those impressions are immediately dispelled.

I was invited to the house of a university professor for dinner while I was in Rangoon. The whole meal was served on traditional red, black and green lacquer plates. We ate Hilsa fish, an oily fish which is very bony but is cooked over a period of twelve hours so the bones soften and can be eaten. This was garnished with little onions and tomatoes. Courgettes were stuffed with pork and prawns and steamed; there was a pork curry, drumstick soup, and plenty of rice. We finished the meal with strawberries, and homemade ice cream.

Hand on heart I can say that Burmese hospitality is boundless and we felt immensely privileged when we were invited to share our last meal in Burma with U Saw N Paw and his family. His wife, Rebecca, gave us fish fritters, pork balls, spring rolls with a chilli sauce, and Burmese sausage (a close relation to the Chinese variety but smaller). Next came the second favourite national dish – *oh-no khaukswe*, a chicken curry in plenty of turmeric-coloured coconut sauce with noodles and accompaniments of hard-boiled egg, chopped onion, and chilli oil (recipe page 85). Finally we ate bananas and drank tea before bidding the family and Burma our fond farewells. Will the bell at the Schwedagon summon me back, I wonder? I'd like to think so.

HINCHO
Clear soup with powdered shrimp and vegetable

This soup is to be drunk at the same time as eating rice and curry.

*2.25 litres/4 pints chicken stock, made
    from carcasses left from chicken curry
    (see page 89)
50 g/2 oz dry powdered shrimp*

*2-3 tablespoons fish sauce (see page 234)
2-3 courgettes, coarsely grated and
    sprinkled with salt*

1. Bring the stock to the boil in a large pan. Add the powdered
   shrimp, then simmer for 10 minutes. Add the fish sauce.
2. Rinse and drain the courgettes and stir into the soup 3-4 minutes
   before serving.

Serves 8

HSAN BYOKE
Fish broth

*350 g/12 oz fish fillet, skinned and
    cubed
1 tablespoon soy sauce
salt and pepper to taste*

*1.75 litres/3 pints prepared fish stock
    (see page 40)
50 g/2 oz long grain rice*

Choose 350 g/12 oz vegetables from the following, with attention to
colour and texture:

finely shredded Chinese leaves, spinach, coarsely grated carrot, white radish, beans

1. Place the fish cubes in a bowl with the soy sauce and seasoning.
2. Pour the fish stock into a large saucepan and add the rice. Bring
   to the boil and cook for 10 minutes.
3. Add the fish to the pan, bring back to the boil and cook gently
   for 3 minutes. Add the vegetables and cook briskly for only 3-4
   minutes. Taste for seasoning and serve.

Serves 8

MOHINGA
Fish curry with noodles

In Burma mohinga has pieces of banana trunk in it, but I have substituted bamboo shoot as a more realistic alternative.

1.4 kg/3 lb huss (rock salmon), skinned but left on the bone

6 stems lemon grass

5 cm/2 in fresh ginger, scraped

2 teaspoons salt

3–4 tablespoons fish sauce (see page 234)

6 onions (approx 550 g/1¼ lb) peeled and quartered

6 cloves garlic, crushed

4–6 chillies, deseeded

2–3 teaspoons ground turmeric, or 5 cm/2 in piece fresh turmeric, scraped and pounded

100 ml/4 fl oz peanut or groundnut oil for frying

1.75 litres/3 pints coconut milk (see page 231)

50 g/2oz rice flour

50 g/2 oz gram or chickpea flour (besan)

540 g/19 oz can bamboo shoot, drained and diced

fresh coriander leaves

2 × 450 g/1 lb packet rice (lai fan) or egg noodles

CHILLI OIL

4 tablespoons oil

2 tablespoons chilli powder

ACCOMPANIMENTS

6 hard-boiled eggs, shelled and cut into wedges

2 onions, peeled and finely sliced

2–3 lemons or limes, cut into wedges

1 bunch spring onions, trimmed and finely shredded

pork crackling (chicaron – see page 235)

½ bunch coriander, chopped

crispy fries (see page 104)

balachuang (see page 100)

fried fish fritters (see page 102)

bitter melon relish (see page 103)

1. Rinse the fish and place in a large pan with sufficient water to cover. Trim the root ends from 4 of the lemon grass stems, then bruise the fleshy ends with a rolling pin.
2. Bruise half the ginger and add to the pan with the bruised lemon grass stems, salt and 2 tablespoons of the fish sauce. Bring to the boil and simmer for 10 minutes, then lift out the fish on a draining spoon and leave to cool.

3. Strain and measure the fish stock. There should be approximately 2 litres/3½ pints. Discard any bones from the fish, flake the flesh into small pieces and set aside.

4. Pound the lower part of the 2 remaining lemon grass stems with the remaining ginger, the onions, garlic, chillies and turmeric to a smooth paste. Heat the oil and fry the pounded ingredients to bring out the flavour, stirring throughout. Draw from the heat, stir in the flaked fish and set aside.

5. Add the coconut milk to the measured fish stock and make up to 4.5 litres/8 pints with water. Blend the rice flour and gram flours together to a smooth thin paste with some of this liquid.

6. Pour the remaining liquid into a very large pan, stir in the flour paste and continue stirring till the mixture has thickened slightly to a thin cream.

7. Add the bamboo shoot along with the spicy fish mixture and bring to the boil, stirring gently all the time. Taste for seasoning and add the remaining fish sauce. Set aside till required.

8. Make up the chilli oil: heat the oil in a small frying pan, then stir in the chilli powder. Stir for 2 minutes over a very gentle heat then draw aside and leave to cool. Drain off the oil into a small jug discarding any sediment. Drizzle this oil over the mohinga just before serving and scatter with the coriander leaves.

9. Serve mohinga with noodles (see below) and put the suggested accompaniments in small bowls.

Serves 10–12

NOODLES

1. Bring a large pan of salted water to the boil. Break up the noodles from one packet into approximately 10 cm/4 in lengths then add them to the pan. Return to the boil, then draw from the heat and leave on one side for 8 minutes.

2. Drain through a colander and rinse well under cold running water. Drain well again, lifting with your hands to get rid of excess water.

3. Repeat with another packet of noodles and serve on a large platter. Guests take some of the noodles, top with hot mohinga and surround with spoonfuls of the various accompaniments.

OH-NO KHAUKSWE
Curried chicken with noodles

1¾ kg/4 lb chicken, jointed into 4
salt
2 large onions, peeled
4 red chillies, deseeded
3 cloves garlic, peeled
2–3 teaspoons ground turmeric or 5 cm/
  2 in piece fresh turmeric, scraped and
  pounded

200 ml/7 fl oz groundnut oil
450 g/1 lb rice noodles (lai fan)
600 ml/1 pint prepared coconut milk
  (see page 231)
4 tablespoons gram flour (besan)
2 tablespoons fish sauce (see page 234)
seasoning

TO GARNISH
chilli oil (see page 83)　　　　　　*shredded spring onion*

ACCOMPANIMENTS
same as mohinga (see page 83)

1. Place the chicken in a large pan with the salt and add water to cover. Bring to the boil, cover and cook for ¾–1 hour or until the chicken is tender. Cool a little.
2. Lift the chicken out of the pan. Remove the meat from the bones, and cut into bite-sized pieces, discarding bones and skin. Measure the stock and reserve 1.5 litres/2½ pints.
3. Pound the onions, chillies and garlic with the turmeric until fine.
4. Heat 120 ml/4 fl oz of the oil in a wok or large pan and fry 50 g/ 2 oz of the rice noodles. They will become puffy and crisp in just a few seconds. Drain on absorbent kitchen paper and reserve.
5. Now fry the onion mixture in the remaining oil to bring out the flavour. Stir in the stock and coconut milk and simmer for 10–15 minutes.
6. Ten minutes before serving blend the gram flour with water to make a thin cream. Add a few spoonfuls of the mixture from the pan to this paste, then stir all back into the pan to thicken slightly. Simmer for 5 minutes before adding the chicken and the fish sauce. Taste for seasoning, drizzle over the chilli oil and scatter with the spring onion.

7. Cook the remaining rice noodles as for mohinga (see page 84). Place a helping of noodles first into deep bowls, top with the khaukswe and garnish with the crispy noodles and other accompaniments.

Serves 8

SHAN KHAUKSWE
Shan noodles

Pork bones – ask the butcher for bones for soup

3 onions, peeled – cut one into quarters and thinly slice the other two

salt

350 g/12 oz pork fillet, thinly sliced

1 teaspoon turmeric or 2.5 cm/1 in piece fresh turmeric, scraped and pounded

100 g/4 oz piece pork fat

2 eggs, whisked with 2 tablespoons water

seasoning

2 soya bean wafers, or 25 g/1 oz chickpeas

½ bunch spring onions

2 chillies, deseeded and shredded

3 large tomatoes, peeled and chopped

375 g/12 oz rice noodles (lai fan) cooked as for mohinga (see page 84)

soy sauce to taste

ACCOMPANIMENTS

coriander leaves

lemon or lime wedges

garlic chips

1. Bring the pork bones to the boil in a pan with water to cover. Skim, add the quartered onion and the salt, and simmer gently for one hour, then strain, reserving the stock.
2. Sprinkle the pork fillet with the turmeric and leave to one side. Fry the pork fat in a heavy frying pan over gentle heat until the fat runs. This will take several minutes. Discard the fat, keep the rendered oil.
3. Season the egg mixture then make one or two thin omelettes in half the pork oil, cooking on one side only, and roll up. Slice thinly and reserve.
4. Toast the soya bean wafers or chickpeas in a moderate oven (180°C, 350°F, Gas Mark 4) for 10–15 minutes. Check every

few minutes to make sure they are browning rather than burning. Grind to a powder and reserve.

5. Trim the ends from the spring onions. Shred the tops and reserve to add to the strained soup.
6. Place the coriander leaves, lemon or lime wedges and garlic chips in little bowls. Everything is now ready for the stir frying.
7. Fry the onions in the chilli-flavoured oil in the wok. Add the pork and turmeric and cook quickly, stirring all the time until the meat is cooked. Toss in the chopped tomato, then the noodles, toss well.
8. When hot add the soy bean powder or chickpea powder, spring onion bulbs and some of the omelette strips. Add soy sauce to taste.
9. Serve on a hot platter garnished with more omelette strips and the accompaniments. Serve the clear pork soup alongside, garnished with the spring onion tops.

Serves 4–5

NGA HIN
Fish curry

900 g/2 lb cod fillets, skinned
1 teaspoon salt
1 teaspoon ground turmeric or 2.5 cm/1 in piece fresh turmeric, scraped and pounded
4 cloves garlic, peeled
1 large onion, peeled
2.5–4 cm/1–1½ in fresh ginger, peeled and sliced

2 red chillies, deseeded, or ½–1 teaspoon chilli powder
6 tablespoons groundnut oil
400 g/14 oz can chopped tomatoes
300 ml/½ pint water
2 tablespoons fish sauce (see page 234)
seasoning

TO GARNISH
3–4 spring onions, finely shredded

1. Sprinkle the cod fillet with the salt and the ground or fresh turmeric. Cut into bite-sized pieces and set aside.

2. Chop or pound the garlic, onion, ginger and chilli.
3. Heat half the oil in a wok and fry the fish cubes for only 1–2 minutes, turning gently to seal in the juices and taking care not to break up the fish. Lift out on a draining spoon and set aside.
4. Add the remaining oil to the pan. When hot fry the pounded ingredients to bring out the full flavour. Add the tomatoes, water, and fish sauce and simmer gently without a lid for 15 minutes.
5. Five minutes before serving return the fish pieces to the wok and bubble gently so that the fish pieces remain whole. Taste for seasoning. Scatter with the spring onion and serve with rice.

Serves 6–8

PAZUN HIN
Prawn curry

675 g/1½ lb prawns, fresh or frozen
2 medium onions, peeled
4–6 green chillies, deseeded
4 cloves garlic, peeled
1½ teaspoons ground turmeric, or 2.5 cm/1 in fresh turmeric, scraped and pounded

6–8 tablespoons groundnut oil
few sprigs fresh coriander
2 tablespoons fish sauce (see page 234)
400 g/14 oz can chopped tomatoes
150 ml/5 fl oz fish stock or water
salt

1. Thaw the prawns if necessary.
2. Chop or pound the onion, 3 or 5 of the chillies, garlic, and turmeric to a fine paste. Fry in the hot oil for a few minutes to bring out the flavour, stirring throughout, then draw from the heat.
3. Remove a few leaves from the coriander for garnish and chop the remainder fairly finely.
4. Return the pan to the heat, add the chopped coriander, fish sauce, chopped tomatoes, fish stock or water and salt. Bring to the boil then reduce to a simmer and cook for 5–10 minutes.
5. Add the prawns and cook for a further 3–5 minutes. Meanwhile

finely shred the reserved green chilli and use to garnish the curry together with the reserved coriander leaves.

Serves 6

KYETHA HIN
Chicken curry

2 × 1.6 kg/3½ lb chickens	*50 g/2 oz piece fresh ginger, scraped and*
1 tablespoon sugar	*sliced*
2 teaspoons salt	*8 red chillies, deseeded, or 1½*
2 teaspoons ground turmeric or 5 cm/2	*tablespoons chilli powder*
in piece fresh turmeric, scraped and	*100 ml/4 fl oz groundnut oil*
pounded	*450 ml/¾ pint chicken stock or water*
2 tablespoons light soy sauce	*2 × 400 g/14 oz cans chopped tomatoes*
4 stems lemon grass	*3–4 teaspoons fish sauce, or to taste (see*
3 large onions, peeled and quartered	*page 234)*
6 cloves garlic, peeled	

1. Divide each chicken into eight portions with the skin left on, i.e. each leg into two, and each breast and wing into two. Make a good chicken stock from the back of the carcass to use in this recipe and for the Hincho (the soup I suggest to serve with the meal – see page 82).
2. Sprinkle the chicken portions with the sugar and salt in a large bowl and toss with hands to release the juices. Sprinkle with turmeric and mix again so that the chicken is evenly coated. Wash hands immediately as the turmeric will stain. Spoon over the soy sauce and set aside whilst preparing the other ingredients.
3. Trim the root from the lemon grass, then cut the lower 7.5 cm/3 in of each stem away and pound with two of the onions, the garlic, ginger, chillies or chilli powder. Bruise the top of the stems and reserve. Finely slice the remaining onion and set aside.
4. Heat the oil in a large wok then fry the pounded paste for a few minutes to bring out the flavour, turning the mixture constantly.
5. Now add half the chicken pieces turning to seal all over. Lift out into a dish and seal the remaining chicken pieces in the same way, ensuring that they are well coated with the spice mixture.

6. Add the remaining onion to the pan and cook for 2–3 minutes. Return the chicken to the wok with the tomatoes and enough chicken stock to almost cover the chicken.
7. Push the bruised stems of lemon grass amongst the chicken pieces to add flavour, cover and simmer gently for 40–50 minutes or until the pieces are tender but not falling off the bone.
8. Taste for seasoning, add the fish sauce and serve with freshly cooked rice. If the curry is prepared a day ahead or even on the morning of your party, cook for only 35–40 minutes. Just before you are ready to eat, bring it to the boil, reduce to a simmer and cook gently for 20 minutes before serving.

Serves 8 generously, 12–16 if part of a buffet

DUCK CURRY

This curry can be made a day in advance as long as you do not overcook it and remember to reheat it thoroughly. Any excess fat can be skimmed from the curry before serving, but this oil is highly regarded in Burmese cuisine.

2 kg/4½ lb duckling
2 teaspoons salt
1 teaspoon ground turmeric, or 2.5 cm/
   1 in fresh turmeric scraped and
   pounded
2 tablespoons soy sauce

3 onions, peeled
4 cm/1½ in piece fresh ginger, peeled
4 cloves garlic, peeled
25 g/1 oz fresh chillies, deseeded
4 tablespoons groundnut oil

1. Cut the duckling into 4 even-sized portions, legs and breast. Place in a bowl and sprinkle with the salt, turmeric and soy sauce. Mix well together and set aside for 30 minutes.
2. Place the carcass of the duckling into a large pan with 1 of the onions and ½ in piece of the ginger, bruised, and water to cover. Bring to the boil, skim, season then simmer gently for ¾–1 hour to make a good-flavoured stock.
3. Slice one onion finely and set aside. Chop or pound the remaining onion, ginger, garlic and chillies. Heat the oil in a wok and

fry the spicy mixture to bring out the full flavour, turning constantly.

4. Now add the duck portions, turning over to seal the meat on all sides. When the duck is a good brown colour, add the sliced onion and 600 ml/1 pint of the prepared duck stock. Bring to the boil then simmer gently for about 1 hour or till the duck pieces are tender.

Serves 4

WETTHA HNAT GYET
Pork curry

The recipe given to me for this curry had a great deal more oil in it, which I have drastically reduced. Authentic Burmese curries are judged by the rich oil which floats on the surface.

1 kg/2¼ lb belly pork, rind removed – ask the butcher for fairly lean meat with the ratio ¾ lean to ¼ fat

2 teaspoons ground turmeric or 5 cm/2 in fresh turmeric, scraped and pounded

½–1 tablespoon salt

4 cm/1½ in prepared ngapi (blachan – see page 228)

50 ml/2 fl oz groundnut oil

½–1 tablespoon chilli powder

3 stems lemon grass

2.5 cm/1 in fresh ginger, scraped

2 teaspoons garam masala

4 cloves garlic, peeled and cut in half lengthwise

225–350 g/8–12 oz tiny onions, peeled, or larger onions peeled and quartered

1. Trim the meat into 2.5 cm/1 in cubes and put in a large bowl. Add the turmeric, salt, prepared ngapi, oil and chilli powder and mix well.

2. Trim the roots from the lemon grass. Cut through the whole stem lengthwise and bruise the fleshy ends, then put the stems in a 2.75 litre/5 pint flameproof casserole or heavy-based pan. Add the meat mixture and water to cover. Bring to the boil, reduce to a simmer and cover.

3. Meanwhile pound the ginger very finely. When the pork has been cooking for an hour add the ginger, garam masala, garlic and onions to the pan.

4. Bring to the boil again. Cover and simmer for a further hour till the pork is quite tender. Remove the lemon grass stems before serving if liked.

Serves 6

BUFFADOO
Duck cooked with spices

2 kg/4½ lb duckling	*2 medium onions, peeled and quartered*
4 cardamom pods	*2 cloves garlic*
6 cloves	*4 tablespoons groundnut oil*
a little mace	*2 tablespoons soy sauce*
small piece cinnamon	*10–12 tiny onions, peeled*
¼ teaspoon each peppercorns and	*150 ml/5 fl oz coconut cream or 25 g/1*
* allspice*	* oz creamed coconut (see page 231)*
	225 g/8 oz okra

1. Wipe the duckling and cut each leg and breast portion into two. Make a stock from the rest of the carcass, strain and reserve 600 ml/1 pint.
2. Dry fry the cardamom pods, cloves, mace, cinnamon, peppercorns and allspice gently to bring out the flavour. Remove the seeds from the cardamom pods and grind all the spices to a powder. Now add the quartered onions and garlic and blend to a paste.
3. Heat the oil and fry this spicy mixture to bring out the full flavour. Reduce the heat and push the mixture to the side of the pan so that the oil separates out. Increase the heat, add the pieces of duck and brown them all over.
4. Pour in the duck stock, soy sauce and the little onions. Half cover and cook for 1¼–1½ hours or until the duck is tender.
5. Add the coconut cream and the okra, then cook uncovered for a further 5–8 minutes. Taste for seasoning. Serve with rice or, as a Burmese friend suggested, roast potatoes and peas!

Serves 4

WET-THANI
Golden pork

2 medium onions, peeled
1 corm of garlic, peeled
175 g/6 oz fresh ginger, scraped
85 ml/3 fl oz groundnut oil

1.4 kg/3 lb pork suitable for casseroling,
   cut into 2.5 cm/1 in cubes
salt

TO GARNISH
crispy fried onions (see Burmese vegetable platter, page 96)

1. Pound the onions, garlic and ginger until very fine. Turn into a muslin-lined sieve and squeeze out as much juice as you can. Reserve both juice and purée.
2. Heat the oil and fry the meat cubes to a golden brown. Pour in the onion, garlic and ginger juice, which should be about 200 ml/⅓ pint, and add salt, with 200 ml/⅓ pint water. Bring to the boil, reduce heat, cover and cook for one hour.
3. Take out half a teacupful of the meat and pound briefly in a food processor. Return to the pan with the onion, garlic and ginger mixture, and continue cooking for a further ¾–1 hour till tender. The pounded mixture thickens the curry.
4. Serve garnished with crispy fried onions.

Serves 8, or 12 as part of a buffet

A-MER-THA-HIN
Mild beef curry

1 kg/2¼ lb best stewing steak, in one
   piece
2 large onions, peeled
2 cloves garlic, peeled
5 cm/2 in piece fresh ginger, scraped
1 teaspoon salt

¼ teaspoon ground turmeric
1 teaspoon chilli powder
4–6 tablespoons groundnut oil
2 teaspoons thick soy sauce
300 ml/½ pint beef stock or water

TO GARNISH
1 red chilli, deseeded and shredded

1. Trim the beef and cut into slices, then into 2.5 cm/1 in strips.
2. Pound the onions, garlic and ginger finely with the salt, turmeric and chilli powder.
3. Fry the meat in half the oil till it begins to brown. Remove from the pan.
4. Fry the onion mixture in the remaining oil to bring out the flavour. Return the meat to the pan and stir in the soy sauce and stock.
5. Cook over a gentle heat until the beef is tender, about 1½–2 hours. Add more water if necessary. Serve garnished with fine shreds of chilli.

Serves 6

TAUNG-BHO-HMO
Burmese-style mushrooms

225 g/8 oz button mushrooms	*¼–½ teaspoon ground turmeric*
2 medium onions, peeled	*3 tablespoons oil*
3 cloves garlic	*seasoning*
2 stems lemon grass, lower 6 cm/2½ in of stem sliced – reserve top	*juice of ½ lemon or lime*

1. Wipe the mushrooms. Leave whole but remove and discard the stems.
2. Slice one onion finely and reserve. Pound the other onion with the garlic and the sliced lower part of the lemon grass. Stir in the turmeric and salt.
3. Heat the oil and fry the spice paste to bring out the flavour. Add the mushrooms and reserved sliced onion, cover and cook for 5 minutes until the mushrooms are tender.
4. Taste for seasoning and squeeze over the lemon or lime juice. Finely shred the lemon grass tops and scatter over the mushrooms before serving. Serve warm or cold.

Serves 8 as part of a buffet

HIN-THEE HIN-YWET HIN
Mixed vegetable curry

3 potatoes, peeled and cubed	*4 cloves garlic, peeled*
1 aubergine	*2 red or green chillies, deseeded*
3 carrots	*½ teaspoon turmeric*
100 g/4 oz French beans	*6 tablespoons groundnut oil*
½ small cauliflower	*75 g/3 oz salt fish (optional)*
100–175 g/4–6 oz okra	*400 g/14 oz can chopped tomatoes*
1 onion, peeled	*300–450 ml/½–¾ pint water*
4 cm/1½ in fresh ginger, peeled and	*salt*
* sliced*	*6 sprigs fresh coriander*

1. Place the potato cubes in a bowl of water. Trim the aubergine and slice thickly then cut into bite-sized pieces and place in the bowl with the potatoes.
2. Peel and slice the carrots evenly. Trim the ends from the beans and cut into 2.5 cm/1 in lengths. Break the cauliflower into florets and then slice into small pieces.
3. Trim the stem end of the okra only. Do not cut into the okra because if cut they become slimy when cooking.
4. Pound the onion, fresh ginger, garlic, chillies and turmeric. Heat the oil in a wok then fry this spicy mixture to bring out the full flavour, stirring all the time.
5. Cut the salt fish, if using, into small cubes and add to the pan. Cook for 1 minute. Add half the tomatoes, half the water and the potato cubes, and cook gently for 10 minutes then add the drained aubergine, carrots and beans and cook for 5 minutes. Stir from time to time.
6. Add the cauliflower pieces and the okra with the remaining tomato, salt, and a little extra water if required. Cook for 5 minutes. Finally add the chopped coriander stems (reserve the leaves), and turn in the pan once or twice, being careful not to break up the vegetables. Serve at once, scattered with coriander leaves.
7. This curry should not be too moist, so use your judgement on the addition of water.

Serves 8 as an accompaniment

HIN-THEE HIN-YWET PYOAT
Burmese vegetable platter

A variety of vegetables can be used – this is perhaps a typical selection but all vegetables in season would be suitable. Colour and texture are important. Tiny cherry tomatoes could be used as a garnish.

1 small cauliflower
450 g/1 lb peeled carrots
225 g/8 oz French beans
100–175 g/4–6 oz okra
1 tablespoon vinegar
1 teaspoon sugar

1 large onion, peeled, finely sliced and
   dried on kitchen paper
oil for frying – you will need at least
   150 ml/5 fl oz
sesame seeds

1. Break the cauliflower into small even-sized florets. Slice the carrots diagonally. Trim the beans and cut in half if very long. Snip the stem end from the okra but do not cut open otherwise they will become slimy.
2. Blanch the vegetables one by one in a pan of salted boiling water, to which the vinegar and sugar have been added. Allow 2–3 minutes for each vegetable then lift out on a draining spoon and immediately put in iced water which will halt the cooking and set the colour. Drain well and pat dry on kitchen towel if necessary.
3. Meanwhile fry the onion slices in oil till crisp, turning all the time. Place the onion in a sieve over a bowl to collect the excess oil, add the oil from the pan to this and reserve.
4. Dry fry the sesame seeds over a medium heat till golden. Arrange the vegetables attractively in groups on a dish. Drizzle over the reserved onion oil then scatter over crispy onion and sesame seeds. Serve cold.

Serves 6–8

A-SEIN THANAT SOHN
Vegetables with tomato dip

DIP

1–2 beefsteak tomatoes, depending on size

1 green chilli, deseeded and finely sliced
a little salt and sugar

VEGETABLES

225 g/8 oz cauliflower, divided into florets

100 g/4 oz okra

100 g/4 oz French beans, cut into finger lengths

1 tablespoon vinegar
4 spring onions

1. Char the skin of the tomato over a gas flame or under the grill and remove. Chop the tomato very finely to a pulp with the chilli. A food processor will make the dip too liquid. Season with salt and sugar, turn into a small bowl and chill.
2. Blanch the cauliflower, okra and beans one by one in a large pan of salted boiling water to which you have added the vinegar. Allow 1 minute per vegetable then rinse with very cold water and drain. Do not cook the spring onions – cut into lengths.
3. Arrange all the vegetables attractively on a platter with the tomato dip in the centre. Guests take a selection of vegetables and a spoonful of the dip on a plate.

Serves 6–8

KHA-YAN-THEE-HNAT
Stuffed aubergines or courgettes

3 large, chunky aubergines or 6 chunky courgettes, weighing about 675 g/ 1½ lb

salt

50 g/2 oz dried prawns, soaked in water for 15 minutes and drained

225 g/8 oz onions, peeled

2 cloves garlic, peeled

1 cm/½ in fresh ginger, scraped

1 red chilli

½ teaspoon turmeric

1–2 tablespoons fish sauce (see page 234)

50 ml/2 fl oz groundnut oil

TO GARNISH

chopped spring onion

1. Cut the aubergines into rings about 4–5 cm/1½–2 in deep. Scoop a tablespoonful of flesh out of the top of each one and reserve. If using courgettes cut in half lengthwise and half again then scoop out a little of the flesh from the centre so that it resembles a boat and reserve. Sprinkle the aubergines or courgettes with salt.
2. Pound the drained prawns finely and turn into a bowl. Then pound the onions, garlic, ginger and chilli with the scooped-out flesh fairly finely. Add the prawns, turmeric and fish sauce to taste.
3. Rinse the aubergines or courgettes. Drain and dry them then spoon the filling into the vegetables.
4. Place in a shallow frying pan, pour the oil into the pan with a little water, bring to the boil then reduce to a simmer.
5. Cover and cook for 30 minutes or until the vegetables are tender. Serve warm or cold sprinkled with chopped spring onion.

Serves 8 as an accompaniment

NGA LETHOK
Fish salad

Lethok is the Burmese word for salad and literally means mixed by hand. The essential point is that though the ingredients can be prepared in advance the salad should be put together at the last moment so that all the flavours retain their identity.

675 g/1½ lb cod or haddock fillet,
   skinned
salt and pepper
2 medium onions, peeled and finely
   sliced

oil for frying
25 g/1 oz dried chickpeas
2 stems lemon grass
fish sauce (see page 234)
juice of 1 lime or lemon

1. Pound the fish with the salt and pepper to a fine paste. With wetted hands form into 24 even-sized balls.

2. Bring a large pan of water to the boil. A deep frying pan or wok would be ideal. Drop in half the balls, making sure that the water keeps bubbling, and cook for 3–4 minutes or until they rise to the surface. Lift out on a draining spoon and cook the remainder in the same way. Leave to cool.
3. Meanwhile fry one of the onions in hot oil till crisp and golden then turn into a sieve set over a bowl to catch the draining oil, and reserve.
4. Roast the dried chickpeas in a moderate oven (180°C, 350°F, Gas Mark 4) for 15 minutes then pound to a coarse powder in a pestle and mortar.
5. Cut the root end from each of the lemon grass stems, strip away any coarse outer leaves, and shred finely. Reserve.
6. Cut the fish balls into slices and place on a serving dish. Pour over the oil from frying the onion, the fish sauce, pounded chickpeas, and lime or lemon juice. Toss well then top with the raw and fried onions and shredded lemon grass.

Serves 6, or 10 as part of a buffet

KHA-YAN-KYIN THEE THOKE
Green tomato salad

This recipe is a real find. It complements so many curry recipes because of the sharpness from the green tomatoes combined with the other distinctive textures and flavours.

6 unripe tomatoes
1 medium onion, sliced
5 tablespoons oil
25 g/1 oz salted peanuts, crushed
1 green chilli, deseeded and shredded

few stems fresh coriander, coarsely
chopped
3 teaspoons fish sauce (see page 234)
juice of ½ lime or lemon

1. Cut the tomatoes into eight wedges, or slices if preferred.
2. Fry the onion in the oil and reserve the oil (see Burmese vegetable platter, page 96).
3. At the last minute mix the tomato, crispy onion and oil with the peanuts, chilli and coriander. Toss well (or mix with hands in

authentic style), then add fish sauce and lime or lemon juice to taste.

Serves 6–8 as part of a buffet

THA-KHWA-THEE SHAUK-THEE THOKE
Cucumber and grapefruit salad

*1 cucumber, cut in half and seeds
  removed*
salt
1–2 grapefruit, depending on size

1 small onion, peeled and thinly sliced
1–2 green chillies, deseeded and shredded
sorrel, spinach or lettuce leaves
1–2 tablespoons fish sauce (see page 234)

1. Using a potato peeler, peel away a thin strip of cucumber rind – shred for garnish. Sprinkle the cucumber with the salt, leave for 20 minutes, then rinse and cut into small chunks.
2. Cut the grapefruit over a large bowl to catch the juice, and remove the segments with a sharp knife. Toss the cucumber, grapefruit and onion together with a little of the chilli.
3. Use the green leaves to line a bowl and fill with the salad. Spoon over the fish sauce and reserved grapefruit juice to taste. Garnish with the remaining chilli and the cucumber rind.

Serves 6–8

BALACHUANG
Burmese relish

The all-time-favourite spicy relish which is loved by all Burmese. No meal is complete without it.

If you happen to live in some far-off sunny place the onions can be left in the sun for a few hours before frying. Fried garlic flakes are now available from oriental stores which you might find useful, but these will obviously not need to be sliced and fried.

1 whole corm garlic, peeled and very
  finely sliced, or 25 g/1 oz garlic flakes
450 g/1 lb onions, peeled and very finely
  sliced
300 ml/½ pint groundnut oil
175 g/6 oz powdered shrimp (see page
  234)

2–3 teaspoons dried chilli powder
1 teaspoon powdered turmeric
2.5 cm/1 in prepared ngapi (blachan –
  see page 228)
1 teaspoon tamarind soaked in 50 ml/2
  fl oz warm water and strained
salt to taste

1. Spread out the onion and garlic slices on a roasting tin or large tray lined with crumpled kitchen paper. Leave for at least 30 minutes to get rid of excess moisture, then fry separately in the groundnut oil till crisp and golden. Lift out on a draining spoon and leave to cool.
2. Fry the shrimp in the same oil along with the chilli powder and turmeric, then draw from the heat.
3. Crumble the prepared ngapi into a bowl and make into a paste with the strained juice from the tamarind. Stir into the shrimp mixture and when cold add the crisp onion and garlic, and salt to taste.
4. Use as an accompaniment to most Burmese curries. Any left over can be stored in a screwtop jar in a cool place for several weeks.

Serves 12–14 as part of a buffet

PAZAN DOK NGAPI GYAW
Fresh prawn balachuang

According to a Burmese friend this is far more delicious than the recipe made with powdered shrimp but it won't keep for long and should be used up within a few days. Made with the tomato it becomes a piquant relish.

If you cannot get fresh or frozen uncooked prawns you can use the cooked variety. Chop and just add to the mixture without cooking. If you want to cut a corner on this recipe both garlic chips and crisp onion can be bought from oriental supermarkets. However, the flavour of the dish might not be so good as the onion-flavoured oil will not be included; the quantity of oil should be reduced by half in this case.

225 g/8 oz fresh or frozen uncooked
    prawns
450 g/1 lb onions, peeled and finely
    sliced
1 corm garlic, each clove peeled and
    finely sliced, or use garlic chips
175 ml/6 fl oz groundnut oil
1 cm/½ in prepared ngapi (blachan –
    see page 228)

2 tablespoons tamarind paste dissolved
    in 75 ml/3 fl oz warm water then
    strained
1 tablespoon chilli powder
1 teaspoon turmeric
1 beefsteak tomato, skinned and finely
    chopped

1. Peel the prawns and chop coarsely on a board – or very briefly in a food processor.
2. Spread the onions and garlic out on a tray lined with plenty of crumpled kitchen paper to absorb the liquid. Leave for at least 30 minutes.
3. Pat dry and fry first the onions and then the garlic in batches in the oil till crisp. Drain in a sieve, catching the draining oil in a bowl below and reserving with the rest of the cooking oil.
4. Mix the ngapi to a paste with a little of the tamarind juice and then add the remainder.
5. Reheat the oil and fry the chilli and turmeric in it. Add the chopped prawns and fry for 30 seconds. Now add the tomato and the ngapi and tamarind mixture. Remove from the heat and leave to cool. Stir in the crisp onion and garlic and serve.

Serves 12–14 as part of a buffet

NGA LETHOKE
Fried fish fritters

450 g/1 lb cod fillet, skin and bones
    removed

salt and pepper
oil for frying

1. Pound the fish to a smooth paste with the seasoning and a tablespoon of the oil.
2. Shape into 12 even-sized fritters. Fry in hot oil till brown on both sides, then drain on kitchen paper.

3. Slice each one into four and serve as yet another accompaniment to mohinga (see page 83).

Makes 12

KHA-WE-THEE THANAT
Bitter melon relish

The unusual bitter flavour combines perfectly with mohinga. Bitter melons (carilla) can be found in oriental stores. They look like very knobbly, small cucumbers – bright green when young, turning yellow as they ripen.

2 bitter melons (carilla)
2 teaspoons salt
1/4 teaspoon turmeric
1 medium onion, peeled
3/4 teaspoon chilli powder
3 tablespoons groundnut oil

1 large beefsteak tomato, peeled and chopped
2 teaspoons powdered shrimp (see page 234)
1–2 teaspoons fish sauce (see page 234)

1. Using a potato peeler, strip off the outer blisters of the bitter melons. Cut the fruit in half lengthwise and then into thin slices across.
2. Sprinkle with the salt, set aside for ten minutes, then rinse, drain and sprinkle with the turmeric.
3. Pound the onion and chilli powder finely. Fry in the oil to bring out the flavour, stirring throughout.
4. Add the bitter melon and chopped tomato. Mix well then allow to cook gently for 10–15 minutes or until the melon is tender.
5. Draw from the heat, add the powdered shrimp and fish sauce to taste. Cool, then transfer to a glass jar with cover and store in the refrigerator.

Serves 8–10 as part of a buffet

AK YAW
Crispy fries

Serve as an accompaniment to mohinga.

1 tablespoon dried yellow split peas
2 tablespoons dried green split peas
pinch bicarbonate soda
100 g/4 oz rice flour

½ teaspoon ground turmeric
approx 175 ml/6 fl oz water
oil for frying

1. Soak the split peas in water with the soda for at least four hours, then drain.
2. Mix the rice flour and turmeric to a paste with a little of the water, then stir in the remaining water to make a creamy mixture.
3. About one hour before serving the mohinga heat the oil in a frying pan.
4. Drop dessertspoonfuls of batter into the pan to make little round fritters, and while they are still liquid scatter a few drained peas into the centre.
5. When the fritters are quite set turn over and fry till crisp on the other side.
6. Drain on kitchen paper. Repeat till all the mixture is used up.

Makes about 16

SAN WIN MA KIN
Baked semolina pudding

A very popular dessert made with coconut milk, which is cut into diamond or square shapes and eaten cold.

600 ml/1 pint coconut milk (see page 231)
75 g/3 oz semolina
pinch salt
50 g/2 oz golden granulated sugar

1 egg white, lightly whisked
50 g/2 oz sultanas or raisins
25 g/1 oz butter or margarine
12 split blanched almonds
1 teaspoon sesame or poppy seeds

1. Pour the coconut milk into a pan rinsed with cold water and heat gently. When warm sprinkle in the semolina and salt then stir all the time till the mixture thickens.

2. Stir in the sugar, cool slightly then add the whisked egg white, sultanas and raisins. Add the butter or margarine cut into small pieces and mix well.
3. Turn the mixture into an oblong ovenproof dish 18 x 25 cm/7 x 10 in. Arrange the almonds on top and sprinkle with the sesame or poppy seeds.
4. Bake in a cool oven (150°C, 300°F, Gas Mark 2) for one hour till golden brown. Allow to cool then cut into square or diamond shapes before serving.

Serves 8

NGA-PYAW-THEE-PYOAT OHN-NO HTA-NYET
Bananas in syrup

8–10 small bananas

225–350 g/8–12 oz muscovado or molasses sugar (the darkest you can find)

450 ml/15 fl oz water

600 ml/1 pint coconut milk (see page 231)

1. Peel the bananas and either leave them whole or cut in half if liked.
2. Dissolve the sugar and water over the heat in a wide frying pan then add the bananas. Bring to the boil, then add half the coconut milk.
3. Cook gently without cover for 20–30 minutes then lift the bananas into a serving dish.
4. Reduce the syrup for 5 minutes and pour over the bananas. Serve warm or cold with the remaining coconut milk.

Serves 8

MYE-PÉ PYIT
Peanut Brittle

175 g/6 oz golden granulated sugar   *100 g/4 oz peanuts*

1. Lightly oil an 18 cm/7 in square baking tin or ovenproof dish.
2. Melt the sugar in a heavy-based pan over medium heat, shaking the pan from time to time until the sugar is liquid and golden.

3. Meanwhile crush the peanuts very lightly either in a pestle and mortar or in a food processor. Add to the melted sugar and turn immediately into the prepared tin. Leave to set.
4. Break up into pieces and serve at the end of a meal.

LEPET or LAPET
Pressed tea leaf

This is an authentic way to end a Burmese feast – the only problem being that the preserved green tea leaf is not obtainable in the UK. However, I can remember when fresh ginger and coriander were in the same category, so who knows, lepet might yet become another exotic item on the oriental shelf.

Lepet is served on almost all occasions from a wedding to a wake. Even for a christening party portions of lepet are sent as substitutes for invitation cards.

The beautiful lacquerware boxes with divisions are an attractive way to present lepet. I put the tea leaf mixed with a little sesame oil and salt in the centre. Two containers hold peanuts, two toasted sesame seeds, one crisp garlic and the other crisp onion flakes. Dried shrimps may also be used and dried peas which have been fried till crisp.

Each person takes a *little* of each of the ingredients, moulds it with the fingers and pops it into the mouth. Drink with plenty of black tea. It's quite a novel experience.

Thailand

The Thai greeting or *wai*, made with hands lightly clasped together, fingers touching and the head bowed as if in prayer, is very likely to be your welcome to Thailand, often referred to as the 'Land of Smiles'. This reputation is well deserved. Even in the hustle and bustle of Thailand's capital, Bangkok, where five million of the country's fifty million people live, this greeting ritual with the word *sawasdee* is performed with a shy smile which is enchanting.

Thai means 'free', which is very apt. The Thais are justly proud of never having been colonized by the European powers. The migration of the Tai tribes from South-West China over the centuries gave birth to the Thai people of today. They are truly one nation, and a rural nation at that. The majority live in the villages and towns, following traditional ways, but as you drive from the airport towards Bangkok you might suspect that the whole Thai population is travelling in your direction. At every traffic light the taxis, buses, motor bikes and tuk tuks (three wheelers) line up as if on the starting grid. Lane discipline is a joke, and to be a pedestrian is to take your life in your hands.

Bangkok was built without a plan and the city has grown out of all recognition. The *klongs* (canals) used to be the veins and arteries of the city leading into the Chao Phya river (the River of Kings) but many of them have now been converted to roads, adding greatly to the congestion. However, it is still possible to find little oases of peace and calm in the temples, or *wats*, dotted all over the city.

Bangkok has been called the 'Venice of the East' and as many as a million people live and work along its waterways. An early-morning ride along the *klongs* gives a fascinating glimpse into life as it has been for years, with its floating markets and restaurants, laundries with 150 pairs of trousers drying in the sun and a backdrop of coconut palms, mango trees and banana plants (not trees). The wooden houses on stilts, each with its verandah bench for watching the world go by in the evening hours, are a buzz of activity by 7 A.M., as produce from the gardens behind is bought and sold. Coconuts, mangoes, bananas, pineapples, pomelos, durian, papaya, vegetables galore, and a breathtaking array of orchids are on offer from girls wearing the famous lampshade hats. As is ever the case in the whole of South-East Asia, food is available round the clock, from a hearty bowl of noodles to fried bananas or a drink of coconut juice. I watched the purveyor of a noodle breakfast perched in her boat as she plunged the noodles into a cauldron of bubbly stock just to warm them, followed by a few prepared vegetables. Noodles and vegetables are scooped into a bowl topped with a little chopped pork, some basil and coriander leaves, a dash of sauce made from pounded chillies and fish sauce, plus the odd whole chilli to enhance the flavour. Food like this is nutritious and cheap, costing a mere eight *baht* (twenty pence).

There are several floating markets; the best known and some would say the most commercialized is the Thonbiri, which is fun and very photogenic, or try the Damnern Sadnak, which is about an hour from central Bangkok and lasts till mid-morning. It's a lot less crowded but equally picturesque.

At the weekend market in Chatuchak Park everything is arranged so attractively that it's hard to resist. Marvellous chillies – from the bird's eye type (the smallest and hottest) in brilliant, glossy red and green colours, to the larger green variety – sit next to juicy limes and masses of fresh coriander leaves, all laid out on banana-leaf-lined baskets. Fruits of every kind are on display, including mangosteen, limes, jackfruit, oranges, guava, custard apple, and rambutan, as are innumerable vegetables, dried fish, dried prawns, and tiny garlic (for pickling). Fresh fish, meat, sugar cane and an infinity of flowers, especially orchids, are also available.

To reach the Grand Palace, Bangkok's most glittering spectacle, you are obliged to walk through a busy, bustling street market awash with colour. Huge baskets piled high with baby cucumbers, aubergines – the pale green-white ones the size of pingpong balls – yardbeans, winged beans, baby sweetcorn, glorious red chillies and oyster mushrooms, look so inviting. Bags of peanuts, peanut brittle and *krupuk* (prawn crackers) sit atop stools and tables made from old sewing machines and covered with bright cloths. A boy tends the family stall where the little cooked fish in groups of three sit in the bamboo steamers all ready to take away for the evening meal. Fish is the main source of protein in the Thai diet. Every household along the *klong* and river is geared to catch some of the daily supply of catfish, carp or gourami. The ubiquitous fish sauce, a whisky-coloured condiment, is made from the tiny *pla katak* fished from the Gulf of Thailand. It is used to enhance almost every savoury dish you can think of, from curries to the equally famous *nam prik* sauce.

The fabled Grand Palace is an amazing walled complex of temples and palaces with red and green tiled roofs, topped with golden spires in classic Thai architecture. A huge, gold-clad stupa reaches into the sky. In all this magnificence are the eight 'prangs' which look like corncobs on the temple of the Emerald Buddha, Wat Phra Keo, the Royal Temple, where the king comes three times a year to change the Buddha's clothes. This is Bangkok's most stunning temple, a sacred place for all Buddhists and to most visitors their most vivid and lasting memory.

Buddhism in Thailand, as in Burma, is a way of life. Young boys and men become monks for a few weeks, months or for life. Many in the rural areas take the opportunity to honour their obligation during the rainy season. At the various temples I visited I saw groups of shaven-headed, saffron-robed boys listening attentively to a senior monk. At dawn these young boys would have been out with their alms bowls collecting food which they would share at a communal meal before midday. The rest of the day is spent in learning, prayer and meditation. Women earn their merit towards their future existence by giving alms and food to the monks. Giving is a key part of the Buddhist philosophy. For instance, if a person is poor they can 'give' time to build a new temple or repair an old one. Every one of Thailand's Buddhists will make their contribution. Intertwined with their faith is a belief in spirits to bring good luck and astrologers to forecast auspicious days for weddings, journeys and starting new businesses.

At the Pramane ground I joined a group of people watching a girl make up a country-style salad in a huge wooden pestle and mortar. First in went the chillies, with one or two yardbeans snapped into short lengths, and a little sugar. All this was pounded together, then came a dash of lemon juice, fish sauce, a few crab claws, and dried prawns. More pounding. Finally a quartered tomato and a handful of shredded green papaya were tossed in and the whole spooned out onto plates for the customers seated on a colourful rug on the ground. It looked quite delicious and I have given a recipe on page 140, substituting babaco for the green papaya. Salads take on a whole new dimension in Thailand. Curiously the Thai word *yam* (salad) means precisely the same as *lethok* in Burma – 'to mix by hand'. In each country the salad is a spontaneous blending of tart, crisp fruit or vegetables – the latter frequently served with a hot, spicy sauce such as *nam prik*. Salads with fruit – pineapple, crisp apples and green mangoes – are popular. They might have a few prawns or shredded pork added to enhance the blend of flavours. The dressing, added at the last moment, is a combination of the tart (lemon or lime juice), sweet (brown sugar) and salt (fish sauce) – three flavours beloved of the Thais.

As you might expect, Thailand has its annual fairs, festivals and ceremonies. The Pramane ground, the Royal Field also known as the Sanam Luang, is the scene for the annual ploughing ceremony in early May on a date named by the Brahman priests to mark the beginning of the rice-planting season. The seeds are blessed and distributed by the king for good luck. A ceremonial plough breaks the ground and the priests predict the success of the harvest. In April, Thais celebrate the Buddhist New Year with the Songkran Festival. *Khao Chae*, ice-cold rice scented with floating jasmine, is traditionally served at this celebration, with an assortment of delicate savoury nibbles such as shrimp paste balls, stuffed peppers, fried crispy white radish and crisp fried beef. Noodles are also popular party fare; long noodles convey a wish for a long life and much happiness. At this time of year family gatherings are arranged. Scented water is poured over the hands of the older and revered members of the family, who pass on blessings for the New Year.

On my last visit to Bangkok I had the good fortune to go to the Oriental Hotel's Thai Cookery School – a low, wooden building in Thai style surrounded by a maze of verandahs festooned in flowers and plants. Overlooking the courtyard are window boxes full of basil, sweet balsam and mint, all favourite herbs in Thai cuisine as well as lemon grass, coriander, ginger, turmeric and chillies.

The school director, Khun Chalie Amatyukul, is an expert on Thai food. Having travelled all over the world he is passionate about food in general and Thai cooking in particular, and conveys this love for his native cuisine in his demonstrations, held in a carefree and relaxed atmosphere. The five-day course covers every aspect of Thai cuisine from soups, curries and salads to the secrets of fruit carving. Visits to markets are included in the programme, which is a thoroughly enjoyable way to enhance one's knowledge of one of the world's most delightful cuisines.

Our tastebuds were delighted with the pork, beef and chicken satay (recipe page 148), intrigued by the *mee krob* – a national dish of noodles with sweet and sour flavours coming through – and enthused by the stir-fried chicken with balsam leaves followed by herb-steamed fish.

The cookery school is owned by the Oriental Hotel, which was originally a two-storey, colonial-style building built in 1876. New wings have recently been added, but the atmosphere in the old building, approached from the river by an orchid-lined path, is one of grace and elegance, like stepping back half a century. High ceilings lend a sensation of space, while the tall, feathery bamboo growing indoors extends a cool, green, tropical touch. The lobby features a number of huge bamboo bird cages, all set at different heights, which turn out to be lampshades. The hotel is very stylish and proud of its past. A string of literary luminaries have stayed there and now have suites named after them: Joseph Conrad, Somerset Maugham (he stayed at Raffles Hotel in Singapore too), Graham Greene, Captain Anderson, John le Carré and, more recently, Barbara Cartland. Jim Thompson, reviver and promoter of Thai silk, stayed here before he mysteriously disappeared in the Cameron Highlands in Malaysia, never to be seen again. After a day in the hurly-burly of Bangkok, sip a sundowner on the terrace of the Oriental as the orange sun slips low in the sky, with lights twinkling on the river, and soak up the past as the 'ex-pats' used to do at this very place as they gathered to collect their mail after a hard day at the office.

Once out of Bangkok travellers pass through acres and acres of *padi* fields, which are harvested by uniformly clad, straw-hatted farmers. Thailand is now the rice bowl of the world and rice is the number one export. Water buffaloes puddle and fertilize and then plough the *padi* fields before planting is done in May. Two-thirds of all the agricultural land is used for growing rice, the best quality coming from the central plains which are watered by the network of rivers that flow through this area.

An invitation to a meal – *rappatan arhan* – means 'come and eat rice'. Rice is not only Thailand's biggest export earner but its staple food. It is renowned for its delicate perfume which pervades the kitchen like no other. There are many schools of thought on the cooking of rice but basically there are two different types: long grain which is served with every meal in the south of Thailand, and short grain or glutinous rice which is more popular in the north as the staple food, as well as being used in the preparation of desserts all over the country.

Little villages of houses set on stilts look as if they have been there for ever. The houses, made of bamboo or teak, are cool and airy with a wide verandah and steep, thatched roofs to cope with the torrential monsoon rains. Flowers and plants grow all around – papaya and mango trees, banana plants and coconut palms give fruit and shade. Close by is the vegetable patch. Ducks, pigs and chickens seek shelter under the house in the heat of the day after foraging for food when the temperature is cooler. When the *padi* fields are flooded there is an abundant supply of fish, making life in the rural areas as near self-sufficient as you will ever get. Indeed, the tempo of life for most Thais is a far cry from the frenzied pace of Bangkok. To drive a mere fifty miles is to be transported to a pastoral pace yet the industriousness of the people is still evident. Like the rural Burmese they still have time to greet friends and passers-by.

First thing in the morning Thai housewives prepare rice and food for the family and for the monks who call by to collect their daily offering, bringing merit to the housewife and her family. After a breakfast of, perhaps, rice porridge, husbands and wives go out into the *padi* fields, whilst children go to school. Families are closeknit so a grandmother or an aunt might stay behind to prepare food for the rest of the day. Noodles are popular for lunch and even out in the villages the noodle seller calls by, providing a nourishing meal. In the cool of the evening the family sits in a circle on the verandah and eats the main meal, usually soup, a fish, beef or chicken curry called *kaeng*, which means something with a sauce, soup or gravy. Vegetables are prepared either as a salad (*yam*) or blanched, and served with the fiery *nam prik* sauce (page 143), plus of course a huge pile of heavenly perfumed homegrown rice. *Nam prik* sauce made from *kapi*, the fermented fish paste, dried prawns, garlic, chillies, coriander, fish sauce, sugar and lime juice, is the hallmark of a good cook. The Thais hate to be pinned down to hard and fast quantities in cooking so there are as many recipes for this famous sauce as there are cooks. Even when times are hard the sauce will still be on the table and may suffice stirred into a substantial helping of plain cooked rice.

Thai food is prepared with love and attention to detail. It must look good as well as taste good, and satisfy the appetite. There is in general a sophistication in the cooking which is absent in other regions of South-East Asia. This undoubtedly comes of never having been colonized, coupled with the pragmatic attitude of the Thais and their ability to absorb and develop new ideas yet produce a dish which is particularly their own. The use of coconut milk is a case in point. Throughout the whole region coconut milk is used in the curries of each country in much the same way as Western cooks add stock, producing a marvellously subtle blend of flavours from a spicy paste and rich coconut milk. In Thai cooking the same ingredients might be employed but their method is quite different. The coconut cream which floats to the top of the milk is spooned into the wok in lieu of oil and the spice paste is fried in this till the flavours of the spices are developed, then the prawns or fish are added, along with the remaining coconut milk, to make the sauce. Another method is used when making a beef curry. The meat is cooked in the milk till tender, then a ladleful of the cooking liquid is spooned into a clean wok and the spice paste cooked in this to develop the full flavour of the spices rather than frying them in oil which would be the normal method in Malaysian, Indonesian and Burmese curries. Curiously, a similar method to the Thai one is used for making beef *rendang* in Indonesia, except that there the spices are added at the outset and not cooked separately at the end.

Thai curries enjoy a reputation for being fiercely hot; the Thais like them that way but many restaurants will tone things down a little for the uninitiated. Those tiny, innocuous-looking chillies are in fact sheer fire, yet I have often seen people eating them whole with great relish.

Rice forms the basis of the meal and a variety of curries will be served in small, deep bowls alongside. The rice is placed onto the plate first and surrounded with a selection of curries spooned round the edge, with a clear soup served at the same time. In Thailand food is eaten with a spoon and fork off pretty blue and white china, which I always feel shows food off so well.

There are many noodle dishes which serve to illustrate links with Chinese cuisine, like the *mee krob*, where the noodles are fried till crisp (recipe page 150), or *pad Thai* – noodles stir-fried with prawn, (or chicken and pork), beansprouts, spices and peanuts (recipe page 144), plus a variety of soups where noodles are an important element. Noodles in many guises are immensely popular. It is no coincidence that *khai soi*, a chicken curry soup with noodles, is served; it is a close relation of the Burmese *panthe* or *oh-no khaukswe* (recipe page 85), which illustrates the point that food has no borders or boundaries.

Food does, however, vary from region to region, as you would expect in a huge country like Thailand, which is about the same size as France. The shape of the country is sometimes likened to the head of the white elephant with the slim, southern stretch resembling the trunk. In the cooler, mountainous, northern area with its fertile valleys, pearly lychees and succulent strawberries are grown. The north-eastern region, a rolling, semi-arid plateau next to the country of Laos, shares half of the broad Mekong river as its border. River fish feature high on the menus, with catfish, which can grow to a massive size, being very popular. Glutinous rice, the sticky variety, is preferred, and eaten with the fingers as it rolls up into a ball with ease. Chicken dishes are popular, such as *gai yang* (recipe pages 130–31), and, hardly surprisingly in this truly rural area, there are also a number of highly acclaimed duck (and some goose) recipes such as *laap pet*, a spicy duck salad, and a variety of crab dishes, eel soups and crispy fried frogs.

Fish is important to everyone in Thailand, but nowhere more so than in the southern region, which straddles the Gulf of Thailand on the east and the Andaman Sea on the west, stretching down to its borders with Malaysia. This part of the country has the highest rainfall, which accounts for the rain forests, the plantations of rubber and coconut palms, and the fruit orchards. At its broadest this trunklike strip of land is only 100 miles wide, with coves, bays and the idyllic holiday island of Phuket. Sea mullet, fried fish with noodles, squid, crabs, mussels, oysters, all can be enjoyed in the many seafood restaurants, or try *tod mun pla* (recipe page 124), which are fried fish cakes from many street vendors. *Kao yam pak Thai* (recipe page 141) is an interesting rice salad made up from a selection of finely chopped and attractively arranged beansprouts, lemon grass, spring onions, with the green and white parts separately shredded, carrot, dry-fried coconut, ginger, shredded, deep-fried balsam or basil leaves and a little pounded dry chilli, all arranged round a pile of rice in the centre of the platter. Toss all together and top with sauce made from chillies, lime or lemon juice and the inevitable *nam prik* sauce.

On my last visit to Bangkok we ate a delicious meal at a restaurant called Lemon Grass. To start we had *goong som*, butterfly prawns cooked in lime juice and coconut cream (see page 128). They were arranged in a wheel shape on the serving platter with a garnish of shallot and chilli.

Our noodle dish, *woonsen kai kem*, was a salad of beanthread noodles, salted egg, spring onion and beansprout, followed by an irresistible roast duck curry (recipe page 134). Magrut leaves featured here, as well as baby aubergines, green curry paste, coconut cream, plus the roast duck which we ate with steamed fluffy Thai rice. With this we drank weak China tea, but Thai beer would also be a good choice.

Puddings or desserts do not rate highly on Thai menus. There is a coconut-flavoured custard – a close relation of the Malaysian *serikaya* (recipe page 71) – or perhaps fried banana, or, when mangoes are plentiful, one of Thailand's favourite desserts, *Khao niew-mamoung* (recipe page 152), a sticky rice cooked in coconut milk and served with slices of mango, surely one of creation's most beautiful and exotic fruits.

Fruit and vegetable carving is another area where the Thai delight in presentation is shown. Young girls learn this skill from an early age, producing almost lifelike specimens of crabs from pieces of ginger, carving melons to resemble baskets, onions to resemble chrysanthemums, and chillies to resemble lilies.

Another memorable meal was served to us at the Thanying, a stylish, rather grand family house. To begin we had a salad of finely shredded beans, carrots and chicken, with beansprouts served with chilli sauce and garnished with sesame seeds (recipe page 138). Small stuffed crabs, *pu-ja*, (measuring 15 cm/6 in across) came next. Pork meat and ginger was mixed with the crabmeat, returned to the shells and steamed. Finally the whole is dipped in beaten egg and deep fried then garnished with coriander leaves and shreds of chilli. This was served with a chilli fish sauce accompaniment. (I prefer to serve the crabs steamed – recipe page 125). Prawns and pineapple made an amazing combination of texture and flavours in a curry. The curry sauce was made from red curry paste with the addition of tiny cherry tomatoes and a few basil leaves to contrast in colour (recipe page 127).

Another Thanying speciality is a salad *nam prik long rua*. The sauce is a variation on the basic *nam prik* (recipe page 143) with the addition of ground pork, dried shrimp, spring onion, and some palm or molasses sugar, which is an interesting combination of flavours offset by the attractive array of crisp and often beautifully sculpted vegetables such as cucumber and carrot, plus crisp lettuce heart, yardbeans, cherry tomatoes and maybe roast belly of pork or pork crackers.

At the well-respected fish restaurant, the Koom Luang – which is something akin to the famous willow pattern scene, with bridges linking the various parts of the restaurant and lights sparkling in the water – we ate squid marinated in lime juice then dressed with fish sauce, coriander leaves, chilli, spring onion, lemon grass and garlic, all set on shredded lettuce leaves (recipe page 137). *Tom yam kung* is served all over Thailand (recipe page 121), and is a fish soup with as many variations as there are cooks. Lemon grass and lime leaves give it an authentic flavour.

The traditional ground beef salad *laab nuea*, with a north-eastern influence, is appealing (recipe page 138). Powerful flavours are blended together: the ground beef is stir fried without oil; toasted, pounded rice, *kha* (*lengkuas*), spring onion, chillies, mint leaves, fish sauce and lime juice are tossed together with the meat, then served on a bed of lettuce leaves and an assortment of vegetables, including cucumber to add crunch to the salad.

Large prawns are immensely popular, and the ones we ate had been shelled, head removed but the tail left on, then dipped in salt and deep fried for seconds only.

Finally at the Koom Luang a crab curry was served in a mild curry sauce. Huge pieces of crab meat were wonderfully succulent in the rich coconut sauce.

Our last meal in Bangkok was at the Sala Rim Naam restaurant run by the Oriental and next to the cookery school. A selection of little nibbles – a deep-fried rice cup, filled with courgettes, with coconut cream on top, yardbeans tied in a love knot, deep-fried catfish threads, and an oriental fish salad – were followed by red rice and duck curry. Pounded pork with a ginger mixture was cooked in bamboo stems. We drank a soup rich with lemon grass, ginger and tamarind, and finished our meal with a kind of *gula melaka* (recipe page 69), a pudding which crosses many borders in South-East Asia.

The development of Thai cuisine with its historical and culinary influences from China, its noodle dishes, and its stir fry and steaming techniques, has been a long and subtle process. From Arab and Indian merchants the Thais adopted the use of dry spices, i.e. coriander, cumin, nutmeg, cloves and turmeric, as used in the Mussa-man curry. This gave a new dimension to the work of the talented cooks of the rich and famous, eventually developing into what is today one of the world's most exciting cuisines. Perhaps the most significant import was the chilli, which was brought East by the Portuguese. Its place in the cooking of Thailand is undisputed but, having said that, it is the clever way that the different flavours are married together which makes Thai food so unique.

Fresh coriander, one of the mainstays of Thai cooking, is now widely available (or grow your own). Not only are the leaves used in cooking and as garnish but the stems are pounded as part of a spice paste. Lemon grass, ginger, lengkuas, lime leaves, ginger, mint, basil and balsam leaves, as well as coconut milk, all play their part as you will see from the following recipes and from the descriptions in the glossary.

Food is a compulsive topic of conversation in the Land of Smiles at any time of day or night. For me my next visit just can't come too soon.

TOM YAM KUNG
Thai fish soup

One of the best-loved soups with its interesting blend of flavours and tartness which the Thais so enjoy. Every recipe is different. Indeed, recipes are hard to come by in Thailand, as cooks will tell you. They taste as they go along, adding a little more of this and that as their tastebuds dictate.

225 g/8 oz cooked prawns can be used in this recipe instead of raw prawns but it will be necessary to make up a well-flavoured fish stock in advance using white fish bones. Cover the bones with water, add a piece of bruised ginger, a celery stick and seasoning. Bring to the boil, skim, then simmer gently for 20 minutes. Strain, add the flavouring ingredients, and cook as below. Add the prawns just before serving to allow time to heat through.

225 g/8 oz raw prawns
1.5 litres/2½ pints water
2 stems lemon grass, root trimmed
1 cm/½ in piece kha (lengkuas), scraped
3 chillies, deseeded
few sprigs coriander

salt
3 lime leaves
2–3 tablespoons fish sauce (see page 234)
4 tablespoons lemon or lime juice
425 g/15 oz can straw mushrooms,
   drained

1. Shell the prawns and place the shells and heads with the water in a large pan.
2. Bruise the lower part of the lemon grass stems. Add to the pan with the bruised kha.
3. Pound two of the chillies with the stems of the coriander, reserving the leaves, and add to the pan with the salt and two of the lime leaves torn into small pieces. Bring to the boil and simmer for 15–20 minutes, then strain this stock into a clean pan.
4. A few minutes before serving, bring the stock to the boil, add the prawns, and cook for 3 minutes only. Add the fish sauce, lemon or lime juice and straw mushrooms. Taste for seasoning. It should have quite a tangy flavour.
5. Serve in bowls with strips of the remaining chilli, shredded, the

remaining lime leaf, torn, and the coriander leaves floating on top.

Serves 6

GAENG JUED LUKE CHEEN
Clear soup with fish balls

FISH BALLS

450 g/1 lb piece cod or haddock fillet, skin and bones removed	*1 egg white*
	1 teaspoon fish sauce (see page 234)
few sprigs coriander	*salt and pepper to taste*
2 cloves garlic, crushed	

SOUP

2 litres/3½ pints chicken stock	*salt and pepper*
1 cm/½ in fresh ginger, scraped and bruised	*4 spring onions, trimmed*
	fish sauce to taste

1. To make the fish balls, pound the fish briefly in the food processor with the coriander stems (reserve the leaves), the garlic, sufficient egg white to bind, the fish sauce and seasoning. With wetted hands shape the fish mixture into 24 small balls and refrigerate till required.
2. Bring the chicken stock to the boil with the bruised ginger, seasoning and the chopped white parts of the spring onions (reserve the green tops). Cook for 10 minutes, then remove the ginger.
3. Cook the fish balls for 3–4 minutes in the boiling stock. When they have floated to the surface, cook for a further 2 minutes.
4. Serve in bowls garnished with the coriander leaves and shredded spring onion tops.

Serves 8

GUAY TIAW NUEA SOD
Beef soup with noodles

Popular hearty fare from hawkers' stalls all over Bangkok. Real beef stock is best for this recipe, but for convenience consommé or stock cubes may be used.

225 g/8 oz rib fillet of beef
2 litres/3½ pints beef stock made from 2 295 g/10 oz cans condensed consommé and water OR from beef stock cubes and water
5 sprigs fresh coriander
1 bunch spring onions, trimmed and chopped
1 cm/½ in kha (lengkuas), bruised
1 cm/½ in piece cinnamon stick

2 tablespoons groundnut or vegetable oil
2 cloves garlic, crushed
2 tablespoons fish sauce (see page 234)
1 tablespoon thick soy sauce
1–2 tablespoons vinegar
freshly ground black pepper
225 g/8 oz dried rice noodles or 450 g/ 1 lb fresh kway teow flat noodles (see page 239)
100 g/4 oz cleaned beansprouts

To serve
1 red or green chilli deseeded and shredded finely, or chilli oil (see page 83), optional

1. Cut the beef into fine strips across the grain and then into thick, matchstick pieces and set aside.
2. Pour the stock into a pan, crush the coriander stems (reserve the leaves for garnish) and add to the pan with half the spring onions, the kha and cinnamon stick. Bring to the boil and simmer for 20 minutes. Then remove the kha and cinnamon stick.
3. Meanwhile heat the oil, fry the garlic and add the beef strips, stirring till they change colour. Pour in the beef soup. Add the fish sauce, soy sauce, vinegar and pepper to taste. Slowly bring to the boil and cook for 5 minutes.
4. Meanwhile bring a large pan of water to the boil. Add the dried noodles, allow to come back to the boil then turn off the heat and set aside for 5–8 minutes. Drain the noodles. Rinse and drain again in a colander. If using fresh noodles just cut into fine strips and scald with boiling water in a colander.
5. When ready to serve divide the noodles and beansprouts between serving bowls and top up with the soup. Garnish with the

reserved coriander leaves, the remaining spring onions and the chilli if using. Real chilli addicts like to add a little chilli oil – stir well – to give the soup a kick.

Serves 8

TOD MUN PLA
Thai fish cakes

675 g/1½ lb cod or haddock fillet, skin and bones removed
3 lime leaves
2 teaspoons green curry paste (see page 147)
1 tablespoon soy sauce

2 tablespoons cornflour
handful of green beans, very finely sliced
beaten egg to bind
freshly ground black pepper
oil for shallow frying

To garnish

mint and coriander leaves   *chunky pieces of cucumber*

1. Cut the fish into pieces and pound briefly in the food processor.
2. Wash the lime leaves and shred finely, then add to the fish with the green curry paste, soy sauce, cornflour and beans.
3. Bind the mixture together with sufficient beaten egg and season with the pepper. Form into 16 fish cakes. Chill if time allows.
4. Fry in hot oil on both sides for 3 minutes or till crisp and cooked through. Serve garnished with coriander and mint leaves and eat with chunky pieces of cucumber.

Makes 16 small fish cakes

PLA PRIEW-WARN
Sweet and sour fish

1 sea bass, red fish or red mullet (1.5 kg/3¼ lb), cleaned and scaled but head and tail left on
1 tablespoon seasoned flour
300 ml/½ pint oil for frying
1 clove garlic, crushed
1 onion, peeled and finely sliced
1 cm/½ in fresh ginger, scraped, sliced and finely shredded

200 ml/⅓ pint water
2 tablespoons rice vinegar or white wine vinegar
5 tablespoons tomato ketchup
2 tablespoons fish sauce (see page 234)
4 Chinese mushrooms, soaked for 15 minutes then drained
1 teaspoon cornflour blended to paste with water

To garnish
sprigs fresh coriander
1–2 red chillies, deseeded and finely shredded

fresh pineapple wedges

1. Rinse the fish and dry well. Coat lightly in the seasoned flour.
2. Choose a wok or frying pan large enough to hold the whole fish, or cut it in half. Heat the oil, lower in the fish and cook for 5–7 minutes on each side or till cooked through. Lift out and keep warm.
3. Spoon 4 tablespoons of the oil into a clean pan and fry the garlic, onion and ginger to bring out the flavour.
4. Blend the water, vinegar, tomato ketchup and fish sauce together and pour into the pan. Finely slice the Chinese mushroom, discarding stalks, add to the pan and cook for 3–4 minutes. Thicken with the cornflour paste then pour the sauce over the fish and serve garnished with the coriander, chilli and fresh pineapple.

Serves 4, or 8 as part of a buffet

PU-JA
Stuffed crabs

Many fishmongers and supermarkets with a fish counter are selling little crabs already dressed, which might make this recipe more appealing! A 150 g/5 oz crab is an ideal size to serve to each person and they taste good either steamed or fried – though I have a preference for the steamed version.

4 small cooked crabs (dressed if
　　available), weighing 150 g/5 oz each
175 g/6 oz pork, finely minced
6 sprigs coriander, stems finely chopped
1 cm/¹/₂ in piece fresh ginger, scraped
　　and pounded

2 cloves garlic, crushed
1¹/₂ tablespoons fish sauce (see page 234)
freshly ground black pepper
1 egg, separated

Sauce

3 chillies, deseeded and pounded
6 tablespoons fish sauce

2 tablespoons groundnut oil

To serve

finely chopped crisp lettuce leaves

1. If the crab is not dressed remove the claws and place each crab on its back with the head away from you. Use your thumbs to push the body from the main shell. Discard the stomach sac and lungs (often called dead men's fingers) and any green matter.
2. Scoop all the edible meat into a bowl and add the meat from the cracked claws. Add the pork, the coriander stems and some of the leaves, the ginger, garlic, fish sauce, and pepper.
3. Whisk the egg white lightly and stir into the mixture. Spoon back into the crab shells neatly. Brush the egg yolk over the stuffing to seal.
4. Prepare the sauce by blending the pounded chillies with the fish sauce and oil. Pour into a sauceboat or small jug.
5. Deep fry the crabs in hot oil, shell side down, for 4–5 minutes, OR steam over hot water for 10–15 minutes if you prefer.
6. Serve hot, garnished with the remaining coriander leaves, on a bed of shredded lettuce. Hand round the sauce to drizzle on top of each crab.

Serves 4

GAENG KHUA GOONG
Prawn and pineapple curry

This delicious curry was served at the Thanying restaurant in Bangkok. The blend of flavours is typically Thai with sweet and sour followed by a slightly salt taste. To be really authentic use the tiny bird's eye chillies (*prik khee noo*) which are the hottest variety.

As an alternative to the prawns you might like to substitute 450 g/ 1 lb white fish, skinned and cut into bite-sized pieces.

8 large prawns, or 225–375 g/8–12 oz smaller ones

600–750 ml/1–1¼ pints coconut milk (see page 231)

1 red and 1 green chilli, deseeded and sliced in half lengthwise

2 tablespoons red curry paste (see page 146), or to taste

1 tablespoon powdered prawn (see page 234)

2 tablespoons fish sauce (see page 234)

1 teaspoon tamarind paste with 3 tablespoons warm water

4–6 cherry tomatoes

1 thick slice fresh pineapple, cut into small pieces

a few basil leaves

1. Peel the prawns and remove the black spinal cord if very obvious. The shells and heads can be added to a fish stock for future use.
2. Spoon the top third of the coconut milk, i.e. the cream, into a wok and bring to the boil, stirring all the time. Add the chillies and red curry paste and fry to bring out the full flavour.
3. Add the powdered prawn, fish sauce, strained tamarind juice and cherry tomatoes, then stir in the remaining coconut milk and bring to the boil very gently.
4. Taste for flavour then add the prawns and pineapple. Cook for a further 3–4 minutes, garnish with basil leaves and serve immediately with a bowl of fluffy rice.

Serves 4

GOONG PAHD GRATIEM
Prawns with garlic

225 g/8 oz medium prawns, shells
   removed
2–3 tablespoons light soy sauce
freshly ground black pepper

1–2 teaspoons sugar
a little vegetable oil
2–3 cloves garlic, thinly shredded

TO SERVE
½ lime, cut into wedges   a few coriander leaves

1. Arrange the prawns attractively like the spokes of a wheel in an ovenproof dish.
2. Mix the soy sauce, pepper, sugar and oil together and pour over the prawns. Top with the garlic pieces.
3. Place in a hot oven (220°C, 425°F, Gas Mark 7) for 5 minutes till prawns are just cooked. Garnish with the coriander leaves and serve with the lime wedges.

Serves 2 as a starter

GOONG SOM
Prawns in coconut cream

The shells and heads, which are discarded in this recipe, can be used to make a good fish stock. Wash, then cover with cold water and add a little salt. Bring to the boil and add a knob of bruised ginger. Cook for 20 minutes then strain.

8 large raw prawns, weighing about 50
   g/2 oz each (thaw if frozen)
juice of 1 lime or 1 small lemon
1 teaspoon sugar

a little salt to taste
150 ml/5 fl oz coconut cream (see page
   231)

TO SERVE
2–3 shallots, finely sliced, and 1 red chilli, shredded

Wayside Malaysian fruit and vegetable stall, selling spiky durian, avocado, green coconut and (hanging) mangosteen

Kuala Lumpur – Ah Moi *(left)* selects a fish for supper from the van man

Left: Typically cheerful Penang laksa (soup) seller

Below: Burma – a view of majestic Pagan, on the banks of the Irawaddy, bathed in evening sunshine

Right: Elegant Burmese
selling the country's
favourite food, mohinga

Below: Burma – sugar
lumps in woven baskets
for sale by the roadside
near Prome

Typical Bangkok market scenes. Colourful umbrellas shade the produce (including oyster mushrooms displayed on a banana leaf, tomatoes, chayote, chilli and winged beans) from the hot sun

Right: Exotic buffet presentation in Bangkok's prestigious Oriental Rim Naam restaurant

Below: Display of dishes outside one of Bangkok's many market restaurants

One of Thailand's typical take-away dishes – pancakes with sweetened coconut filling

The King's summer palace at Bang-pa-in, about 50 miles north of Bangkok

Right: Indonesian lady making tempe for market, sealing the packet of soya beans over a flame before fermentation

Below: The lobby of the celebrated Oriental Hotel with its hanging birdcage lampshades

Left: Colourful display of fruit in Jakarta's Cikini market – starfruit, rambutan, papaya, banana, mangosteen, lime, Malay rose apples and sapodilla plums

Below: Magnificent selection of prawns, displayed in the ubiquitous banana leaf, in Jakarta's largest fish market

1. Remove the heads and body shells from the prawns but leave the tails intact. Carefully cut along the curved back of each with a sharp knife from near the tail end to the head, without cutting through. Remove the spinal cord.
2. Open each one slightly and arrange in an ovenproof dish. They will open up further on cooking into an attractive shape. Pour over the lime or lemon juice, sugar, salt, and coconut cream.
3. Cook in a hot oven (220°C, 425°F, Gas Mark 7) for about 5–7 minutes. Garnish with the shallots and chilli and serve at once.

Serves 4 as a starter

KHIAW WAAN GOONG
Green prawn curry

If cooked prawns are used omit stage 1. Add the prawns to the sauce and cook for 2 minutes only.

450 g/1 lb raw prawns
600 ml/1 pint coconut milk (see page 231)
4–5 tablespoons green curry paste (see page 147)

3–4 lime leaves, torn
1–2 tablespoons fish sauce (see page 234)
coriander leaves, some chopped finely, the remainder left whole to garnish

1. Remove the shells from the prawns and place the shells with the coconut milk in a pan. Bring to the boil then simmer for several minutes without cover. Strain the coconut milk and discard the shells.
2. Pour a quarter of the fish-flavoured coconut milk into a wok and slowly bring to the boil. Add the curry paste and cook gently for 1–2 minutes, stirring all the time to bring out the flavour.
3. Gradually add the remaining coconut milk and lime leaves, then cook for a further 3–4 minutes. Add the prawns and fish sauce and cook for a further 3–4 minutes only. Longer cooking will toughen the prawns. Stir in the chopped coriander leaves.
4. Remove from the heat and serve scattered with more coriander leaves. This curry can be made ahead and set aside for a few

hours so that the flavours develop further. Reheat briefly before serving.

Serves 4

GAI YANG 1
'Lemon Grass' barbecued chicken

This is named after the Lemon Grass restaurant in Bangkok.

4 chicken breasts
2 tablespoons soft brown or golden granulated sugar
3–4 red chillies, deseeded and sliced

6 shallots, peeled and sliced
6–8 tablespoons coconut cream (see page 231)
salt to taste

TO SERVE
chunky pieces of cucumber and a few coriander leaves

1. Slash the chicken breasts deeply two or three times with a sharp knife. Sprinkle with the sugar and toss well to start releasing the juices.
2. Pound the chillies and the shallots into a smooth paste. Stir in the coconut cream with salt to taste, then pour over the chicken and leave to marinate for at least an hour before cooking.
3. Place the chicken joints over a barbecue and cook for 20–25 minutes, turning several times till cooked through, OR cook in a hot oven (200°C, 400°F, Gas Mark 6) for 35–45 minutes, or until the chicken pieces are cooked right through and look a rich, red-golden colour.
4. Serve with a few wedges of cucumber and a garnish of coriander leaves.

Serves 4

GAI YANG 2
Thai barbecued chicken

1.5 kg/3¼ lb chicken, or 8 thighs or
  drumsticks
1 tablespoon sugar
1–1½ tablespoons whole black
  peppercorns

2–3 cloves garlic, crushed
4 sprigs coriander
juice of 1 lemon
2 tablespoons fish sauce (see page 234)
2 teaspoons thick soy sauce

To serve

wedges of lime or lemon

1. Cut the chicken into 8 portions (see page 59). Slash each portion, or the thighs or drumsticks if using, with a sharp knife, cutting deep into the flesh so that the marinade will permeate the meat fully.
2. Sprinkle the chicken pieces with the sugar and put in a deep glass or glazed bowl.
3. Grind the black peppercorns, not too finely, then add the garlic and the coriander leaves and stems, and pound together.
4. Add the lemon juice, fish sauce and soy sauce then pour the mixture over the chicken joints. Cover and leave to marinate for several hours, turning the pieces in the marinade once or twice if possible.
5. Cook over a barbecue until the juices run clear and the pieces are golden brown and crisp, OR cook in a hot oven (190°C, 375°F, Gas Mark 5) for 35–40 minutes or till tender. Baste at least once.
6. Serve each portion with a wedge of lime or lemon to squeeze over, and eat with fluffy rice and a salad.

Serves 4, or 8 as part of a buffet

GAI PAAD GA-PROW
Stir fry chicken with basil leaves

2 chicken breasts, boned and skinned
4–5 tablespoons groundnut oil
1 medium onion, peeled and finely
   chopped
15 basil leaves

2–3 bird's eye chillies, deseeded and
   finely sliced
2–3 tablespoons fish sauce (see page 234)
1 teaspoon brown sugar

To garnish

2 chilli flowers made from bird's eye
   chillies (see page 230)

a few basil leaves

1. Cut the chicken into neat, bite-sized pieces. Heat half the oil and quickly fry the chicken pieces, stirring all the time till they have changed colour and are cooked through. Turn out of wok with juices and keep warm.
2. Wipe out the wok, then pour in the remaining oil and fry the onion, the basil leaves and the chillies, stirring all the time. After 3 minutes add the chicken pieces, fish sauce and sugar.
3. Turn into a serving bowl and garnish with the remaining basil leaves. Top with the chilli flowers and serve with plenty of fluffy rice.

Serves 2–3, or more as part of a buffet

MOOH PAHD PRIG KHING
Stir fry pork and prawns with beans

450 g/1 lb beans, trimmed and cut into
   4 cm/1½ in lengths (I use half and
   half wing beans with French beans)
6–8 tablespoons groundnut oil
2–3 tablespoons red curry paste (see page
   146)

225 g/8 oz pork fillet, cut into thin
   strips
4 tablespoons fish sauce (see page 234)
100 g/4 oz peeled prawns
1 tablespoon soft brown sugar, or to
   taste
freshly ground black pepper

To serve

1 red chilli, either shredded or made into a chilli flower (see page 230)

1. Blanch the beans in boiling water for 2 minutes, then drain, plunge into cold water to halt the cooking and drain again.
2. Heat the oil and fry the curry paste to bring out the flavour. Add the pork and fry till it changes colour. Being so thin the pieces will cook very quickly.
3. Add 3–4 tablespoons water, the fish sauce, prawns and beans. Add the sugar and black pepper to taste. Serve at once, garnished with the shredded red chilli or chilli flower.

Serves 3–4

RAAM LONG SONG
Rama's bath

This dish was dedicated to a Thai king – Rama. The presentation on a platter of green leaves represents a bath.

1 kg/2¼ lb good-quality stewing beef
1 litre/1¾ pints coconut milk (see page 231)
1 tablespoon soy sauce
100 g/4 oz peanuts, lightly crushed
6 shallots or 1 medium onion, peeled
6 cloves garlic, peeled
2.5 cm/1 in piece fresh ginger, peeled and sliced
1 stem lemon grass, root trimmed
1 teaspoon chilli powder
1 tablespoon molasses or dark brown sugar
salt

TO SERVE
450 g/1 lb spinach, curly kale or mustard greens

TO GARNISH
1 red chilli flower (see page 230)

1. Cut the beef into thin slices and then into even-sized pieces.
2. Spoon 8 tablespoons of cream from the top of the coconut milk and reserve. Pour the remaining coconut milk into a large pan and allow to come to the boil. Add the meat, soy sauce and half the nuts. Cook gently, stirring from time to time till the beef is tender, allowing about 1 hour.
3. Meanwhile prepare a spice paste by pounding the shallots or

onion, garlic, ginger and the lower 6 cm/2½ in of the lemon grass to a paste with the chilli powder.

4. About 20 minutes before the beef is cooked spoon almost all the reserved coconut cream into a wok and heat gently. Keep the remaining cream. Add the spice paste and cook, stirring all the time to bring out the flavours.

5. Add this mixture to the beef in the pan and continue to cook for 10–15 minutes. Add sugar and salt then taste for seasoning.

6. Blanch the spinach leaves, kale or mustard greens, drain well and arrange on a serving dish. Spoon the meat and sauce onto the greens and scatter with the remaining crushed peanuts. Drizzle over the remaining coconut cream just before taking to the table, and top with the chilli flower.

Serves 6–8

GAENG PED PED YAANG
Roast duck curry

1 small duckling, approximately 2 kg/ 4½ lb
salt
750 ml/1¼ pints coconut milk (see page 231)
2–4 tablespoons green curry paste (see page 147), or to taste
4 lime leaves
2–3 tablespoons fish sauce (see page 234)
2 green chillies, deseeded and sliced in half lengthwise
100 g/4 oz tiny, pea-sized aubergines (optional)
few sprigs coriander, leaves and stems chopped

1. Cut the duckling into 2 breast and 2 leg portions, then prick all over with a fork and lightly sprinkle with salt.

2. Place on a trivet in a roasting tin and cook in a moderately hot oven (190°C, 375°F, Gas Mark 5) for 50–60 minutes or till the flesh is tender and the skin crisp. Take from oven and leave on one side for at least 15 minutes before cutting the meat up into small pieces.

3. Heat the top one-third of the coconut milk, i.e. the cream, in the wok, stirring all the time. Add the curry paste and fry to bring out the flavour, stirring all the time.

4. Tear three of the lime leaves and add to the pan with the rest of the coconut milk, the fish sauce and the chillies. Add the little aubergines if using, then allow to bubble gently for about 20 minutes.
5. Add the pieces of duck to the sauce and cook for a further 10 minutes. Stir in the chopped coriander, which will improve the colour. Serve garnished with the remaining lime leaf, finely shredded.

• Chicken joints can be used instead of duck. Roast in the oven for only 30–35 minutes depending on the size of the joints, or till the juices run clear when tested with a skewer, then proceed as above.

Serves 4, or 8 as part of a buffet

GAENG PED GAI
Green or red curried chicken

600 ml/1 pint coconut milk (see page 231)

2–4 tablespoons green or red curry paste (see pages 147/146), or to taste

1.5 kg/3¼ lb chicken, cut into eight or even sixteen portions (see page 59)

3–4 lime leaves, washed and torn

2 tablespoons fish sauce (see page 234)

425 g/15 oz can straw mushrooms (optional) if using red curry paste

100 g/4 oz tiny aubergines (optional) if using green curry paste

To garnish
1 red chilli, deseeded and shredded for red curry, or chopped coriander or basil leaves for green curry

1. Use a ladle to scoop off 300 ml/½ pint of the cream which has risen to the top of the coconut milk and pour it into a wok. Slowly heat till it bubbles round the edges and has reduced a little.
2. Add the curry paste and fry to bring out the full flavour. Now add the chicken pieces and turn in the curry paste till well coated.
3. Stir in the remaining coconut milk, the lime leaves, fish sauce

and the baby aubergines if using. Simmer gently for 40–45 minutes or until the chicken pieces are tender.
4. Add the drained straw mushrooms at the last minute if using, allowing time just to warm through as they are already cooked. Taste for seasoning, adding more fish sauce if required, then serve in a bowl and garnish with chilli, or with coriander or basil leaves.

Serves 4, or 8 as part of a buffet

GAENG MUS-SA-MAN
Mus-sa-man curry

This recipe shares many similarities with the beef rendang in the Indonesian chapter. Both are authentic recipes, which emphasizes a common thread linking the dishes of the region.

1 kg/2¼ lb good-quality stewing beef, in a piece
1 litre/1¾ pints thin coconut milk (see page 231)
4–6 tablespoons mus-sa-man curry paste (see page 147), or to taste
450 g/1 lb potato, peeled and diced

350 g/12 oz small onions or shallots, peeled
a little oil
2 tablespoons tamarind pulp soaked in 150 ml/5 fl oz warm water then strained
2–3 tablespoons dark brown sugar
juice of ½ lemon or lime

To garnish
1 red chilli, deseeded and shredded

1. Cut the beef into thin strips and then into even-sized pieces. Put in a large pan or wok with the coconut milk, slowly bring to the boil, then simmer without covering for about 45 minutes or until the meat is tender.
2. Lift the meat out on a draining spoon and reserve. Reduce the coconut milk by boiling for a further 2–3 minutes. Add the curry paste and stir for 2–3 minutes to bring out the flavours.
3. Fry the potatoes and the onions in the oil in a separate frying pan till golden, then add to the coconut milk with the meat.

Cook for 20 minutes, then add the tamarind juice, brown sugar and lemon or lime juice to taste, then cook for a further 10 minutes before serving garnished with the shredded chilli.

Serves 6, or 8–10 as part of a buffet

YAM PLA MUEG
Squid salad

450 g/1 lb squid cleaned (see page 52)
  and cut into small rings
juice of 1 large lemon (4 tablespoons)
2 tablespoons fish sauce (see page 234)
1 clove garlic, crushed

1 small red chilli, deseeded and shredded
1 small stem lemon grass, finely
  shredded
4 spring onions
2–3 sprigs fresh mint
2 stems coriander

To serve
lettuce leaves

1. Heat the wok and toss in the squid pieces. Keep stirring for 1 minute then drain well and turn into a bowl. Spoon over the lemon juice, fish sauce, garlic, chilli and half the lemon grass. Cover and refrigerate.
2. Shred the spring onions, some of the tops can be cut into curls for garnish (see page 240). Tear the mint leaves finely, keeping 2 or 3 for garnish, along with the coriander leaves. Line a dish with the lettuce leaves.
3. Add the spring onion, mint leaves and some coriander to the fish salad. Mix well, and turn onto the lettuce-lined dish. Garnish with the remaining lemon grass, spring onion curls, mint and coriander leaves.

Serves 3–4

LAAB NUEA
Ground beef salad

450 g/1 lb lean beef, finely minced

2 tablespoons long grain rice

1 cm/½ in piece kha (lengkuas), scraped and sliced

6 spring onions, trimmed and finely shredded

75 ml/3fl oz fish sauce (see page 234)

juice of 2 lemons

½ teaspoon chilli powder

mint and coriander leaves, half chopped, remainder for garnish

To garnish

few lettuce leaves

1 red chilli, deseeded and shredded or 1 chilli flower (optional) (see page 230)

To serve

cucumber, red and green pepper and celery and carrot, cut into fingers

1. Dry fry the minced beef in a hot wok till it changes colour, stirring all the time. Set aside in a bowl to cool.
2. Wash out the wok and dry, then dry fry the rice till it is golden, stirring all the time. Pound to a fine powder.
3. Pound the kha until fine and add to the cooled meat. Just before serving add the spring onions, fish sauce, lemon juice, chilli powder, chopped mint and coriander plus the finely ground rice.
4. Turn into a bowl lined with the lettuce leaves and garnish with mint and coriander leaves and shredded chilli, if using, or top with the chilli flower if liked. Serve with the vegetable pieces as well as some plain rice.

Serves 4, or more as part of a buffet

YAM THANYING
Thanying salad

225 g/8 oz cooked chicken meat

100 g/4 oz French beans, trimmed and blanched for 2 minutes in salted boiling water

175 g/6 oz carrot, peeled

100 g/4 oz beansprouts

SAUCE

5 cm/2 in piece cucumber, coarsely
  grated
4 shallots, peeled and chopped
1–2 red chillies, deseeded

2 tablespoons brown sugar
4 tablespoons rice wine vinegar
freshly ground black pepper
50 g/2 oz peanuts, finely crushed

TO GARNISH

a few coriander leaves

a few sesame seeds, dry fried (optional)

1. Shred the chicken meat into fine strips. Shred the beans into similar-sized pieces and the carrots into matchstick-like pieces. Snip the brown ends from the beansprouts. Keep all these ingredients separate till just before serving.
2. Make the sauce by grating the cucumber into a bowl. Pound the shallots and chillies together to a paste, then add the brown sugar, vinegar and pepper. Just before serving stir in the peanuts and taste for flavour. It should taste sour, sweet and salty.
3. Toss all the ingredients together with the sauce and serve immediately, garnished with coriander leaves and sesame seeds if using.

Serves 4, or 8 as part of a buffet

NAM PRIK LONG RUA
Pork salad

225 g/8 oz belly of pork, skinned and
  cut into 1 cm/1/2 in slices
seasoning
8 pieces pork crackling (chicaron – see
  page 242)

1/4 crisp cabbage, cut into bite-sized
  wedges
8 cherry tomatoes
6–8 spring onions, trimmed and cut
  into finger lengths

TO GARNISH

mint and coriander leaves

DIP

nam prik sauce (see page 143)

50 g/2 oz finely minced pork

1. Roast, grill or barbecue the seasoned belly of pork, allow to go cold then cut into strips.

2. Arrange the pork strips and the pork crackling on a large platter with the cabbage, tomato and spring onions. Garnish with the mint and coriander leaves.
3. Place the nam prik sauce in a bowl. Dry fry the pork in a wok till it changes colour. Continue to cook for 5 minutes over a gentle heat. Leave to cool, then add to the nam prik sauce, with a little water if necessary. Mix well and serve as a dip with the salad.

Serves 4–6

SOM TUM
Market salad

A new fruit called a babaco is now being grown in Guernsey which closely resembles the papaya. To reproduce the sharp flavours of this salad choose an unripe babaco, cut in half and scoop out the fluffy centre and any seeds before slicing finely. The ingredients for this salad can be prepared ahead of time but it is important to mix just before serving.

450 g/1 lb green papaya or babaco, or crisp green cabbage, shredded
1 red chilli, deseeded
6–8 French beans, trimmed
1 teaspoon sugar
4 tablespoons fish sauce (see page 234)

lime or lemon juice to taste
25 g/1 oz dried prawns, pounded
2 medium tomatoes, cut into eighths
25–50 g/1–2 oz crushed peanuts (optional)
lettuce leaves

To garnish
coriander leaves

1. Peel the papaya or babaco, cut in half, remove seeds and cut into wafer-thin slices by hand, or use the slicer of a food processor. Set aside.
2. Pound the chilli and the snapped green beans with the sugar. Add the fish sauce, lime or lemon juice and mix well, then add the dried prawns and tomato pieces. Turn into a bowl and add the papaya, babaco or cabbage shreds slowly to ensure that all the ingredients are thoroughly mixed.

3. Taste for seasoning, add the peanuts if using and garnish with the coriander leaves. Turn into a lettuce-lined bowl and serve at once. Delicious eaten with barbecued chicken.

Serves 4–6

KAO YAM PAK THAI
Rice salad

225 g/8 oz Thai rice, washed and cooked then left to cool

3 carrots, peeled and coarsely grated

100 g/4 oz wing beans or French beans, blanched and finely chopped

175 g/6 oz wedge of cabbage, finely sliced

1 bunch spring onions, trimmed and finely shredded

2–3 stems lemon grass, trimmed and finely shredded

5 cm/2 in piece ginger, peeled and finely shredded

100 g/4 oz beansprouts, cleaned

100 g/4 oz peanuts, coarsely chopped

basil, balsam leaves or coriander, shredded and deep fried

DRESSING

3–4 red chillies

juice of 3 limes or lemons

3–4 tablespoons fish sauce (see page 234)

1. Arrange all the ingredients in neat piles on a large platter with the rice in the centre, or on two separate platters if preferred.
2. Prepare the dressing by pounding the chillies, with or without seeds depending on how fiery you like the dressing. Slowly add the lime or lemon juice and the fish sauce to taste, then pour into a sauceboat.
3. Guests take a little of each ingredient and drizzle some of the dressing over the top, tossing everything together before eating.

Serves 4, or 8 as part of a buffet

YAM MOO YAANG
Crispy pork salad

350 g/12 oz belly pork with rind, cut into 3 rashers and ½ packet crispy pork crackling (chicaron – see page 242)
6 shallots, peeled and finely sliced
1 cm/½ in fresh ginger, scraped and finely shredded

4 spring onions, trimmed and shredded
1 red or green chilli, deseeded and shredded
3 sprigs coriander, stems chopped and leaves left whole

DRESSING

2 tablespoons oyster sauce (see page 241)
1–2 teaspoons brown sugar
2 tablespoons fish sauce (see page 234)

2 tablespoons lime or lemon juice, or to taste

1. Either grill or deep fry the pork rashers till crisp, whichever you prefer. Slice finely when still hot and leave to cool on kitchen paper. Cut the crispy pork crackling into thin slices.
2. Prepare the shallots, ginger, spring onions, chilli and coriander, reserving a little of the chilli and coriander for garnish. Just before serving toss all together with the crispy pork rashers and the slices of crackling.
3. Mix all the ingredients for the dressing together and add to the salad. Turn onto a serving platter and scatter with the coriander and chilli. Serve at once.

Serves 4

KHANA HAW
Lettuce parcels

Allow the following per person:

2 lettuce leaves from a round soft
* lettuce, washed and dried*
1 paper-thin slice lemon cut into
* quarters*
a few shreds of fresh red or green chilli

a few shreds of fresh ginger
a few salted peanuts
8 small cooked prawns
2 small wedges of lemon

Each person places a lettuce leaf on the plate and places half of the suggested ingredients on this, finishing with a squeeze of lemon juice. Roll up into a neat parcel and eat at once, then repeat with the remaining ingredients.

Guests enjoy making up their own parcels, and of course the great advantage is that they know how much chilli or ginger they like.

NAM PRIK SAUCE WITH VEGETABLES

This is the most famous of all Thai sauces. The quantities in the recipe vary from cook to cook but the ingredients remain fairly constant. The sauce can be served on its own, stirred into a helping of plain cooked rice.

50 g/2 oz dried prawns, soaked in water
* for 15 minutes then drained*
1 cm/1/2 in piece prepared kapi (blachan
* – see page 228)*
3–4 cloves garlic, crushed
3–4 chillies, deseeded and sliced
50 g/2 oz fresh cooked prawns (optional)

few sprigs coriander
8–10 tiny, pea-sized aubergines
* (optional)*
2 tablespoons fish sauce, or to taste (see
* page 234)*
3–4 tablespoons lemon or lime juice
1 tablespoon brown sugar, or to taste

To serve
a platter of fresh vegetables as for crudités, OR a platter of blanched vegetables as
for Burmese vegetable platter (page 96)

1. Pound the soaked prawns, kapi (blachan), garlic and chillies together.
2. Add the fresh prawns if using, plus the coriander stems and leaves. Pound again then add the aubergines, if using, and blend well to incorporate them into the sauce.
3. Add the fish sauce, lemon or lime juice, and sugar to taste. A little water may be added if you feel the sauce should be thinner in consistency.
4. Place in a bowl in the centre of the fresh or lightly blanched vegetables.

Serves 4–6

GUAY TIAW PAD THAI
Thai noodles

450 g/1 lb dried vermicelli rice noodles
2 eggs, beaten with 1–2 tablespoons water
seasoning
4–5 tablespoons oil
8 shallots, peeled and finely chopped
2 cloves garlic, crushed
2 dried chillies, deseeded and pounded, or ½ teaspoon chilli powder

1 tablespoon brown sugar
1 teaspoon tamarind pulp, soaked in 2 tablespoons warm water then strained
1–2 tablespoons fish sauce (see page 234)
225 g/8 oz cooked prawns
175 g/6 oz beansprouts

To garnish

1–2 tablespoons powdered, dried shrimp (see page 242)
25 g/1 oz peanuts, crushed
6 squares fried bean curd (see page 227), sliced

1 red chilli, deseeded and shredded
coriander leaves
spring onions, shredded

1. About 10 minutes before the noodles are required cover with hot water to soften. Drain well and keep covered with a cloth.
2. Season the egg mixture. Heat 1 tablespoon of the oil in a frying pan and make 2 very thin omelettes, cooking on one side only. Roll up into a sausage shape. Cut into slices when cold.

3. Pound the shallots, garlic, chillies or chilli powder to a paste. Heat the remaining oil in a wok and fry the paste without browning. Stir in the brown sugar, strained tamarind and fish sauce.
4. Add the softened noodles and toss well, adding a little water if necessary to keep the noodles moist. Add the prawns and cook over a high heat, tossing all the time. Finally add the omelette strips and a handful of the beansprouts, toss, then remove from heat. Taste for seasoning.
5. Pile the mixture onto a plate. Sprinkle dried powdered shrimp and peanuts over it and arrange the bean curd slices round the edge with the remaining beansprouts. Scatter the chilli, coriander and spring onions round the edge of the dish and serve at once.

Serves 6–8

KHAO PHAD PRIK KHING
Thai fried rice

225 g/8 oz combined weight of pork fillet or breast of chicken and prawns
100 g/4 oz French beans, trimmed and cut into 2.5 cm/1 in lengths
6–8 tablespoons groundnut or vegetable oil
2 medium onions, peeled and finely chopped

1–2 tablespoons red curry paste (see page 146)
2 eggs, beaten
675 g/1½ lb cold cooked rice (using 225 g/8 oz long grain rice)
2 tablespoons tomato ketchup
2–3 tablespoons fish sauce (see page 234)
salt and pepper to taste

To garnish
coriander leaves
3–4 spring onions, trimmed and shredded

1 lime or lemon, cut into wedges

1. Slice the pork or chicken into thin slices and thaw the prawns if necessary.
2. Cook the beans in boiling water for 2–3 minutes only. Drain and plunge into cold water to halt the cooking then drain again.

3. Heat the oil in a wok. Fry the onions till transparent then add the curry paste and fry to bring out the flavour, stirring all the time.
4. Toss in the pork or chicken pieces and fry quickly to seal. Push to one side and let the oil collect. Add the eggs, stirring all the time till they look scrambled.
5. Now add the rice, tossing till the grains are well coated. Add the tomato ketchup, which gives the rice a richer and more authentic colour. Add the beans and prawns. Season with the fish sauce. Taste and adjust the seasoning with salt and pepper.
6. Turn onto a serving platter and garnish with coriander leaves and shredded spring onion. Serve hot and give each person a wedge of lime or lemon to squeeze over each helping.

Serves 4–6

KRUENG GAENG PHED
Red curry paste

Sachets and small cans of ready-made curry paste are available from many oriental supermarkets and you might like to try them, but I'm sure you will find these homemade pastes are excellent in quality and flavour.

10 red chillies, deseeded and sliced, or 1½ tablespoons chilli powder
100 g/4 oz dark red onions or shallots, peeled and sliced
4 cloves garlic, peeled
3 stems lemon grass, lower part of stem sliced and bruised
1 cm/½ in kha (lengkuas), peeled, sliced and bruised

4 sprigs coriander
1–2 tablespoons groundnut oil
1 teaspoon grated magrut, or grapefruit peel
1 cm/½ in square of prepared kapi (blachan – see page 228)
1 tablespoon coriander seeds
2 teaspoons cumin seeds
1 teaspoon salt

1. Pound the chillies or chilli powder, onions or shallots, garlic, bruised lemon grass, kha and coriander stems to a fine paste with the oil. Add the grated magrut or grapefruit peel and the kapi (blachan).

2. Dry fry the coriander and cumin (see page 233) then turn into a pestle and mortar and grind to an aromatic powder. Add to the spice paste with the salt and process briefly.

3. Use as directed. Any leftover paste can be spooned into a glass jar. Cover with clingfilm then a tight-fitting lid and store in the refrigerator till required. It will keep for several weeks. Alternatively freeze the paste in small plastic containers, making a note of the quantity.

GAENG KHIEV WAN
Green curry paste

Use the same ingredients as for red curry paste, but use green chillies in place of the red, white onions instead of red ones, and add the leaves from the coriander to strengthen the colour.

GAENG MUS-SA-MAN
Mus-sa-man curry paste

Use the same ingredients as for red curry paste plus the following:

6 cardamom pods   *½ teaspoon each ground cloves and cinnamon*

1. Lightly fry the chillies with the onions, garlic, bruised lemon grass and kha in a little oil, stirring all the time. This initial frying will enhance the flavours.

2. Turn into a food processor and at this stage add the chilli powder if using and blend to a smooth paste. Add the coriander stems, magrut or grapefruit peel and kapi (blachan). Blend again.

3. Dry fry the coriander and cumin seeds plus the cardamom pods and salt. Remove the seeds from the pods and pound in a pestle and mortar. Add the cloves and cinnamon, turn into the food processor with the spice paste and blend again. Use as directed or store as for red curry paste.

PRIG SOD SAI
Stuffed chillies

In spite of the seeds having been removed, these stuffed chillies are very hot, so serve them with one or two milder dishes and plenty of rice.

12–16 even finger-sized chillies, either red or green
100 g/4 oz lean pork, finely minced
salt
3 tablespoons oil

1 tablespoon red or green curry paste (see pages 146/7)
1–2 tablespoons fish sauce (see page 234)
1 teaspoon sugar

To garnish
2–3 lime leaves, shredded

1. Trim the stalks and caps from the chillies then slit down the length of each one with a sharp knife so that they can be filled with the stuffing, OR leave whole, scrape out the seeds with a small spoon and use a forcing bag fitted with a plain nozzle to fill them.
2. Season the pork with the salt and neatly fill the chillies with this. Bring a small pan of water to the boil and cook the stuffed chillies for 3–4 minutes, then drain.
3. Heat the oil in a wok and fry the curry paste to bring out the flavour. Add the chillies and cook for a further 2 minutes, then add the fish sauce and sugar to taste. Arrange on a plate and garnish with the shredded lime leaves.

Makes 12–16

ORIENTAL SATAY

This is the satay we ate at the Thai Cookery School at the Oriental. The addition of curry powder to the marinade gives a wonderfully warm spicy flavour to the meats, which is complemented by the peanut sauce and the crispness of the cucumber salad.

225 g/8 oz each of chicken breast, pork fillet and tender beef
300 ml/½ pint medium coconut milk (see page 231)
1 teaspoon ground turmeric

1 teaspoon mild or hot curry powder, according to taste
a little salt
1 teaspoon dry-fried cumin seeds (see page 232), finely ground
oil for brushing satay

SATAY SAUCE

350 ml/12 fl oz coconut milk (see page 231)
2 tablespoons red curry paste (see page 146)
2 tablespoons brown sugar

1 teaspoon tamarind pulp soaked in 1 tablespoon warm water and strained
fish sauce to taste (see page 234)
25–50 g/1–2 oz peanuts, coarsely ground

TO SERVE

triangles of hot toast

1. Cut the meats into neat, even-sized pieces keeping the beef separate.
2. Stir the coconut milk with the turmeric, curry powder and a little salt and pour two-thirds of this over the chicken and pork. Add the freshly ground cumin seeds to the remaining mixture and pour over the beef.
3. Leave to marinate for at least 1 hour but several hours will not harm either. Select satay sticks and soak in water till required.
4. Prepare the satay sauce by slowly heating the top of the coconut milk, i.e. the cream, in a wok till hot and bubbling. Add the prepared curry paste and fry to bring out the flavours fully.
5. Now add the sugar, remaining coconut milk, tamarind juice and fish sauce to taste. Add the peanuts at the very last minute before serving.
6. Drain the chicken, pork and beef pieces then thread separately on to the satay sticks and place under a hot grill or over a barbecue, turning frequently till cooked through. Brush with oil as necessary. Serve with the prepared sauce, salad (see over) and hot toast.

Makes 18–20 skewers

SALAD TO SERVE WITH ORIENTAL SATAY

½ cucumber, thinly sliced
6 shallots or 1 small onion, peeled and thinly sliced
1 red chilli, deseeded and shredded
1–2 tablespoons sugar

salt to taste
75 ml/3 fl oz rice vinegar or white wine vinegar
3 tablespoons water
2 tablespoons crushed peanuts (optional)

1. Toss the cucumber, shallots or onion, and chilli together.
2. Blend the sugar, salt, vinegar, and water together, pour over the salad and toss well, then cover and chill. Scatter with peanuts when about to serve, if liked.

MEE KROB
A classic Thai noodle dish

A fun dish to prepare for an informal lunch. Follow it with a selection of fresh fruit.

350 g/12 oz thick rice noodles (lai fan)
oil for deep frying
4 eggs, beaten
1 medium onion, peeled and finely chopped
1 clove garlic, crushed
225 g/8 oz pork fillet, trimmed and very finely sliced
1 chicken breast, very finely diced
7.5 cm/3 in fresh bean curd, rinsed, dried and diced

100 g/4 oz chopped prawns
½ teaspoon chilli powder
6 tablespoons salted yellow beans (from a can)
handful of French beans, ends trimmed and finely sliced
2 strips peel from a small grapefruit, very finely shredded
2 tablespoons fish sauce (see page 234)
4 tablespoons icing sugar
2–3 tablespoons rice wine vinegar

GARNISHES

deep-fried garlic flakes (see page 240)
3 spring onions, trimmed and finely shredded
3 red chillies, 2 deseeded and shredded and the third made into a chilli flower (see page 230)

½ box fresh beansprouts tails removed
a little shredded grapefruit peel
coriander leaves

1. Fry handfuls of the noodles in hot oil (375°F, 190°C). They will immediately puff up so watch carefully and do not allow them to colour. Lift out with a draining spoon onto absorbent kitchen paper on a tray and leave on one side.

2. Carefully pour the equivalent of one egg into hot oil in a very thin stream to form a lacy net. This net is used to drape over the mee krob when serving. Only one net is required so reserve the rest of the egg for the filling. Lift out with two fish slices and place to one side.

3. If using a wok for frying then pour the oil into a suitable container, wipe the base of the wok with kitchen paper to remove any sediment then spoon back 5 tablespoons of the oil and heat through.

4. Make sure that all the other ingredients and the garnishes are ready. Fry the onion and garlic in the hot oil without browning then add the pork and chicken and cook till the meats change colour. Lower heat and cook for a further 2–3 minutes. Now add the diced bean curd to the pan and keep stirring, then add the prawns.

5. Fry for 1 minute, add the chilli powder and yellow beans, then add the green beans and the remaining beaten egg in stages, plus the shredded grapefruit peel. Keep stirring and turning the mixture all the time and do not have the heat too high at this point. Add a little extra oil if necessary.

6. Spoon in the three essential flavours in this dish, salt, sweet and sharp, i.e. the fish sauce, icing sugar and vinegar. Mix in well and set on one side. Remove half the mixture from the pan and crush half the crisp-fried noodles then mix altogether and turn onto a serving platter. Repeat with the remaining mixture and noodles and pile on top.

7. Drape the lacy egg net over the top, arrange garlic flakes, spring onions, shredded chillies, beansprouts, shredded grapefruit peel and coriander leaves around the base attractively, and crown the top with a red chilli flower.

Serves 6

KHAO NIEW-MAMOUNG
Glutinous rice and mango

225 g/8 oz glutinous rice, soaked
  overnight
300 ml/½ pint coconut milk (see page
  231)

50 g/2 oz caster sugar
good pinch of salt
1–2 ripe mangoes

1. Wash and drain the rice and place in steamer lined with wetted muslin. Set over a pan of gently boiling water with cover and steam for 30 minutes or till the rice grains are tender.
2. Stir the coconut milk, sugar and salt together till the sugar has dissolved then stir in the cooked rice.
3. Turn into a serving bowl, cover and leave on one side for 1–2 hours until the rice has absorbed the coconut milk. Meanwhile peel, stone and slice the mango into neat slices.
4. Spoon the rice into individual serving bowls and top with slices of mango.

Serves 8

LYCHEES IN SWEET COCONUT MILK

300 ml/½ pint water
100 g/4 oz white sugar
300 ml/½ pint thin coconut milk (see
  page 231)
567 g/1 lb 4 oz can lychees
3 kiwi fruit, peeled and sliced

15 g/½ oz dry white jelly fungus
  (optional), broken into small pieces
  then washed and soaked either in the
  sugar syrup or in the juice from the
  lychees

1. Place the sugar and water in a pan. Slowly bring to the boil, stirring till the sugar has dissolved, then simmer for 3–4 minutes. Draw from the heat and leave to cool.
2. Mix the syrup and coconut milk together. Add the lychees and juice, with the soaked white jelly fungus if using, plus the kiwi fruit. Serve in a glass bowl.

- Freshly cooked sweetcorn kernels are quite a favourite addition. Use instead of the kiwi fruit.

Serves 6–8

KHANOM MAW GAENG
Thai baked or steamed custard

This was my first experience of topping a dessert with crispy fried onions. If you are unsure, serve the onions separately and scatter over each helping at the table.

175 g/6 oz skinned mung beans, soaked overnight
4 eggs, size 3, beaten

100 g/4 oz soft brown sugar
200 ml/⅓ pint coconut milk (see page 231)

TO GARNISH
crispy fried onions (see page 200)

1. Drain the beans and cook in fresh water to cover for 20 minutes or till soft. Drain and purée in a food processor (makes 450 ml/¾ pint).
2. Whisk the eggs and sugar together, add the bean purée and the coconut milk, and pour into a shallow 1.25 litre/2 pint baking dish or soufflé dish.
3. Bake in a moderate oven (180°C, 350°F, Gas Mark 4) for about 40 minutes, OR steam over boiling water, having covered the dish with foil, and cook for 45 minutes or till set. Leave to cool.
4. Sprinkle the top with the deep-fried onion and serve cut into portions with a sharp knife.

Serves 8

Indonesia

Often referred to as the Spice Islands of the East, this necklace of almost 3,000 islands lies to the West and South-East of Malaysia and is the fifth largest nation in the world. Java, one of the largest islands has a population of 100 million, of which 7 million are in Jakarta, the capital.

The East Indies have a fascinating history. Over the centuries waves of traders and merchants have come in search of valuable spices from these lush, tropical and volcanic islands, leaving an inheritance of culture, religion, customs and cuisine. The Hindus in the 1st century and the Buddhists in the 8th century left a legacy of vegetarianism, along with many beautiful temples, the most famous being the world's largest Buddhist monument at Borobudur near Yogjakarta in the centre of Java. Islam was brought to the islands by the Arab traders in the 15th century and is the faith embraced by eighty-five per cent of Indonesians today, but this has happened slowly and indeed there are islands such as Bali, which is principally Hindu, where pork, the forbidden food of the Muslims, is eaten as a festive food. For most of the 16th century the Portuguese attempted to monopolize the lucrative spice trade and undermine the growing hold of the Muslim faith. To a degree they succeeded, with the conversion of thousands of people to the Catholic faith. Some of these became Protestants during 250 years of Dutch rule, which ended in 1945 when Indonesia became a Republic.

Though Java is the most densely populated island it is by no means the largest. Borneo (of headhunter fame), the world's third largest island, is now three-quarters Indonesian and named Kelimantan. Sumatra is also in the big league, being the fifth largest island in the world, then there is Sulawesi (Celebes) and Maluca (the Moluccas). Irian Jaya is the other half of the island of Papua New Guinea, and is much smaller. But perhaps the best known is the Emerald Island of Bali . . . the jewel in the Indonesian tourist crown.

Jakarta was called Batavia in the early 16th century, a Dutch dream to build an exact replica of Amsterdam in the East which badly backfired. Canals became a perfect breeding ground for the resident mosquitos, which in turn wiped out vast numbers of the population. Most of the old city has been demolished but even today, as you approach from the air, you see a huge area of pretty, red-tiled roofs reminiscent of old colonial buildings, glowing in the evening light and interspersed with palm trees to keep you in mind that you are in the tropics, not in Amsterdam. A more significant reminder is the cultivation of the land to within a whisker of the sea. *Padi* fields (which compete with tea gardens for first prize in orderliness) each have a mud wall walkway, giving the impression from the air of an enormous maze.

Rice is life and is eaten at least twice a day. *Padi* is rice on the stalk, *beras* is hulled rice and *nasi* the cooked result, as in *nasi goreng*. Like Thailand, with the ploughing ceremony and blessing of the grain before planting, there are many ceremonies connected with rice in Indonesia, where most of the land is under cultivation, much of it in *padi* fields. On Bali for instance, where whole communities take part in the planting, holy water is sprinkled over the *padi* fields to ensure a rich harvest, and the oxen run races to entertain the spirits. As harvest time approaches, the shrine of the rice goddess will be presented with offerings of betel nut flowers, coconuts, and women's clothes. Fronds of bamboo with long streamers of white paper can be seen in the fields to indicate that harvest time is near. Two sheaves of rice are tied together to represent father and mother. These are placed in the shrine, prayers are offered and incense burned, followed by a feast with rice as its main ingredient, before the toil of the harvest proper begins. Planting and harvesting are times when the whole village or community work together, their reward being one-fifth of the total which is equally divided between them. There is a delightful story of how this came about. A young man was thought to be cursed so no one was willing to employ him, till one day he told his sad story to an old woman too old to work her own farm who offered him one-fifth of the crop if he would help her. Delighted at last to be given a chance the young man threw himself into the ploughing and planting with enthusiasm. As harvest time drew near the old woman asked daily when the crop was to be cut. The young man was near panic, as he had secretly opened an ear of *padi* to find it empty. He decided he must run away before the old lady discovered the truth. As he looked fondly on the *padi* which he had so lovingly reared he noticed a change in the golden stems rippling in the breeze. For the last time before his intended escape he plucked an ear of *padi* and to his joy found that the grains of rice were grains of gold. The old woman was faithful to her promise and gave the young man one-fifth of the crop. He became a rich and prosperous farmer but always gave the people who helped him this one-fifth share, which still holds good today.

Java is an island the size of England where 100 million people live so the production of food is bound to be of paramount importance. It is, fortunately, a green, pleasant and fertile land and is dotted with volcanoes which dominate the landscape. Those which erupt spew out rich nutrients which fertilize the soil. The variety of crops is wide, as you would imagine: coffee, tea, rubber, oil palm, coconut and cloves have all grown there since the arrival of the Dutch to these islands. As Java was more developed than its neighbouring islands people migrated there in vast numbers. The island is now a huge melting pot of different peoples all with their own languages, customs and cuisines, which makes it a fascinating place to visit for anyone with a keen interest in food.

I was extremely fortunate to meet a delightful Indonesian lady who is passionate about food – Ibu Eri Sudewo, who gives Indonesian cookery demonstrations in Jakarta. She introduced me to the Cikini Market, a riot of colour not only in the array of fruits on display but the colourful batik sarongs of the women and the shirts of the men. Huge banana-leaf-lined baskets were filled to overflowing with bright, lemon-coloured star fruit, which make a beautiful sorbet and are also excellent in chutney or in fruit salads, with their slightly tart flavour. Snakefruit have a glossy, scalelike appearance with sharp, crisp-tasting flesh. Bananas were in abundance, the tiny, chubby-fingered type, *pisang mas*, with their sweet flesh are my favourite. There were also the cooking bananas – the smaller ones known as *pisang kepok* and the larger plantain type as *pisang tandok*. The potato-like sapodilla plum when peeled has a pleasing, honey-flavoured flesh, and the jambu, both large and small, add another splash of brilliant, rose-pink colour. They are commonly known as rose apples and are very crisp and refreshing. Large bunches of rambutans were hanging from a simple wooden structure, as well as papayas, pineapples, mangosteen, watermelons and jackfruit, an important ingredient of a traditional Indonesian dish called *gudeg* (recipe page 184). Originally the recipe came from Jogjakarta and the story goes that before the war there was starvation in the area so the Sultan decreed that everyone had to plant two kinds of tree in their garden. These were the jackfruit (or *nangka*) and belingo trees. The jackfruit is a huge fruit, often much larger than a rugby ball and of course much heavier. It has a tough, densely patterned skin and is often sold cut into sections (as we buy large melons). The flesh is yellow with a strong flavour when ripe. Indonesians don't always wait until it is ripe, when it can be eaten as a fruit, but often cook it when young as a vegetable. The belingo or melingo tree produces nuts which when pounded and dried are fried to serve as a snack or as an accompaniment to a meal. These *emping* are very much smaller than the prawn crackers you may be more familiar with and have a slightly bitter taste, which counteracts the sweetness in some Indonesian dishes.

Moving into the market I found sacks of the different types of rice. Red rice has a very good flavour and is said to have a slightly higher protein and vitamin B content than white rice. On the same stall were many beans, whole and in flour form, peanuts (which are grown widely to make the various peanut-based sauces for dishes such as *sate* and *gado gado*, and Javanese almonds, which are larger than our almonds but can be used in the same way. Close by was the full range of dry spices – coriander, cloves, cardamom, cumin, peppercorns and plastic bags of finely pounded red chilli scooped from a large bowl in the background. Duck eggs are readily available, as are quail's eggs sold in boxes of thirty, plus the preserved egg which is so popular with Chinese communities everywhere, and lots of bottled sauces including *kecap asin*, a thin sauce, *kecap sedang*, the medium-dark type, and *kecap manis*, a very thick, sweet sauce which is a vital ingredient in so many dishes. On the *warungs* – the wayside stalls providing instant meals – *asin* and *sedang* sauces are available along with a tomato chilli sauce to add extra flavour to a bowl of noodles or *nasi goreng*.

The *warungs* provide a tremendous service in the big city. On my first night in Jakarta I remember hearing the *warung* man banging the side of his stall as he cycled along selling sustenance to all the night watchmen who had managed to stay awake. Some attract attention by ringing a bell, others hoot, or strike their handlebars with a piece of hollow bamboo. Soon you get to know whether the *sate* seller, the noodle man or the baker with his garish-coloured cakes is in the vicinity. Throwing impromptu parties or supplementing the meal you have prepared just isn't a problem. The *warung* man or woman (and there are thousands of them in the city) are often immigrants from other islands, or even people from the rural areas who have come to the metropolis to try and improve their lot. Many start out when young as shoeshine boys, and some may even become rich and prosperous, like the supermarket chief of a chain called Ken Chick's, who, as you might have guessed, started out selling chickens around the streets of Jakarta years ago. Most will not achieve such fame and fortune; it's a hard and precarious life, but it's a way of earning a living and gives them the flexibility to return to the country to help their families with the planting and harvesting of the crops. Their stalls vary enormously, from a hand-pushed cart fitted with old bicycle wheels to the bicycle type with huge gourds strapped on the back like saddle bags, perhaps filled with palm wine or a box arrangement containing a pot of *bubor ayam*, like a rice porridge, for breakfast. Slightly more sophisticated stalls may have an awning and even a foldaway bench which can be strapped to the side of the stall for easy transportation, such as the *tunkung baso*, selling meat dumplings in a spicy broth with a few vegetables and rice noodles. For those with a lighter load a bamboo pole is carried across the shoulders. Nicely balanced at either end of the pole might be tins of cooking oil or huge tins the size of an old-fashioned metal dustbin full of *krupuk*, the prawn crackers. These *tunkung warung*, or street hawkers, move around at a cracking pace with such loads – with perishables to sell not a moment can be wasted. They are not exclusive to the city; in every town and village they can be found selling food, fruit, snacks such as peanuts, spicy clove cigarettes, *martabak* (recipe page 173), mats, brooms and brushes, baskets of all shapes and sizes, fish, vegetables, 'Dutch wives' (*kapok*-filled pillows), mattresses, shoes and balloons. People queue up to buy the sweetest of drinks from the 'Jamu girls', made from honey, palm sugar, finely ground rice and spices such as cassia and ginger. This is an Indonesian tonic to cure all ailments, and it is also claimed that it sustains beauty and helps you keep slim!

On a trip to the fish market down by the harbour I watched two strong young men wearing yellow oilskins, Wellington boots and trilby-type hats carry an enormous basket of fish slung over a bamboo pole to the central covered area where the fish was being auctioned. *Ikan merah* (red snapper) was available along with *tengirri*, grouper (sea bass) and the much-sought-after pomfret, which are in danger of being fished out as were our herrings a few years ago. The Chinese consider these fish supreme. As they will serve only the best, availability can be a problem. Over the way, there were also shellfish, cockles, mussels (very large ones with sea-green-coloured shells which are now obtainable in the UK from some fishmongers and supermarkets), clams, eels, squid and oysters. It's hardly surprising that fish plays such an important part in the Indonesian diet, the country being made up of so many islands. Freshwater fish is popular too, and when fresh fish is not available there is always a plentiful supply of dried or salted fish in the markets.

At the market in Bogor I found to my joy fresh nutmegs, which I hadn't seen for many years. The fruit looks rather like a smooth chestnut and, like the chestnut, splits open when ripe, revealing the bright red tendrils of mace which turn orange when exposed to the air. When the mace is removed then the nut is cracked and there you have the nutmeg. In Malaysia the fleshy outer husk is used, nothing ever wasted; it can be either crystallized or pickled, both being eaten as a snack.

A women's extension group I visited in a very rural area way out of Jakarta showed me how they make *abon* which, together with tempe and tofu, is sold by the group for cash in the market down the valley. Chicken (or rabbit or beef) flesh is cooked with water until tender then until the water has evaporated. The flesh is shredded very finely and then deep fried until crisp. It is sold in small packets and is served stirred into a helping of rice or as a side dish. This way of preserving meat at least ensures that some protein is introduced into the diet. However, tempe, a preserved soya bean, is an even richer source of protein. Requiring no refrigeration it is widely available and, much more to the point, greatly enjoyed. The soya beans are first soaked, then the skins are rubbed off and the beans are steamed. When the beans are cooked they are transferred to a large basket and cooled with a fan, then scooped into small plastic bags along with a little fermented soya bean yeast. Each bag is sealed over a paraffin flame then pricked with a bamboo sate stick and left to ferment. The beans form a light-orange-coloured mass over a period of one to two days, depending on the conditions and temperature. Tempe is very versatile, it can be deep fried and served with a spicy sauce, marinated first or cooked with the spicy ingredients before deep frying. Whichever way, it's delicious and with its forty per cent protein content, a godsend to all vegetarians.

Festivals abound in Indonesia, as they do in the other countries of the South-East Asian region, with a party being given on the slightest pretext. Put this down to living in the tropics where every growing thing flourishes and people can be entertained with ease under the tall palms or on the wide verandah round the house. With the world's four main religions being practised on Indonesian soil – Islam, Hinduism, Buddhism and Christianity – there is no shortage of feast days and festivals. Lebaran, the feast day to celebrate the end of Ramadan, is the time when all families come together and a huge, cone-shaped mound of *nasi kuning* (yellow rice – recipe page 195) is the centre piece on the table. This is served with *rendang* (recipe page 185), which is beef cooked in spices with coconut milk. It should be cooked till dry, making it easy to transport. Pilgrims on the *haj* to Mecca would take a supply of *rendang* as it is so highly spiced it has good keeping properties.

On the island of Bali, Hinduism is the main religion and due respect is paid to the spirits who come to take part in the many festivals. A major festival is Galungan, a celebration of the victory of goodness over evil. The date changes from year to year, and the gods spend ten days sharing in the festivities. On the final day vast quantities of food are taken to the temple and offered to the spirits who in turn take the 'essence' of these gifts, the remainder being given back for everyone to eat and enjoy. A suckling pig rubbed with fresh turmeric, lime juice and salt is barbecued over an open fire, and fresh turtle meat from the giant turtle is transformed into *sate*. At the centre of the feast are mounds of home-grown rice which has been lovingly cared for by the rice goddess Dewi Sri.

Perhaps the best known Indonesian meal is the *rijsttafel* or the rice table. The Dutch adopted this essentially Indonesian style of serving a meal, known as *nasi gerar*, which means rice served with countless side dishes. This is frequently served as a hotel 'special meal' once a week. Some restaurants serve it in grand style as a regular feature with the head waiter carrying a huge bowl of rice aloft followed by a long procession of serving boys or girls carrying bowls of the various accompaniments. These dishes go through the whole gamut of textures and flavours, spicy, bland, hot, cold, crisp, soft, sweet and sour. Soup, fish, meat, vegetables, spicy hot *sambals* and crisp and soft fritters feature. This is a perfect meal to serve buffet style and the ideal plate on which to serve it is a wide, old-fashioned soup plate. Each person takes a helping of rice, moistens this with the soup, or *sayur*, and then takes a selection of whichever accompaniments appeal. It is a very flexible meal and accommodates the whole range of appetites with ease. If this sounds like a lot of work it's a comfort to know that many of the spicy dishes can be made in advance and stored in the refrigerator or freezer. As with all Indonesian food a meal such as this is eaten with a spoon and fork, and it's quite permissible to eat meats on the bone with your fingers. When this is the case, a small bowl of water might be placed on the table for rinsing the fingers. Dessert is usually fresh fruit arranged as attractively as possible on a glossy banana leaf. *Nasi-rames* is a one-portion miniature *rijsttafel* which might be four or five accompaniments with a mound of beautiful white rice all on one plate.

Chinese immigrants came to Indonesian shores in considerable numbers early in the 20th century to add to those from years past. Wherever they go these incredibly industrious and enterprising people rapidly introduce their own cuisine and consequently they made their contribution to the food of these islands wherever they have settled. The *wajan*, which is the same as the Chinese wok, is standard equipment in the kitchen, and noodles, bean curd and sweet and sour flavours are all spin-offs from Chinese cuisine.

Indonesian food is as varied and fascinating as the races who people the country. It isn't always 'chilli hot' as you might believe. From island to island there are enormous differences in culture and cuisine, and I hope that I have managed to convey some of this infinite variety here so that you can enjoy real Indonesian fare.

Selamat makan. 'Good eating', as they say in Indonesia.

SAYUR MENIR
Vegetable broth with minced beef

100 g/4 oz beef, finely minced
1 large onion, peeled and finely grated
1 clove garlic, crushed
2 tablespoons groundnut oil
1–2 chillies, deseeded and chopped
1 cm/½ in prepared terasi (blachan –
  see page 228)
3 macadamia nuts, pounded

1 carrot, peeled and finely grated
1 teaspoon brown sugar
salt
1 litre/1¾ pints hot water
225 g/8 oz spinach, washed, drained
  and finely chopped
½ 326 g/11½ oz can sweetcorn
  kernels, drained

1. Prepare all the ingredients before you start cooking. Fry the beef, onion and garlic in the oil, stirring all the time till the meat changes colour.
2. Add the chillies, terasi, nuts, carrot, brown sugar and salt. Gradually add the water, bring to the boil, then simmer for about 10 minutes.
3. A few minutes before serving add the chopped spinach and the drained sweetcorn and heat through.

Serves 6

SAYUR ASAM
Hot-and-sour-flavoured broth

This colourful soup from Jakarta has more than a hint of sharpness from the tamarind, which makes it very refreshing when eaten on its own. When served as part of a meal use it to moisten helpings of rice before placing portions of the other foods on offer around the edge of the rice, so that the individual flavours and textures can be enjoyed.

5 shallots or 1 medium red onion, peeled and sliced

3 cloves garlic, crushed

2.5 cm/1 in laos (lengkuas), peeled and sliced

1–2 red chillies, deseeded and sliced

25 g/1 oz peanuts

tiny piece prepared terasi (blachan – see page 228)

1.25 litres/2 pints well-flavoured stock

50–75 g/2–3 oz unskinned peanuts if you wish to be authentic, but skinned, salted peanuts can be used

1–2 tablespoons dark brown sugar

1 chayote, thinly peeled, seed removed, and finely sliced

100 g/4 oz French beans, trimmed and finely sliced

6 tablespoons sweetcorn kernels (optional)

a handful of green leaves, watercress/rocket or Chinese leaves, finely shredded

1 teaspoon tamarind pulp soaked in 5 tablespoons warm water, then strained

salt to taste

TO GARNISH

1 green chilli, shredded

1. Prepare the spice paste by pounding the shallots or onion, garlic, laos, chillies, peanuts and terasi to a paste.
2. Pour in some of the stock to moisten, then pour this mixture into a pan or wok, adding the rest of the stock. Add the unskinned peanuts and cook for 15 minutes.
3. Add the sugar, then about 5 minutes before serving add the chayote slices, beans and sweetcorn, if using, and cook fairly rapidly, adding the green leaves at the last minute.
4. Add the tamarind juice and taste for salt. The soup should taste slightly salty, sweet and sour. Serve garnished with the chilli.

Serves 4, or 8 as part of a buffet

SOTO AYAM
Indonesian chicken soup

There are two ways of serving this delicious soup. The family way requires beansprouts in the base of a large soup bowl, then the vermicelli, pieces of chicken meat, hard-boiled egg slices, celery, crispy onions, and the potato chips, if using. Top with the hot

chicken broth, placing the fricadelles, lemon wedges, chilli sambal
and the kecap manis to hand so that everyone helps themselves.

For a party arrange all the ingredients attractively on a large
platter or in separate bowls, and put the hot soup in a large tureen.
For hungry families the noodles can be omitted and a helping of rice
placed in the base of each bowl, which turns it into a very substantial
meal.

*4 shallots or 2 small onions, peeled and
    sliced*
*2.5 cm/1 in fresh ginger, scraped, sliced
    and shredded*
4 cloves garlic, crushed
2–3 tablespoons groundnut oil

*1 teaspoon turmeric powder, or 2.5 cm/
    1 in fresh turmeric, scraped and
    pounded*
1 stem lemon grass, bruised
1 cm/1/2 in laos (lengkuas) bruised
1.5 kg/3¼ lb chicken, rinsed and dried
3 lime leaves
salt

FRICADELLES

*450 g/1 lb potatoes, boiled and drained
    well*
100g/4 oz beef, finely minced
1 small onion, peeled and finely chopped

1 egg, lightly beaten
seasoning to taste
shallow oil for frying

SAMBAL

2–3 cloves garlic, crushed
2–3 red chillies, deseeded and sliced
4–6 macadamia nuts

1 tablespoon water
1 tablespoon lemon juice
1 tablespoon brown sugar

GARNISHES

*25 g/1 oz bean-thread vermicelli (see
    page 240), soaked in hot water for 3
    minutes then drained*
2–3 cloves garlic, crushed
2 eggs, hard-boiled, shelled and sliced
3 sticks celery, sliced
*½ box beansprouts, cleaned and ends
    trimmed if necessary*

crispy fried onions (see page 200)
*potato chips, homemade or oven type
    (optional)*
1 lemon, cut into thin wedges
*a small bowl of kecap manis (see page
    244)*

1. Fry the shallots or onion, ginger and garlic in the oil to bring out
   the flavour but do not allow to brown. Stir in the turmeric,

lemon grass and laos, then add the chicken and cover with water (approximately 2 litres/3½ pints).

2. Add the lime leaves and salt, then bring to the boil, reduce to a simmer and cook for about 50–60 minutes, or until the chicken is tender. Do not overcook the chicken; the juices should run clear when a skewer is pushed in.

3. Lift out the chicken and allow to cool, then take the meat from the bones and cut into bite-sized pieces. Strain the broth and leave to cool, skim any fat from it before serving.

4. Meanwhile make the fricadelles by mixing the boiled potatoes with the beef and onion, then bind to a dough with a small amount of beaten egg and season to taste. Form into 24 small balls or patties and leave on a tray dusted with flour in a cool place till required.

5. Now make the sambal by pounding the garlic, chillies and macadamia nuts to a fine paste then stir in the water, lemon juice and sugar to taste. Pour into a small bowl.

6. Cut the drained vermicelli into 5 cm/2 in lengths and cook in boiling water for 1 minute, then drain well. Reheat the broth, add the crushed garlic and taste for seasoning.

7. Assemble eggs, celery, beansprouts, crispy fried onions and chips, if using. Fry the fricadelles in shallow oil for 2 minutes on each side or till crisp and golden.

8. Serve as suggested above, with the sambal, kecap manis and lemon wedges in separate dishes.

Serves 8

SOP BAKSO
Soup with meatballs

This is served on stalls and in many restaurants throughout Jakarta and is a very popular lunchtime dish with the addition of a handful of noodles and plenty of chilli sauce.

MEATBALLS

175 g/6 oz beef, very finely minced
1 small onion, peeled and very finely chopped
1–2 cloves garlic, crushed

salt and freshly ground black pepper
1 tablespoon cornflour
a little egg white to bind, lightly beaten

SOUP

4–6 Chinese mushrooms, soaked in warm water for 30 minutes
1 large onion, peeled and finely chopped
2 cloves garlic, finely crushed
1 cm/½ in ginger, peeled and bruised
2 tablespoons groundnut oil

2 litres/3½ pints chicken or beef stock, including the mushroom soaking liquid
2 tablespoons kecap sedang (see page 244)
100 g/4 oz green leaves, curly kale, spinach or Chinese leaves, shredded

1. Mix the beef with the onion, garlic, seasoning and cornflour, then bind with sufficient egg white to make a firm mixture. Roll with wetted hands into tiny, bite-sized balls and set aside whilst preparing the soup.
2. Drain the mushrooms, reserving the soaking liquid. Discard stalks, slice the caps finely and set aside.
3. Fry the onion, garlic and bruised ginger in the oil to bring out the flavour. Pour in the stock and mushroom soaking liquid when the onion is soft. Bring to the boil and add the kecap and the mushrooms.
4. Simmer for 10 minutes then add the meat balls and cook for a further 10 minutes. Just before serving remove the ginger and add the green leaves. Cook for 1 minute only then serve immediately.

Serves 8

PANGSIT GORENG
Savoury filled wrappers – deep fried

100 g/4 oz pork fillet	*seasoning to taste*
225 g/8 oz prawns, thawed if frozen	*1 tablespoon cornflour*
2–3 cloves garlic, crushed	*1 packet of wonton skins*
2 spring onions, very finely chopped	

SAMBAL KECAP

1–2 red chillies, deseeded and sliced	*3–4 tablespoons lemon or lime juice*
1–2 cloves garlic, crushed	*1–2 tablespoons water*
3 tablespoons kecap manis (see page 244)	

1. To make the pangsit, place the pork fillet in a food processor. When finely ground add the prawns, garlic, spring onions, seasoning and cornflour then process briefly.
2. Place a little of the prepared filling onto each wonton skin just off centre with the skin shaped like a diamond in front of you. Dampen the edges except for the peak of the diamond shape.
3. Lift the corner nearest to you towards the filling, then roll up once more to cover the filling. Turn over. Bring the two extreme corners together, sealing one on top of the other. Squeeze lightly to plump up the filling.
4. Repeat till all the skins and the filling are used up. Any leftover wonton skins can be wrapped and stored in the freezer.
5. Meanwhile prepare the sambal by blending the chillies and garlic together then stir in the kecap manis, lemon or lime juice and water. Pour into a serving bowl.
6. Deep fry the little pangsit for 3–4 minutes in hot oil (190°C, 375°F) then serve on a platter with the bowl of sambal in the centre for dipping.

Makes 40

REMPEYEK
Crisp prawn fritters

100 g/4 oz cooked prawns
seasoning
2 teaspoons coriander seeds, dry-fried
   (see page 233)
1/2 teaspoon cumin seeds, dry-fried (see
   page 233)
3 shallots, peeled and sliced
1 clove garlic, crushed

1 cm/1/2 in fresh ginger, peeled and
   sliced
1 teaspoon salt
150 ml/5 fl oz thick coconut milk (see
   page 231)
1 egg, beaten
100 g/4 oz rice flour
oil for frying

1. Lightly chop the prawns by hand on a board, not in the food
   processor as this will reduce them to a paste. Season with salt
   and pepper and set aside.
2. Pound the coriander and cumin seeds to a powder in a pestle and
   mortar then add the shallots, garlic and ginger, and pound to a
   fine paste. Add the salt.
3. Add the coconut milk to the beaten egg, then slowly add this
   mixture to the rice flour to make a batter. Stir in the spice
   mixture and prawns.
4. Heat the oil in a large frying pan and spoon in teaspoonfuls of
   the mixture, cooking seven or eight fritters at a time. Fry on
   both sides till crisp then drain well on absorbent kitchen paper.
5. Serve cold with a variety of dishes, or simply serve as a snack.
   Any fritters which are left over can be stored in an airtight tin.

Makes 20–25

MARTABAK
Spicy meat-filled snacks

FILLING

225 g/8 oz good-quality minced beef
1 small onion, peeled and finely chopped
1 leek, trimmed, washed, and very
    finely chopped
1 clove garlic, crushed

1 teaspoon coriander seeds, dry-fried and
    pounded (see page 233)
½ teaspoon cumin seeds, dry-fried and
    pounded (see page 233)
salt and freshly ground black pepper
1 egg, beaten

DOUGH

225 g/8 oz plain flour, sifted
1 teaspoon salt

150 ml/5 fl oz water
a little oil or lard for frying

TO SERVE

thin soy sauce (see page 244)

1. Mix the meat with the onion, leek, garlic, coriander, cumin and seasoning, then bind to a soft consistency with the beaten egg. Any leftover egg can be used to seal the edges of the martabak.
2. Prepare the dough by mixing the flour and salt in a bowl, then adding sufficient water to make a soft dough. Knead on a floured worktop till smooth and divide into 16 pieces. Roll each piece into a thin round about 13 cm/5 in in diameter.
3. Divide the filling between each round, and fold side to middle so that the edges just overlap. Brush the edges with either beaten egg or water, and fold the other two edges side to middle in the same way so that you now have a square parcel shape. Make sure that the parcel is as flat as possible to speed cooking.
4. Rub the base of a frying pan with oil and when hot cook several of the martabak at a time, depending on the size of the pan. Cook for 3 minutes on the first side then turn over and cook for 2 minutes before lowering heat and cooking a further 3–5 minutes or till cooked through.
5. Serve hot, cut in two diagonally or in quarters, with a light drizzle of thin soy sauce over each helping.

- Cook as soon as possible after preparing the martabak as the dough will become soft and sticky if left for some time. They can be cooked and then reheated in a moderately hot oven (190°C, 375°F, Gas Mark 5) for 5 minutes before serving.

Makes 16

SATE KAMBING KETJAP
Lamb sate

Goat, beef or pork could be used instead of lamb.

675 g/1½ lb meat from leg of lamb (off the bone)

MARINADE

150 ml/5 fl oz kecap manis (see page 244)

3–4 cloves garlic, crushed

3 tablespoons groundnut oil

salt and pepper

50 g/2 oz peanuts, finely crushed (optional)

SAUCE

1 medium onion, peeled and finely chopped

2–3 red chillies, deseeded and pounded, or 1 tablespoon sambal oelek (see page 197)

150 ml/5 fl oz kecap manis (see page 244)

juice of 1–2 limes or 1 large lemon

50 g/2 oz peanuts, coarsely ground

TO SERVE

wedges of lime or lemon

pieces of peeled onion, or fried onion if preferred

1. Trim the meat and cut into even-sized cubes which are not too thick. Blend the kecap, garlic, oil and seasoning together with the nuts, if using. Pour over the meat and marinate for at least 1 hour, turning the meat in the marinade from time to time. Thread onto soaked skewers, three or four pieces of meat onto each one.
2. Meanwhile prepare the sauce by placing the onion, chillies, kecap and lime or lemon juice in a saucepan. Add a little water,

bring to the boil, then simmer gently for about 5–8 minutes and set aside.

3. Cook the sates under a hot grill or barbecue, turning them frequently till tender. This will vary according to the meat you are using, but allow 5–8 minutes.

4. Serve on a large platter with wedges of lime or lemon, fresh or fried onions, and the prepared sauce to which the coarsely ground peanuts have been added at the last moment.

Makes 24 skewers

REMPAH
Spicy meat patties with coconut

100 g/4 oz freshly grated coconut or desiccated coconut, soaked in 4–6 tablespoons boiling water for 10 minutes

350 g/12 oz beef, finely minced

1/2 teaspoon each coriander and cumin seeds, dry-fried and pounded (see page 233)

1 clove garlic, crushed

salt to taste

beaten egg to bind

1–2 tablespoons plain flour

groundnut oil for frying

TO SERVE

thin wedges of lemon

1. Mix the moist coconut with the beef. Add the spices to the meat mixture with the garlic, salt and sufficient egg to bind.

2. Divide into even-sized portions the size of a walnut and form into pattie shapes. Dust in flour then fry on both sides for 4–5 minutes, or until golden brown and cooked through. Can be served hot or cold and are often served as an accompaniment to rijsttafel (see page 164).

Makes 22

ACAR IKAN
Sweet and sour fish

Indonesian-style sweet and sour fish which looks very pretty and tastes good too.

1 whole fish such as red snapper, weighing 1 kg/2¼ lb, gutted and scaled
salt and pepper
5 macadamia nuts
2 cloves garlic, crushed
2 stems lemon grass, root trimmed, lower 5 cm/2 in sliced
2.5 cm/1 in laos (lengkuas), peeled and sliced
2.5 cm/1 in ginger, peeled and sliced
½ teaspoon turmeric powder
1 tablespoon brown sugar
3 tablespoons cider vinegar
approximately 350 ml/12 fl oz water
2 lime leaves, torn
2 bay leaves
2–3 tablespoons cornflour
oil for frying
4 shallots, peeled and quartered
3 tomatoes, skinned and sliced into wedges
3 spring onions, trimmed and finely shredded
1 red chilli, deseeded and shredded

1. Wash and dry the fish, then sprinkle inside and out with salt. Set aside for 15 minutes while preparing the other ingredients.
2. Pound the macadamia nuts, garlic, lemon grass, laos and ginger to a fine paste, then stir in the turmeric powder. Add the brown sugar, vinegar and water to this, plus the lime leaves, bay leaves and salt and pepper.
3. Coat the fish with the cornflour and fry on both sides in hot oil till almost cooked through, allow 10–15 minutes. Drain on absorbent paper and transfer to a serving dish. Keep warm.
4. Pour off most of the oil from the pan then pour in the spicy liquid, bring to the boil and reduce heat. Cook for 3–4 minutes then add the shallots and tomatoes, followed 1 minute later by the spring onion and chilli. Taste for seasoning.
5. Pour the sauce over the fish and serve at once with plenty of freshly cooked rice.

Serves 4, or more as part of a buffet

IKAN KECAP
Pickled fish

If made a day ahead place straight onto a serving dish after cooking, then pour over the sauce, cover with clingfilm and refrigerate till required.

450 g/1 lb fish fillet – mackerel, carp, cod, red snapper or grey mullet
salt to taste
flour for dusting
a little groundnut oil for frying
1 onion, peeled and roughly chopped
1 small clove garlic, crushed
4 cm/1½ in fresh ginger, peeled and grated

3 red chillies, deseeded and sliced
1 cm/½ in prepared terasi (blachan – see page 228)
4 tablespoons water
juice of ½ lemon
1 tablespoon brown sugar
2 tablespoons kecap manis (see page 244)

1. Rinse and dry the fish, removing any large bones, then cut into serving portions if liked or leave whole. Season with salt, dust with flour and fry in hot oil on each side for 3–4 minutes or till cooked. Lift onto a plate while preparing the sauce.
2. Rinse out the pan and dry. Heat a little more oil and fry the onion, garlic, ginger and chillies to bring out the flavour.
3. Blend the terasi with the water to make a paste and add to the mixture with a little extra water if necessary.
4. Cook for a further 2 minutes then add the lemon juice, sugar and kecap. Pour over the fish in the serving dish and eat hot or cold.

Serves 3–4, or 8 as part of a buffet

CUMI CUMI SMOOR
Spicy squid

Prawns can be substituted for the squid to equal effect. Allow 450 g/1 lb prawns, and if they are already cooked add them for only 1 minute at stage 3.

675 g/1½ lb squid, cleaned (see page   *2 tablespoons kecap manis (see page 244)*
* 52)*   *½ teaspoon ground nutmeg*
6 tablespoons groundnut oil   *6 whole cloves*
1 medium onion, peeled and finely   *juice of ½ lemon or lime*
* chopped*   *150 ml/5 fl oz water*
2 cloves garlic, crushed   *seasoning to taste*
1 beefsteak tomato, skinned and chopped

1. Cut the squid into rings. Heat 2–3 tablespoons of the oil in a wok and toss in the squid, stirring constantly for 2–3 minutes. Lift out and set aside.
2. Heat the remaining oil and fry the onion and garlic till soft and beginning to brown. Add the tomato, kecap, nutmeg, cloves, lemon or lime juice and water. Bring to the boil, then reduce the heat and add the squid and seasoning.
3. Cook for a further 5 minutes without cover, stirring from time to time. Serve hot, warm or cold with freshly boiled rice or as part of a buffet spread.

Serves 3–4, or more as part of a buffet

SAMBAL GORENG

Sambals constitute a full range of sauces and accompaniments in Indonesian cuisine. They can be used as a basic sauce, much as we use white sauce, to which numerous ingredients can be added as I've shown here. Alternatively, they can be smaller (usually fiery) side dishes where only a tiny quantity is necessary – see sambal blachan (p.63).

BASIC RECIPE

8 shallots or 1 medium onion, peeled and sliced

4 cloves garlic, crushed

2.5 cm/1 in laos (lengkuas) peeled and sliced

4 red chillies, deseeded and sliced, or 1 tablespoon sambal oelek (see page 197)

1 cm/1/2 in prepared terasi (blachan – see page 228)

salt

3–4 tablespoons groundnut oil

1 tablespoon tomato purée

2 bay leaves

2 lime leaves

300 ml/1/2 pint stock or water, or coconut milk if you prefer

1 teaspoon tamarind, soaked in 3 tablespoons warm water for 10 minutes then strained

1 tablespoon molasses or soft dark brown sugar

2–3 tablespoons coconut cream or a thin slice of creamed coconut (see page 231)

1. Pound the shallots or onion with the garlic, laos, chillies or sambal oelek, terasi, and salt until smooth.
2. Heat the oil and fry the prepared paste to bring out the flavours.
3. Stir in the tomato purée, bay leaves, lime leaves and stock, water or coconut milk.
4. Choose one of the variations listed below and add the ingredients to the sauce as directed. Finally, stir in the tamarind juice, molasses or sugar, and coconut cream. Taste for seasoning and serve with freshly boiled rice.

SAMBAL GORENG HATI (LIVER IN SPICY SAUCE)

225 g/8 oz calves' liver, rinsed, dried and cut into even-sized pieces

2–3 tomatoes, skinned and chopped

225 g/8 oz potato peeled and cut into dice then fried in hot oil until golden

Add the liver to the sauce and cook gently for 5–8 minutes, then add the tomatoes and the fried potatoes and cook for a further 5 minutes before stirring in the final ingredients.

SAMBAL GORENG KERING TEMPE (TEMPE IN SPICY SAUCE)

Cut 100 g/4 oz tempe into small pieces, thawed if frozen. Add to the sauce and cook gently for 10–15 minutes then add the final ingredients.

Sambal goreng telor (Eggs in spicy sauce)

Cut 4 hard-boiled eggs in half, or use 12 quail's eggs left whole, and add to the sambal goreng. Cook for 5 minutes then leave to stand for a while so that the spices permeate the eggs. Reheat gently before adding the final ingredients plus a few coarsely ground peanuts if liked.

Sambal goreng tomaat (Tomatoes and prawns in spicy sauce)

450 g/1 lb unripe tomatoes and 225 g/8 oz fresh or thawed frozen prawns

Remove the core from the tomatoes, peel if liked, then cut into wedges before adding to the sambal goreng and cook for 5 minutes. Add the prawns just before stirring in the final ingredients.

Sambal goreng kembang kubis (cauliflower in spicy sauce)

Add 1 small cauliflower, trimmed into florets and blanched, to the sambal goreng and cook for just under 5 minutes before adding the final ingredients.

Sambal goreng kacang kedele (Soya beans in spicy sauce)

175 g/6 oz soya beans, 2 large ripe tomatoes, skinned and cut into even-sized pieces

Soak the soya beans in water overnight. Drain and cover with plenty of fresh water then cook for about 2 hours or till tender. Add to the sambal goreng with the tomato pieces and cook for 5 minutes before adding the final ingredients.

Serves 3–4, or 8 as part of a buffet

SAMBAL GORENG PETIS TELOR
Spicy eggs

This is a quite different recipe from the previous one in spite of its similar-sounding name.

4 eggs, hard-boiled
1 small onion, peeled and sliced
1 cm/½ in laos (lengkuas), peeled and sliced
1 clove garlic, crushed
1 cm/½ in prepared terasi (blachan – see page 228)

2–3 tablespoons groundnut or vegetable oil
1 teaspoon dark brown sugar
200 ml/7 fl oz coconut milk (see page 231)
juice of ½ lemon
salt to taste

To Garnish

celery leaves

1. Shell the eggs, cut them in half, and arrange on a serving dish.
2. Pound the onion, laos and garlic to a fine paste, using a pestle and mortar rather than a food processor, as this is a very small quantity. Add the terasi and pound again.
3. Heat the oil and fry the paste to bring out the flavour, but do not allow to brown. Keep the mixture moving all the time.
4. Stir in the sugar and then gradually add the coconut milk and continue to cook without cover, stirring from time to time till the sauce is creamy and the flavours are well developed.
5. Add the lemon juice and salt if necessary, then pour over the eggs. Garnish with celery leaves. This dish can be eaten hot, warm or cold and can be made a day ahead if liked.

Serves 8 as part of a buffet

AYAM KECAP
Chicken with spices and soy sauce

A very simple recipe which tastes even better when gently reheated the following day.

1.4 kg/3 lb chicken, jointed and cut into 16 pieces (see page 59)

3 onions, peeled and sliced

3 cloves garlic, crushed

4 red chillies, deseeded and sliced, or 1 tablespoon chilli powder

3–4 tablespoons oil

½ teaspoon ground nutmeg

6 whole cloves

1 teaspoon tamarind purée, soaked in 3 tablespoons water and strained

2–3 tablespoons kecap manis or kecap asin (see page 244)

salt to taste

1. Place the chicken in a large pan with 1 litre/1¾ pints water just to cover, plus one of the onions. Bring to the boil then reduce the heat and simmer for 20 minutes.
2. Meanwhile pound the remaining onion with the garlic and chillies to a fine paste, then fry in the oil in a wok to bring out the flavour but do not allow to brown.
3. When the chicken is half-cooked after the 20 minutes, lift out of the stock in the pan on a draining spoon and put straight into the spicy mixture. Toss over a fairly high heat so that the spices permeate the chicken pieces.
4. Add the nutmeg, cloves, tamarind juice and kecap to the chicken and cook for a further 2–3 minutes, then add 300 ml/½ pint of the stock the chicken was cooked in. Taste for salt and cook uncovered for a further 25–35 minutes or until the chicken pieces are tender.

Serves 4, or 8 as part of a buffet

AYAM BAKAR
Grilled chicken

1.5 kg/3¼ lb chicken

4 cloves garlic, crushed

2 stems lemon grass, root removed and lower part of stem sliced

1 cm/½ in laos (lengkuas), peeled and sliced

1 teaspoon turmeric powder

salt to taste

3–4 bay leaves

3 tablespoons each kecap manis and thin soy sauce (see page 244)

50 g/2 oz butter or margarine

1. Cut the chicken into 8 portions (see page 59). Slash the fleshy part of each portion twice and set aside.

2. Pound the garlic, lemon grass, laos, turmeric and salt to a paste in a pestle and mortar. Rub the paste into the chicken pieces and leave for at least 30 minutes. Wear rubber gloves for this as the turmeric will stain heavily, or wash your hands immediately after mixing.
3. Transfer to a wok, add the bay leaves and pour in 450 ml/¾ pint water. Bring to the boil, cover and cook gently for 30 minutes, adding a little more water if necessary. Stir from time to time.
4. Add the two soy sauces to the pan and the butter or margarine. When the chicken is well coated and the sauce reduced, transfer the chicken pieces to a grill, barbecue or moderately hot oven (190°C, 375°F, Gas Mark 5) to complete the cooking. Allow 10–15 minutes or till cooked through. Baste with the sauce during cooking.
5. Serve with plenty of freshly cooked rice and Acar bening (see page 189), or as part of a buffet or rijsttafel (see page 164).

Serves 4, or more as part of a buffet

AYAM OPOR
Chicken cooked in coconut milk

1.5 kg/3¼ lb chicken	2 stems lemon grass root, trimmed and
4 cloves garlic, peeled	fleshy part bruised
1 medium onion, peeled and sliced	3 lime leaves
4 macadamia nuts	2 bay leaves
1 tablespoon ground coriander	salt to taste
3 tablespoons oil	1 teaspoon sugar
2.5 cm/1 in laos, (lengkuas) peeled and	600 ml/1 pint coconut milk (see page
bruised	231)

To garnish
crispy fried onions (see page 200)

1. Cut the chicken into eight pieces (see page 59).
2. Pound the garlic, onion, macadamia nuts and coriander to a fine

paste. Heat the oil and fry the pounded mixture to bring out the flavour. Do not allow to brown.

3. Add the chicken pieces to the wok with the laos, lemon grass, lime leaves, bay leaves, salt, sugar and coconut milk.

4. Bring to the boil then reduce heat and simmer for a further 40–45 minutes without cover, or until the chicken is tender and the coconut sauce is reduced. Serve sprinkled with crispy fried onions.

Serves 4, or 8 as part of a buffet

GUDEG
A chicken and jackfruit dish from Jogjakarta

1.5 kg/3¼ lb roasted chicken

565 g/1 lb 4 oz can young green jackfruit in brine

1 bunch chard or 450 g/1 lb spinach or 1 head of Chinese leaves

2 tablespoons dry-fried coriander seeds, freshly ground (see page 233)

10 shallots, peeled and sliced

5 cloves garlic, crushed

4 macadamia nuts

2.5 cm/1 in prepared terasi (blachan – see page 228)

1 tablespoon muscovado sugar

salt

450 ml/15 fl oz thin coconut milk (see page 231)

450 ml/15 fl oz medium coconut milk (see page 231)

4 slices laos (lengkuas), peeled and lightly bruised

6 bay leaves

6 hard-boiled eggs, shelled and cut in half

100 g/4 oz fried bean curd (see page 227)

1. Strip the meat from the chicken and cut into neat pieces. Drain the jackfruit and cut into thin slices. Wash the leaves and dry. Tear if very large, otherwise leave whole.

2. Pound the coriander, shallots, garlic, macadamia nuts, terasi, sugar and salt together to make a paste. Divide this paste between the coconut milks.

3. Line the base of a heavy pan or a flameproof casserole with half the green leaves, all the laos and the bay leaves. Make layers of the jackfruit, chicken, halved eggs and bean curd.

4. Pour over the thin coconut milk with spices and cover with the remaining green leaves. Cover and cook over a low heat till the

liquid has almost disappeared and the jackfruit pieces are tender – about 30 minutes.

5. Bring the medium coconut milk with the spices to the boil then simmer till it has the consistency of cream. This is served as a sauce with the gudeg in the pan or casserole and can be poured over the gudeg before serving or spooned over each helping.

Serves 8

BEEF RENDANG
Beef curry from Padang

This recipe is much moister than a traditional rendang and is a firm favourite in my repertoire.

1 kg/2¼ lb good-quality beef, in one piece

2 onions, or the equivalent in shallots, peeled and sliced

4 cloves garlic, crushed

2 cm/¾ in laos (lengkuas), peeled and sliced

2 cm/¾ in ginger, peeled and sliced

4–6 red chillies, deseeded and sliced

1 stem lemon grass, root trimmed and lower part sliced

1 teaspoon turmeric, or 2.5 cm/1 in fresh turmeric, scraped and pounded

1 teaspoon coriander seeds, dry-fried and pounded (see page 233)

1 teaspoon cumin seeds, dry-fried and pounded (see page 233)

2 lime leaves, torn

750 ml/1¼ pints thin coconut milk (see page 231)

1 teaspoon tamarind purée soaked in 4 tablespoons water and strained

2 tablespoons kecap sedang or thin soy sauce (see page 244)

salt to taste

8 small new potatoes, well-scrubbed (optional)

a little stock or water (optional)

TO GARNISH
crispy fried onions (see page 200) and a chilli flower (see page 230)

1. Trim the meat into long strips and then into even-sized pieces and place in a bowl.
2. Pound the onions, garlic, laos, ginger, chillies, lower part of lemon grass and turmeric to a fine paste. Spoon over the meat

and mix well with your hands, or with a spoon to prevent staining your hands.

3. Spoon the ground coriander and cumin over the meat and mix well then add the lime leaves. Leave to marinate whilst preparing the other ingredients.

4. Pour the coconut milk and the tamarind juice into a wok or flameproof casserole and turn in the spiced meat and the kecap. Taste and add salt if necessary, then stir till the liquid comes to the boil, reduce heat and simmer gently without cover for about 1½–2 hours, or until the meat is tender and the liquid reduced.

5. If using the new potatoes, add them to the rendang about 20–25 minutes before the end of the cooking time. These absorb a lot of the rendang sauce so be ready to add a little stock or water to compensate for this if you prefer the rendang to be rather more moist than it would be served in Indonesia.

6. Transfer the rendang to a serving bowl and garnish with crispy fried onions and a chilli flower.

Serves 6–8

PERGEDEL DJAWA
Meat balls

450 g/1 lb good-quality minced beef
1 large onion, peeled and finely chopped
1–2 red chillies, deseeded and sliced
2 cloves garlic, crushed
1 cm/½ in prepared terasi (blachan – see page 228)
1 tablespoon coriander seeds, dry-fried and pounded (see page 233)

1 teaspoon cumin seeds, dry-fried and pounded (see page 233)
2 teaspoons kecap manis (see page 244)
salt and freshly ground black pepper
1 teaspoon dark brown sugar
juice of ½ lemon
beaten egg to bind
oil for frying

1. Place the meat in a large bowl. Chop the onion, chillies and garlic in a food processor if liked with the terasi so that it is well distributed throughout. Do not over-chop or the onion will become wet and spoil the consistency of the meat balls.

2. Add to the meat together with the pounded coriander and

cumin, the kecap, seasoning, sugar and lemon juice. Bind with sufficient beaten egg and shape into small, even-sized balls.

3. Chill briefly if liked, then fry in shallow oil, turning often till cooked through. This will take 4–5 minutes depending on the size.

4. Drain on absorbent kitchen paper and serve in a bowl as an accompaniment, or in a sambal goreng sauce (see page 178), or take on a picnic with sate sauce (see page 174).

Makes 24

BABI PANGGANG
Barbecued spareribs

Pork spareribs are sold in packs from many supermarkets but be sure to look for meaty ribs and chunky shapes, which are easier to cook in this recipe. Beef ribs can be cooked in the same way but you may have to brush with oil on the grill or barbecue, which should not be necessary with the pork.

900 g/2 lb pork spareribs
85 ml/3 fl oz kecap manis (see page 244)
1 medium onion, peeled and finely chopped
2 cloves garlic, crushed
2.5 cm/1 in fresh ginger, peeled and finely shredded

1–2 red chillies, deseeded and chopped, or 1 tablespoon sambal oelek (see page 197)
salt and pepper
1 teaspoon tamarind pulp soaked in 75 ml/3 fl oz water for 10 minutes then strained
1–2 tablespoons dark brown sugar
2 tablespoons groundnut oil

1. Wipe the ribs and place in a wok or wide frying pan.
2. Blend the kecap, onion, garlic, ginger and chillies or sambal oelek together in a bowl or in a food processor. Add the seasoning, strained tamarind juice, sugar and oil, then pour over the ribs and toss till they are well coated.
3. Slowly bring to the boil then reduce to a simmer, stirring frequently and adding a little water if necessary. Cook without cover

for 30 minutes. Transfer to a grill or barbecue and continue cooking till the ribs are tender. Baste as necessary with the sauce.
4. They can also be finished off set on a grid over a roasting tin in a hot oven (200°C, 400°F, Gas Mark 6) for a further 20 minutes depending on the thickness of the ribs. Turn from time to time.

Serves 6

CHAH KANGKUNG
Stir-fried greens

2 bunches kangkung, chard or spinach, or 1 head Chinese leaves, or 450 g/ 1 lb curly kale

3 cloves garlic, crushed

1 slice ginger, peeled and shredded

3–4 tablespoons groundnut oil

100 g/4 oz chicken breast, pork fillet or a mixture of both, very finely sliced

12 quail's eggs, hard-boiled and shelled

1 red chilli, deseeded and shredded

2–3 tablespoons oyster sauce (see page 241)

1 tablespoon brown sugar

salt to taste

2 teaspoons cornflour mixed to a paste with 50 ml/2 fl oz cold water

1. Wash the leaves well and shake dry, then strip the tender leaves from the stems and tear into pieces. Discard the lower, tougher part of the stems but slice the remainder evenly.
2. Have all the other ingredients ready, then fry the garlic and ginger in the oil for 1 minute without browning. Add the chicken or pork or both and keep them moving in the wok till the meat changes colour.
3. When the meat looks cooked add the sliced stems first and cook quickly, then add the torn leaves, quail's eggs, and chilli. Spoon in the oyster sauce and a little boiling water if necessary, cover and cook for 1–2 minutes only.
4. Remove cover, stir, add the sugar and salt and taste. Stir in the cornflour and toss thoroughly till glossy and well coated. Serve at once whilst the greens are still very hot and the colours positively jewel-like.

Serves 4

ACAR BENING
Mixed vegetable pickle

This can be served as an accompaniment to any Indonesian or Malaysian meal. Any leftovers should be used within a few days rather than weeks, to retain crispness.

1 small cucumber, peeled, deseeded and sprinkled with salt
1 onion, peeled, thinly sliced, and sprinkled with salt
1 small ripe pineapple
1 green pepper, deseeded and chopped
2 firm tomatoes, skinned, deseeded and cut into wedges

1 large ripe tomato, skinned, deseeded and chopped
2 tablespoons golden granulated sugar
3–4 tablespoons cider vinegar or white wine vinegar
120 ml/4 fl oz water
salt to taste

1. Rinse the cucumber, dry then cut into even-sized pieces. Rinse the onion, dry and place in a large bowl with the cucumber.
2. Peel the pineapple, removing all the eyes by cutting from top to bottom. Slice thinly, then core and cut the slices into neat pieces. Add to the bowl with the green pepper and all the tomatoes.
3. Heat the sugar, vinegar and water over a gentle heat till the sugar dissolves, then draw from the heat and cool quickly.
4. When cold add a little salt then pour over the fruit and vegetables. Cover and chill in the refrigerator till required.

Serves 8

CUCUR BAWANG
Savoury vegetable fritters

A little chopped chilli, a few prawns or some pounded spices can be added to these fritters as a variation on the theme.

*100 g/4 oz white cabbage, very finely
  shredded*
*75 g/3 oz carrots, peeled and finely
  grated*
*50 g/2 oz green beans, trimmed and
  shredded*
1 stalk celery, finely chopped
2 large spring onions, shredded

100 g/4 oz plain flour
2 cloves garlic, crushed
*3 shallots or 2 small onions, peeled and
  finely chopped*
seasoning to taste
2 eggs, beaten
75 ml/3 fl oz water
oil for shallow frying

1. Mix the cabbage, carrots, green beans, celery and spring onions
   together.
2. Sift the flour into a bowl, stir in the garlic, onions, and seasoning
   and make into a batter with the beaten eggs and water.
3. Stir in the chopped vegetables and drop dessertspoonfuls of the
   batter into hot oil in a frying pan. The batter should hold its
   shape when fried in flat fritters. Allow 2 minutes to cook on each
   side till crisp and golden.

Makes 30

TAHU GORENG KETJAP
Bean curd and cucumber salad

1 small cucumber
salt
1 square fresh bean curd

oil for frying
100 g/4 oz beansprouts

DRESSING

1 small onion, peeled and grated
2 cloves garlic, crushed
*1–1½ teaspoons sambal oelek (see page
  197)*
*2–3 tablespoons kecap manis (see page
  244)*

*1–2 tablespoons cider vinegar or rice
  vinegar*
½ tablespoon dark brown sugar
salt to taste

TO GARNISH

celery leaves

crispy fried onions (see page 200)

1. Trim the ends from the cucumber then cut into neat dice. Sprinkle with salt and set aside while preparing the remaining ingredients.
2. Fry the bean curd in hot oil on both sides until golden, then drain on absorbent kitchen paper and cut into cubes. Trim the brown tails from the beansprouts, wash and drain thoroughly.
3. Prepare the dressing by blending the onion, garlic and sambal oelek together, then stir in the kecap, vinegar, sugar and salt to taste. This can be done by shaking in a screwtop glass jar if liked.
4. Just before serving rinse the cucumber dice under cold water and drain thoroughly. Toss the cucumber, fried bean curd and sprouts together and pour the dressing over.
5. Garnish with celery leaves and crispy fried onions and serve at once.

Serves 4–6, or more as part of a buffet

GADO GADO
Indonesian salad with peanut sauce

VERSION A: COOKED VEGETABLE SALAD

Individual servings of this salad can be prepared instead of putting everything onto a large platter. It's a perfect recipe for lunch or an informal gathering.

450 g/1 lb cabbage, spinach and bean-sprouts in roughly equal proportions

½ cucumber, cut into wedges, salted and set aside for 15 minutes

1 square bean curd OR 100 g/4 oz piece tempe, thawed if frozen, and a squeeze of lemon juice

oil for frying

6–8 large krupuk and 24 emping (see pages 236/234)

225 g/8 oz cooked waxy potato, sliced and diced

2–3 eggs, hard-boiled, shelled, and sliced or cut into quarters

a few crispy fried onions (optional – see page 200)

1. Wash and cut the cabbage and spinach into shreds. Trim the brown tails from the beansprouts if liked. Have a large pan of salted boiling water ready, then plunge the cabbage, spinach and beansprouts in separately for just a few seconds to blanch. Lift out and run under very cold water or leave in iced water for 2 minutes. Drain thoroughly.

2. Rinse the cucumber pieces and drain well. Cut the bean curd into dice or the tempe into 8 thin slices. Soak the tempe slices in a little water with the lemon juice for 5 minutes. Lift out and dry on kitchen paper. Fry the bean curd or tempe in hot oil till crisp on both sides, then drain on kitchen paper.

3. Add a lot more oil to the pan then deep fry the krupuk one or two at a time and the emping in two lots. Reserve on a tray lined with kitchen paper.

4. Arrange the potatoes, green vegetables and beansprouts attractively on a platter with the cucumber, hard-boiled eggs, bean curd or tempe, emping, and onions if using.

5. Just before serving make the peanut sauce. The fried krupuk can be handed round separately.

Serves 6–8

PEANUT SAUCE (SIMPLE METHOD)

2–4 red chillies, deseeded and pounded, or 1 tablespoon sambal oelek (see page 197)

300 ml/½ pint coconut milk (see page 231)

½ 340 g/12 oz jar crunchy peanut butter

1 tablespoon molasses, or dark brown sugar

1 teaspoon tamarind pulp soaked in 3 tablespoons warm water, then strained

salt to taste

a few coarsely crushed peanuts if liked

1. Pound the chillies and add to the coconut milk in a pan. Add the peanut butter and heat gently stirring till there are no lumps of peanut butter.

2. Allow to bubble gently as the sauce thickens, then add the sugar, tamarind juice, salt and crushed peanuts. Serve hot in a sauce-boat. Guests help themselves to the salad and spoon the sauce on top.

VERSION B: FRUIT AND RAW VEGETABLE SALAD

A banana leaf which can be bought from oriental stores (see page 226) can be used to line the platter for a special occasion.

crisp lettuce leaves, washed and shredded

1/4 cucumber, seeds removed, sliced and salted

3 small tomatoes, cut into wedges

2–3 slices fresh pineapple, core removed and cut into wedges

175 g/ 6 oz wedge bangkuang (see page 226), peeled and cut into matchstick pieces, or use 2 unripe pears, peeled and sliced at the last moment

1–2 apples, cored and sliced at the last moment, but not peeled

2–3 eggs hard-boiled and shelled, or 12 quail's eggs, hard-boiled and shelled

175 g/6 oz cold, cooked egg noodles, chopped

fried krupuk and emping, cooked as for version A

crispy fried onions (see page 200)

peanut sauce (see above)

1. Just before serving arrange all the vegetables and fruit attractively on a flat serving platter. A banana leaf or the lettuce can be used to form a bed for the salad.
2. Slice or quarter the hard-boiled eggs (if using quail's eggs leave them whole), and add them to the salad with the chopped noodles, krupuk, emping and crispy fried onions. Serve at once with the peanut sauce.

Serves 6

NASI GORENG
Indonesian fried rice

A very popular recipe which is again a perfect lunch or supper dish. Cooked meats and leftovers can be substituted for the fresh pork and chicken.

350 g/12 oz long grain rice, cooked and
   left to cool
1 medium onion, peeled and finely
   chopped
2 cloves garlic, crushed
1 cm/½ in prepared terasi (blachan –
   see page 228), optional but
   recommended
1–2 red chillies, deseeded and chopped
2 eggs
salt and freshly ground black pepper

1–2 tablespoons water
225 g/8 oz pork fillet or chicken breast,
   or a combination of both
6 tablespoons oil
100 g/4 oz prawns
2 tablespoons tomato ketchup
1 tablespoon kecap manis (see page 244)
2 tablespoons kecap asin or thin soy
   sauce (see page 244)
a little sesame oil

To garnish
6 spring onions, trimmed and chopped   chilli flower (see page 230)

To serve
prawn crackers (krupuk), cooked in hot oil (see page 236)

1. Fork through the rice so the grains are separate. Pound together
   the onions, garlic, terasi and chillies to make a spice paste, and
   make sure all the other ingredients are ready.
2. Beat the eggs with the seasoning and water and make 1 or 2
   omelettes in a lightly oiled frying pan, cooking on one side only.
   Roll up tightly and set aside. When cold cut into fine strips.
3. Fry the pork or chicken slices or both in half the oil till the meats
   change colour, stirring all the time. Lift out of the wok and
   reserve with the prawns.
4. Heat the remaining oil, then fry the spice paste for 2 minutes to
   bring out the flavour, stirring all the time.
5. Stir in the cold rice, mix well then add the tomato ketchup,
   kecap manis and thin soy sauce. Stir in the meats and prawns
   and a little sesame oil, then toss thoroughly together.
6. Turn the nasi goreng on to a hot platter and garnish with the
   spring onions, the omelette strips and the chilli flower. Serve
   with prawn crackers.

Serves 6

NASI KUNING
Yellow festive rice

Usually served on special occasions such as a wedding, a birthday or a farewell gathering. Even today it is traditional for guests to pray for God's blessing before helping themselves to this festive dish. The rice is very rich, being cooked in a good proportion of coconut milk. It will not be as separate and fluffy as normal rice because of the high coconut milk content.

450 g/1 lb long grain rice
1 teaspoon turmeric powder
450 ml/³/₄ pint water
2 stems lemon grass, root trimmed and fleshy part bruised
1–2 lime leaves

1–2 pandan leaves, tied into a knot
1–2 curry leaves if available
salt to taste
600 ml/1 pint coconut milk (see page 231)

GARNISHES
omelette strips (see page 199)
fricadelles (see page 168)
basil leaves
celery leaves

small chunky pieces of cucumber and tomato
fried peeled peanuts or salted peanuts
1 red chilli flower (see page 230)

ACCOMPANIMENTS
sayur menir (see page 166)
abon (see page 225)
beef rendang (see page 185)

acar bening (see page 189)
coconut sambal (see page 63) or sambal katjang (see page 198)

1. Wash the rice several times in fresh water and transfer to a large pan. Add the turmeric powder, water, lemon grass, lime leaves, pandan leaves and curry leaves plus salt to taste.
2. Bring to the boil then stir in the coconut milk, lower the heat and cook gently for 5–8 minutes until the surface of the rice is pitted with holes and the rice is partly cooked.
3. At this stage transfer the rice and the leaves to a muslin-lined steamer and continue cooking gently with cover for 30 minutes or till the rice is tender. If a steamer is not available the rice can be cooked in a large, covered ovenproof casserole in a moderately

hot oven (190°C, 375°F, Gas Mark 5) for 20–30 minutes or till tender and the grains are separate.

4. Remove the leaves from the yellow rice, leave the rice covered until ready to serve, then pile into a cone shape on a large serving platter and garnish round the base with the omelette strips, fricadelles, basil and celery leaves, cucumber and tomato pieces and peanuts. Topped with a chilli flower.

5. Serve with the suggested accompaniments. Usually guests will help themselves to rice in a large broad-brimmed soup plate. They moisten the rice with a little of the sayur menir then take portions of the accompaniments and garnishes. The beauty of this meal is that everyone gets exactly what they like and feels free to return to the table for second helpings, which they invariably do.

Serves 8

BAMIE GORENG
Fried noodles

This is a wonderfully accommodating dish. Within this basic recipe you can, if you wish, substitute other vegetables such as mushrooms, chayote, tiny pieces of broccoli, leeks, or beansprouts. Like fried rice you can use whatever you have to hand but do bear in mind the colours and flavours of the end result.

450 g/1 lb dried egg noodles, soaked for 10 minutes in warm water	*100 g/4 oz calves' liver, finely sliced (optional)*
2 eggs, beaten	*100 g/4 oz peeled prawns*
seasoning	*100 g/4 oz spinach or Chinese leaves*
6 tablespoons oil	*2 celery stalks, finely sliced*
25 g/1 oz margarine	*4 spring onions, trimmed and shredded*
2 cloves garlic, crushed	*kecap manis and thin soy sauce to taste (see page 244)*
1 chicken breast, finely sliced	
100 g/4 oz pork fillet, finely sliced	

To garnish

crispy fried onions (see page 200)   *celery leaves (optional)*

To serve

acar bening (see page 189)   *chilli sauce (optional)*

1. Cook the noodles in boiling salted water for 2 minutes (see page 239) then drain, rinse with hot water and drain again. Set aside till required.
2. Season the beaten eggs, then heat 1 teaspoon of the oil with the margarine in a small pan till melted. Stir in the eggs and keep stirring till scrambled. Set aside.
3. Heat the remaining oil in a wok and fry the garlic and meats till they have changed colour. Being very thin slices they will cook very rapidly. Add the prawns, spinach or Chinese leaves, celery and spring onions, tossing well.
4. Now add the cooked and drained noodles and toss again so that all the ingredients are well mixed. Add the kecap and soy sauce to taste and finally stir in the scrambled egg.
5. Turn out immediately on to a hot serving platter, scatter with crispy fried onions and garnish with celery leaves if available. Acar bening is an attractive crunchy accompaniment to the noodle dish and many people enjoy drizzling a little chilli sauce on top of their helping and stirring in before eating.

Serves 6–8

SAMBAL ULEK or OELEK
Chilli paste

This is made from finely pounded chillies with the addition of salt. In South-East Asia it can be bought in small plastic bags from the van man who comes to call, or from the supermarkets or markets where customers can buy as much or as little as they want from a huge bowl, scooped onto a banana leaf or into a plastic bag. If you make this at home make up a good quantity as it will store well in the refrigerator for two weeks in a glass jar. First cover with clingfilm and then a screwtop lid. In the freezer it will keep for a couple of months. Remember when storing in the freezer to package in small containers and mark each one giving some indication of the number of chillies in the container. It is available in glass jars from

oriental supermarkets but if you would like to make your own here
is the recipe. You can always halve the quantity, of course.

225 g/8 oz fresh red chillies   *2 teaspoons salt*

1. Count the chillies so that you know roughly how many there are
   in each container if you decide to freeze the paste.
2. Discard the stalk end of the chillies. Cut from stem end to tip
   with a sharp knife and scoop out the seeds under running water.
   This prevents the vicious oils escaping which make you cough
   and splutter! If you like really powerful chilli flavours then some
   of the seeds can be left in.
3. Cook the chillies in a pan of boiling water for 6–8 minutes then
   drain. Pound with the salt to a fine paste and use as directed in a
   recipe or store as indicated above.
4. Use a stainless steel or plastic spoon for measuring the sambal
   ulek for recipes. Do take care not to rub your eyes with your
   fingers when preparing the chillies and do wash your hands
   thoroughly in soap and water when the preparation is complete.

Makes 225 g/8 oz jar

SAMBAL KATJANG
Chilli and peanut accompaniment

This can be made a day or two ahead, which makes it a very good
candidate when serving an Indonesian meal.

175 g/6 oz salted peanuts
*2 onions, peeled, finely sliced and fried
    till crisp (see page 200)*
3 cloves garlic, crushed
*1 cm/¹/₂ in laos (lengkuas), peeled and
    pounded*
1 teaspoon chilli powder
*3–4 tablespoons oil (use the oil from
    cooking the onions, if available)*

*1 cm/¹/₂ in prepared terasi (blachan –
    see page 228)*
*1 teaspoon tamarind purée, soaked in 3
    tablespoons water then strained*
*200 ml/7 fl oz thick coconut milk (see
    page 231)*
1 tablespoon soft dark brown sugar
salt to taste

1. Roughly chop the peanuts. This can be done in a food processor
   but take care not to chop them too finely.

2. Prepare the crispy onions and set aside.
3. Fry the garlic, laos and chilli powder briefly in the oil for 1 minute but do not allow to brown. Draw from heat.
4. Blend the terasi with the strained tamarind juice and stir into the fried ingredients. Pour in the coconut milk and sugar and stir till the mixture comes to the boil. Reduce to a simmer and cook without cover for 5 minutes.
5. Add the onions and the peanuts and continue to cook gently for about 10 minutes or until the liquid has evaporated and the mixture is dry. Add salt to taste.
6. Serve with plain boiled rice, or as a sambal as part of a rijsttafel or gado gado. Keep any leftovers in a screwtop jar in the refrigerator or a very cool place.

Makes 500 g/1 lb 4 oz jar

OMELETTES

Omelettes are used throughout Indonesia and Malaysia not only as a garnish but often as an integral part of a noodle or rice dish available from the hawker's stall. I have also seen the omelette strips added to a sambal goreng, which is a very quick and simple lunch snack to have up your sleeve if you just happen to have some leftover sambal goreng sauce in the refrigerator or freezer.

2 eggs beaten   *2 tablespoons water*
salt and freshly ground black pepper   *1–2 teaspoons oil or lard for frying*

1. Beat the eggs, seasoning and water together.
2. Heat the oil in a frying pan, a very large pan will make 1 omelette, a 20 cm/8 in one will make two.
3. Flood enough of the egg mixture into the pan to cover the base and cook till nicely brown on the underside.
4. Draw from the heat and with a palette knife roll up from one end to the other in a tight roll. Turn onto a board or plate to cool then slice thinly. Repeat with the remaining egg mixture.

BAWANG GORENG
Crispy fried onions

These are used extensively as a garnish in Indonesia and also in Burma, especially in the famous Balachuang (see page 100). It is worthwhile making a quantity of these onions and storing them.

450 g/1 lb onions   *oil for deep frying*

1. Peel the onions, then slice as finely as possible. I use the slicing blade of the food processor.
2. Spread out on absorbent kitchen paper to dry for ½–1 hour. In sunny climes this can be done in the sunshine but a dry, airy place will suffice.
3. Heat the oil then fry the onions in batches till crisp and golden. Drain very well and leave to cool. Store in an airtight container. In Burmese recipes the oil in which the onions have been fried is often reserved and used as a dressing for salads and vegetable dishes.

LONTONG
Compressed glutinous rice

Traditionally lontong, or ketupat as it may also be called, is made from white glutinous rice and is cooked in little basket containers made from plaited strips of palm fronds and then secured with the rib of the frond. Sometimes a banana leaf is used which is first held over a flame or scalded with boiling water to make the leaf supple so that it can be made into a parcel for the rice before cooking. Cooked in this way the rice takes on a pleasing flavour from the banana leaf too. The end result is a plump cushion of rice which is then left to cool and cut into diamond shapes. It is often served as an accompaniment to the sate served all over Indonesia and Malaysia.

I have found that the boil-in-the-bag rice is a useful alternative, especially when 2–3 pandan leaves are added to the pan whilst cooking to give that extra dimension in flavour.

100 g/4 oz packet boil-in-the-bag rice   *2–3 pandan leaves (optional)*

1. Place the bag of rice in a pan of boiling salted water with the pandan leaves if using and cook for 1¼ hours, making sure that the rice is covered all the time.
2. Allow to cool completely before stripping off the bag and cutting into neat cubes, which are served with sate or barbecue foods.

Serves 4 as an accompaniment to sate

SRI KAYA
Banana and coconut custard

450 ml/¾ pint thin coconut milk
25 g/1 oz sugar
3 eggs, beaten
25 g/1 oz bean-thread noodles (see page 240), soaked in boiling water for 2 minutes

4 ripe bananas or 2 ripe plantains
2 pandan leaves, stripped through with a fork and tied into a knot
pinch of salt

1. Add the coconut milk and sugar to the beaten eggs and whisk well. Strain into a 1.75 litre/3 pint soufflé dish.
2. Drain the noodles, cut into small pieces and add to the mixture with the bananas or plantains cut into small pieces. Add the pandan leaves and stir in the salt.
3. Cover with foil and cook in a steamer for about 1 hour or till set. Serve hot or cold, on its own or topped with ice cream.

Serves 8

DADAR GULUNG
Pancakes filled with sweet coconut

Traditionally the green colour in the batter for these pancakes was made with the juice of pandan leaves, which must have been a real labour of love. Mrs Sudewo suggests using green colouring and vanilla essence as today's alternative to what must have been a lengthy process.

175 g/6 oz soft dark brown sugar
450 ml/3/4 pint water
1 pandan leaf, stripped through with a fork and tied into a knot

175 g/6 oz desiccated coconut
a little salt
oil for frying

PANCAKE BATTER

225 g/8 oz plain flour, sifted
2 eggs, beaten
2 drops green colouring

few drops vanilla essence
450 ml/3/4 pint water
3 tablespoons groundnut oil

1. Dissolve the sugar in the water with the pandan leaf in a pan over a gentle heat, stirring all the time, then increase the heat and boil gently for 3–4 minutes until the mixture just becomes syrupy. Do not let it caramelize.
2. Turn the coconut into a wok with the salt. Pour the prepared sugar syrup over it and cook over a gentle heat, stirring frequently till the mixture becomes almost dry; this will take 15–20 minutes. Set aside until required.
3. Make up the batter by blending together the flour, eggs, colouring, vanilla essence, water and oil. Rub an 18 cm/7 in frying pan with oil and cook the pancakes on each side till all the batter is used up. It should make about 16.
4. Fill each one with a generous spoonful of the coconut mixture, roll up and serve hot.

Serves 8

Vietnam and Cambodia

It's hard to believe that in these war-torn countries eating might be for more than just survival. Yet the cooking and presentation of food has always been and continues to be an important part of life.

Though the Chinese influence is very marked and eating with chopsticks is the norm, the Vietnamese have many special characteristics in their cuisine, which appeals to those who love good food, attractively presented. The French influence is not to be overlooked either. After all, the French ruled Vietnam for eighty years, and with their expertise in culinary matters it is no wonder that many of their basic foods such as baguette, wine, glorious vegetables, and pâté still play a prominent part in the cuisine of Vietnam today. Indeed Paris claims to have the best Vietnamese food outside Vietnam. Following the massive exodus of people from Vietnam after the war, restaurants are springing up wherever the refugees find a haven. Like the Chinese, the Vietnamese are committed to taking their food with them wherever they go, convinced that it is the best in the world.

It is said that the people of Vietnam came originally from Indonesia, Malaysia, Thailand and the southern part of China over the centuries. Despite almost 1,000 years of Chinese occupation the Vietnamese language and customs and a fierce pride in the national identity still prevail.

Vietnam is divided by a mountain range in the centre and shares a long stretch of border with landlocked Laos and, for the latter third, with Cambodia. From north to south, a distance of a thousand miles, the whole of the east coast provides a wealth of fish from the ocean. These are turned into a wonderful variety of dishes, from soups and stir fry to sweet and sour dishes, pâtés and omelettes. From the cooler north comes a famous fondue dish in which cubes of beef are cooked in a beef broth and served with a white radish and carrot pickle – shades of the Mongolian firepot style of cooking but with its own local interpretation. The central area, seat of the ancient royal capital, Hue, is perhaps the least prosperous but claims *bun bo hue* (a noodle soup) and a wealth of fish dishes to its credit. The rich fertile south, with the Mekong delta and its *padi* fields stretching as far as the eye can see, is the area where fruits and vegetables of every kind grow in profusion and these feature extensively in the diet. Spicy food is appreciated and here coconut milk is used, which is a real departure from the Chinese influence.

Many dishes are served all over the country, though the Vietnamese from each region might still claim a particular dish as being from their own area. Rice, soup and *nuoc cham* are the three staples of the cuisine. Rice is served for both lunch and the evening meal along with other dishes such as chicken, meat, or pork, which is a real favourite ('they use all but the squeal' could happily apply to the Vietnamese), offal of all kinds, vegetables, or fish from the rivers and sea. Breakfast is very often a bowl of soup. This can be the famous *pho* (pronounced 'foe'), a beef soup which is available from itinerant hawkers or in little coffee shops and restaurants, or a pork soup again with noodles and some green leaves. Green leaves, be they lettuce, mint or coriander, are used everywhere for wrapping up neat little morsels which are then dipped into the famous *nuoc cham*, a sauce made with garlic, chilli, sugar, lemon or lime juice and fish sauce. The Vietnamese are very patriotic about their fish sauce, and there is even a joke which claims that the Vietnamese can endure all trouble and pain save being without their fish sauce! It is made by a process of fermentation with salt, and the real connoisseurs reckon that, like good malt whisky, the sauce must mature for ten years, although the normal period is closer to six months. Fish sauce is a vital ingredient in *nuoc cham*, which is served at every opportunity in the same way that the Burmese serve *balachuang*, the Thais *nam prik* and the Malays and Indonesians *sambals*.

The celebrations which bring families together each year are *Tet*, the Lunar New Year, the Festival of the August Moon, and *Trung thu*, in which children receive gifts of games, toys and sweets. Then there is the thanksgiving for the harvest; two crops a year are the norm.

A friend of mine, Philip Tran, who left Vietnam a number of years ago, recalls how it was customary for families to go out in a boat into the centre of the Perfume River at Hue in the hot season in order to catch any cooling breeze that might prevail. This weekend activity was a popular way of relaxing with family and friends. There were hundreds of little boats, each one selling something delicious to eat, and if you wished to order some particular dish or even a group playing music then you ran up a flag and the people offering whatever you ordered would scurry to your boat. It was also possible to order a whole meal, course by course, from the hawkers who passed by the house during the evening. As in Jakarta, each one was recognized by his bell or gong or by simply calling his wares. Similarly it was possible to go to a restaurant renowned for its soup, fish dishes, pancakes or *cha gio* (spring rolls) and spend the evening moving from place to place till you had had your fill.

Philip told me that in a well-to-do home there would always be an ancestors' shrine, a sacred place. Vietnam is a Buddhist country and the people are very devout. Behind the shrine would be the bedrooms, to the sides there would be a sitting room and a dining room for everyday use. The kitchen was always separate, the place for women and children, never the men. Flowers abounded all round the house and the well-swept yard at the front would be used for drying the rice. Animals such as buffalo would be kept to one side of the house and a car, carts, or other machinery to the other side. Near the kitchen at the back there would be a garden for all the herbs and leaves so essential to Vietnamese cuisine, particularly as salads are much enjoyed. Orchids of many different kinds lodged in the cracks in the tree bark, and at the back of the house you would find a bamboo hedge enclosing palm trees, lychees, jackfruit, banana, guava, custard apples, pomelo, mango, and citrus fruit trees, making the family almost self-sufficient.

In the kitchen a small type of wok is used called a *chao*; for soups and steaming a pot called a *noi* is used, which looks like a tureen in shape. The barbecue is a very popular mode of cooking throughout the country and is perfect for cooking those little morsels wrapped in leaves, which are peculiarly and enchantingly Vietnamese.

Cambodian houses also have the kitchen set at the back of the home but within easy reach of the sitting area, where a great deal of socializing goes on. Many of the houses are on sturdy pillars which not only make the house cooler but provide a shady area where people can sit more comfortably. As in Vietnam flowers are abundant and every house will have its garden where leaves for the various soups and salads are grown. Each home will have many fruit trees, and mango is a special favourite. Slices of underripe mango are lightly spread with a paste made from *blachan*, fish sauce, pounded chilli and sugar, which I am told is a revelation though I have yet to try it.

Rice is the number one food, the premium type being grown and harvested in the Battambang valley, a major rice-growing region. Freshwater fish come principally from the Mekong river and its tributaries as well as a huge lake called the Tonle Sap.

Much of the cultural heritage of this beautiful country has been destroyed by the ravages of war. I hope that one day the people who have been forced to flee and live in camps beyond the borders of their own country will be free to go home to a life of peace and personal freedom, such as we in the West take so much for granted. Let us hope too that one day the once-glorious cuisine of Cambodia can be rediscovered for us all to emulate and enjoy.

CANH CUA
Crab and asparagus soup

The asparagus is a reminder of the French influence on the cooking of this part of the world, where it is often referred to as Western bamboo.

6 shallots, chopped, or the lower white part of spring onion, chopped
2–3 tablespoons cooking oil
340 g/12 oz can asparagus spears, drained and coarsely chopped
100 g/4 oz crabmeat, fresh or canned
900 ml/1½ pints homemade chicken stock, or a stock cube and water

1 tablespoon cornflour, mixed to a paste with water
2 tablespoons fish sauce (see page 234)
salt and freshly ground black pepper to taste
1 egg, lightly beaten
spring onion tops or chives, shredded

1. Fry the shallots in the oil, stirring all the time. Do not allow to brown. Add the asparagus pieces, the crab broken up into small pieces, and stock. Bring to the boil.
2. Cook for 3 minutes, then draw from the heat and spoon some of the liquid into the cornflour mixture. Return all to the pan and stir till the mixture thickens slightly.
3. Add the fish sauce and seasoning, then pour the beaten egg into the almost boiling soup, stirring round and round so that the egg forms threads in the soup. Finally stir in the shredded spring onion tops or chives and serve immediately.

Serves 4–6

CANH CA
Sour fish soup with pineapple

4 Chinese mushrooms, soaked in warm
   water for 20 minutes
1 medium onion, peeled and finely
   chopped
2 cloves garlic, crushed
3 tablespoons peanut oil
175 g/6 oz crabmeat
1.25 litres/2 pints fish stock (see page
   40)
1 slice fresh pineapple, finely chopped

1 piece canned bamboo shoot, cut into
   matchstick pieces
3 tablespoons tamarind puree, soaked in
   9 tablespoons water for 10 minutes
   then strained
seasoning to taste
2 spring onions, finely shredded
a few sprigs coriander, stems chopped
225 g/8 oz rice noodles (lai fan) cooked
   and drained (see page 239)

1. Drain the mushrooms, discard the stalks and slice the caps. Reserve the soaking liquid.
2. Fry the onion and garlic in the oil without browning until soft and transparent. Add the crabmeat, mushroom slices and fish stock, plus the soaking liquid from the mushrooms. Bring to the boil then simmer for 5 minutes.
3. Add the pineapple and the bamboo shoot to the pan; cook only briefly then stir in the strained tamarind juice and seasoning to taste. The soup should have a sharp flavour.
4. Add the spring onions, coriander stems and leaves just before serving. Spoon some cooked noodles into serving bowls and pour the soup over the top.

Serves 6–8

MI QUANG
Pork and noodle salad soup

This is a traditional soup from an area south of Hue in South-Central Vietnam. It is an ideal dish for entertaining as everything can be prepared in advance. In addition there is no end to the variations on the theme. Beef stock and strips of beef, crabmeat and squid with fish stock, or chicken meat and chicken stock can all be used instead of the pork to ring the changes.

PORK STOCK

450 g/1 lb pork bones
1 onion, peeled and quartered
1 cm/½ in piece ginger, peeled and
    bruised

fish sauce to taste (see page 234)
salt and pepper

SOUP

225 g/8 oz lean belly pork, rind
    removed
100 g/4 oz pork liver
3 tablespoons oil
1 medium onion, peeled and finely
    chopped

25–50 g/1–2 oz dried prawns or
    shrimp, soaked in water for 10
    minutes then drained
2–3 tomatoes, skinned and chopped
salt and pepper to taste

SALAD

100 g/4 oz beansprouts, any brown tails
    removed
¼ cucumber, diced

a few crisp lettuce leaves, washed, dried
    and shredded
mint and coriander leaves

NOODLES

100 g/4 oz rice noodles (lai fan) – or use double the quantity for hearty eaters

TO GARNISH

25 g/1 oz salted peanuts, lightly crushed   2 tablespoons onion oil or red sauce (see
    below)

1. Prepare the homemade pork stock, which makes an enormous difference to this soup. It can be made a few days ahead and stored in the refrigerator or freezer if you prefer. Wash the bones well, then place in a pan of water to cover (2–2.25 litres/3½–4 pints approx.) and bring to the boil. Skim well, adding more water if necessary to cover, and add the onion quarters, ginger, fish sauce and seasoning.

2. Reduce the heat and simmer for 1–2 hours to obtain a good-flavoured stock. Skim off any fat when the stock has cooked, then set aside till required.

3. To prepare the soup, cut the pork belly into thin strips, and then into tiny pieces. Wash and dry the liver and cut into similar-sized pieces. Heat the oil, then fry the pork and liver to seal on all sides.

4. Add the onion and keep stirring till it has softened, then add the soaked prawns or shrimp, the tomatoes and the prepared pork stock made up to 2 litres/3½ pints with water if necessary. Bring to the boil and simmer for 30–35 minutes while preparing the other ingredients. Taste for seasoning before serving.

5. Place all the salad ingredients on a platter then prepare the noodles: bring a large pan of salted water to the boil, add the rice noodles, return to the boil, then draw from the heat and set aside for 8 minutes. Drain, rinse and drain again thoroughly, then turn into a serving bowl.

6. Now everything is ready to serve. Guests spoon some of the salad ingredients into the bottom of their bowl, followed by a helping of noodles, then the hot soup. Finally sprinkle over a few nuts and drizzle a little onion oil or red sauce over the top. Use chopsticks and a soup spoon to eat this wonderful soup.

Serves 8

ONION OIL

The onion oil can be strained and used as suggested here, or leave the onions in the oil and use within a few hours as an accompaniment/garnish.

6–8 spring onions, chopped   *6 tablespoons oil*

1. Put the spring onions in an ovenproof basin. Heat the oil and pour over the onions, then leave to cool.

2. Strain and use as directed above. The oil can also be drizzled over omelettes and lots of other dishes just before serving. Any leftovers can be kept in a screwtop jar for future use.

Philip Tran gave me the following recipe as an accompaniment instead of the onion oil, to serve with the noodle salad soups which are so popular in Vietnam:

NUOC MAU
Red sauce

2 small onions, or shallots (50 g/2 oz), peeled and finely chopped
2 cloves garlic crushed
2 tablespoons groundnut oil
1/2–1 teaspoon chilli powder

1/2 teaspoon paprika
1 tablespoon tomato purée
85 ml/3 fl oz coconut milk (see page 231)
85 ml/3 fl oz fish, pork or chicken stock
seasoning to taste

1. Fry the onion and garlic in the oil without browning. Stir in the chilli powder and paprika and cook to bring out the flavours, then stir in the tomato purée and cook till almost dry over a very gentle heat.
2. Now add the coconut milk and stock. Stir then cook gently but do not allow to boil. The red oil will float to the top when the sauce is ready. Season to taste.

TRUNG HAP
Steamed egg or omelette

3 Chinese mushrooms, soaked in water for 25 minutes and drained
25 g/1 oz fine rice noodles (beehoon), soaked in boiling water for 2 minutes and drained
100 g/4 oz lean pork, finely minced

2 spring onions, finely shredded
50 g/2 oz prawns or crabmeat
5 eggs, beaten
1 tablespoon fish sauce (see page 234)
salt and freshly ground black pepper
a little onion oil (see page 212)

TO SERVE

lettuce, mint and coriander leaves

nuoc cham sauce (see page 223)

1. Slice the mushrooms and cut the noodles into short pieces. Place in a bowl and add the pork, spring onions, prawns or crabmeat, beaten eggs, fish sauce and seasoning.
2. Either turn into a greased 20 cm/8 in ovenproof dish, cover with

foil and steam very gently over boiling water for 15–20 minutes, OR heat a little oil in a 20 cm/8 in frying pan and cook the mixture like an omelette on one side only.

3. Place under a hot grill just to brown the top if liked and drizzle with the onion oil. The omelette or steamed egg is served in pieces wrapped in a lettuce leaf with a few mint leaves and coriander and the ever-popular nuoc cham sauce.

Serves 6–8 as a starter or 2 as a light lunch, or take on a picnic

GOI CUON
Rice paper parcels with black bean sauce

Rice paper wrappers come in small and large rounds. They are very brittle, so purchase with care. They soften when brushed with warm water. Any casualties can be used for patching other papers. Wrappers are great fun for a party where everyone folds up his or her parcel, some more successfully than others. Buy from an oriental supermarket.

2 litres/3½ pints water
1 small onion, peeled and sliced
a few coriander stems

fish sauce (see page 234) and freshly ground black pepper to taste
225 g/8 oz piece belly pork, boned and rind removed

TO SERVE
50 g/2 oz fine rice vermicelli (beehoon)
225 g/8 oz box beansprouts, drained
1 crisp lettuce, leaves separated carefully then washed, drained and dried

mint and coriander leaves
175 g/6 oz cooked prawns, or more if liked
16 large rice papers

BLACK BEAN SAUCE

2 cloves garlic, crushed

1 red chilli, deseeded and sliced

1–2 tablespoons groundnut oil

4–5 tablespoons fermented black salted
  beans (from a can)

1 tablespoon fish sauce (see page 234)

1 teaspoon vinegar

2–3 teaspoons brown sugar

1 tablespoon crunchy peanut butter

1 tablespoon sesame seeds, dry fried (see
  page 233)

1 teaspoon sesame oil

85 ml/3 fl oz fish, pork or chicken stock

1. Put the water into a saucepan with the onion, coriander stems, fish sauce and pepper. Bring to the boil. Add the pork and cook for 20–30 minutes, turning the pork from time to time, till tender when tested with a skewer.

2. Lift the pork from the pan and allow to cool before slicing into thin strips. The stock can be strained and reserved for a soup or other dish.

3. Prepare the black bean dipping sauce: fry the garlic and chilli in the oil to bring out the flavour. Add beans, fish sauce, vinegar, sugar, peanut butter, sesame seeds and oil. Stir well and add the stock. Taste for seasoning. Transfer to a blender and process for a few seconds. Pour into a serving bowl and leave to cool.

4. Cook the beehoon (rice vermicelli) for 2 minutes in boiling water, drain and transfer to a serving bowl. Turn the drained beansprouts into a separate dish. Prepare the lettuce (each leaf can be torn in two) mint and coriander leaves, and arrange on a large platter. Transfer the prawns to a bowl.

5. When almost ready to serve, place the rice papers two at a time on a teatowel and brush both sides with warm water to soften them. Transfer very carefully onto individual serving plates.

6. Each person places a piece of lettuce on the wrapper at the end closest to them. Top with some of the noodles, beansprouts, mint and coriander leaves and 1–2 slices pork. Fold the edge of the rice paper towards the centre then roll fairly firmly once.

7. Place a few prawns on the open part of the wrapper and continue rolling into a neat parcel. As the rice paper is almost transparent you will see the green leaves and the pink prawns clearly through the wrapper which looks very pretty. Dip the parcel into the

sauce before eating then repeat with another wrapper and the remaining ingredients.

Makes 16 parcels

CHA CA TOM
Vietnamese fish loaf

This is a marvellous starter or light lunch dish. Each slice makes 2 'parcels' per person. The slice is cut in half then each half is placed on a whole crisp lettuce leaf with coriander and mint leaves, and rolled up into a neat parcel. This is then dipped into nuoc cham sauce before eating. The crispness of the lettuce with the flavours of the leaves and the fish loaf make a wonderful combination.

450 g/1 lb fresh cod fillet, skinned,
*   boned and cut into cubes*
50 g/2 oz pork fat, chilled in the
*   refrigerator then cut into tiny pieces*
4 spring onions, white part only
3 cloves garlic, crushed
2 tablespoons fish sauce (see page 234)
freshly ground black pepper

3 egg whites, lightly beaten with a fork
6 or 8 medium prawns or crab claws
1 tablespoon rice wine
small piece fresh ginger, crushed
*   (optional)*
coral from the crab, if available, and 1
*   egg yolk*

To serve
lettuce, mint and coriander leaves   *nuoc cham sauce (see page 223)*

1. Chill the fish in the refrigerator for at least thirty minutes with the pork fat and the bowl from the food processor so that everything is cold, then process the fish, pork fat pieces, spring onions, 2 of the garlic cloves, fish sauce and pepper till smooth.
2. Pour in the egg whites slowly until incorporated into the mixture. This will take less than 30 seconds.
3. Season the prawns or pieces of crab with the rice wine, the third clove of garlic, pepper and a little crushed ginger if liked.
4. Spoon half the fish and pork mixture into a 750–900 ml/1¼–1½ pint ovenproof dish and arrange the prawns or pieces of crab across the centre, then spoon the remaining mixture on top.

5. Cover with foil and place in a steamer over gently boiling water for 15–20 minutes, or till just firm when tested with a skewer. Remove from the steamer and lift off the foil. Use kitchen paper to mop up any moisture which may have collected round the edge of the loaf.
6. Blend the coral of crab, if available, to a brushing paste with a little beaten egg yolk, or simply use the beaten egg yolk to brush over the surface of the fish loaf, then replace in the steamer away from the heat for a few minutes to set. Cool.
7. Serve cold, cut into slices, with nuoc cham sauce and a selection of lettuce, mint and coriander leaves.

Serves 8 as a starter

PA KHING
Grilled or steamed fish à la Cambodgienne

675 g/1½ lb snapper, grey mullet, bream or carp, gutted but head and tail left on
6 spring onions, green tops chopped for stuffing and garnish, white bulbs chopped for sauce
2.5 cm/1 in fresh ginger, peeled and shredded
juice of ½ lemon or lime
seasoning to taste
a little oil (optional)
2 tablespoons groundnut oil
1 red chilli, deseeded and shredded
2 tablespoons light soy sauce
1 tablespoon sesame oil

TO SERVE
green leaves

1. Wipe the fish and slash the body 3 times on each side. Fill the body cavity with half the spring onion tops and half the ginger and close up the cavity with fine skewers.
2. Squeeze over the lemon or lime juice, season then drizzle with a little oil if grilling. This will not be necessary if steaming.
3. Either place under a grill and cook for 7–8 minutes on each side or till cooked through, turning carefully half way through the cooking, OR place on a suitable platter or sheet of foil, put in a

steamer (depending on the size of the steamer the fish may have to be cut in half) and cook for 15–20 minutes.

4. Meanwhile prepare the sauce by heating the groundnut oil and gently frying the chopped spring onion bulbs and the remaining ginger. Do not allow to brown. Draw from the heat, add the chilli, then stir in the soy sauce and lastly the sesame oil.

5. Place the fish on a serving dish lined with any green leaves and flood the hot sauce over the top. Garnish with the remaining spring onion tops.

Serves 3

KOY PA
Fish salad à la Cambodgienne

450 g/1 lb white fish fillet, skinned and
   cut into finger-length strips

juice of 2–3 lemons or limes (approx. 7
   tablespoons)

SAUCE

1 clove garlic

1 small onion

1 cm/½ in lengkuas

2–3 coriander stems, chopped

1 tablespoon groundnut oil

1 teaspoon sugar

1–2 tablespoons fish sauce (see page 234)

seasoning to taste

50 g/2 oz peanuts, lightly crushed

VEGETABLES FOR SERVING

½ box beansprouts

½ daikon (moolie), peeled and cut into
   matchstick pieces, or coarsely grated

1–2 stems lemon grass, lower part very
   finely shredded

½ red pepper

½ green or yellow pepper

½–1 bunch spring onions, cut into fine,
   finger-length pieces

coriander leaves

1 lettuce washed and dried, leaves left
   whole or shredded if preferred

a handful of mint leaves

TO GARNISH

25 g/1 oz peanuts, lightly crushed

1. Place the fish pieces in a glass or stainless steel bowl and cover with the lemon or lime juice. Marinate for at least 3 hours, or

longer if possible. The fish will turn milky white and firm up. Drain and reserve the juices for the sauce.

2. Thread the unpeeled garlic, onion and lengkuas on a skewer and hold over a gas flame to cook the outside lightly, or place under a grill if more convenient. Cool a little then skin before pounding to a paste with the coriander stems.

3. Lightly fry this spice paste in the oil, without browning, to bring out the flavours. Add the lemon or lime juice marinade and cook gently for 2 minutes only, then add the sugar, fish sauce, and seasoning. Remove from the heat. Just before serving add the peanuts, plus sufficient water to make the sauce thinner, but it must still be tangy in flavour, so add the water little by little and taste as you go.

4. When ready to serve mix the fish strips with the beansprouts, daikon and shredded lemon grass. Pile into the centre of a serving platter and scatter with the peanuts for garnish.

5. Arrange the pepper slices, spring onions, coriander leaves, lettuce leaves and mint round the edge of the dish and serve the sauce in a separate bowl.

6. Each person takes a lettuce leaf or some shredded lettuce and tops it with some of the fish and other ingredients, then drizzles some of the sauce on top.

Serves 6–8, or more as part of a buffet

GOI DUA LEO
Vietnamese salad

750 ml/1¼ pints water
2 shallots, peeled and sliced
1 clove garlic, crushed
1 stem lemon grass, the whole bruised
strip of rind from magrut, if available,
    or lime or grapefruit
2 tablespoons fish sauce (see page 234)
freshly ground black pepper
salt
few coriander stems

225 g/8 oz belly pork in a piece, boned
    but rind left on
4 squid, cleaned (see page 52) but left
    whole
50 g/2 oz prawns (optional)
1 cucumber
1–2 red chillies, deseeded and shredded
50 g/2 oz peanuts, coarsely ground
a few mint and coriander leaves
2–3 tablespoons fish sauce
lettuce leaves

TO SERVE

nuoc cham sauce (see page 223) – use
    some of the stock in the sauce instead
    of water

24 prawn crackers (krupuk) fried in oil
    (see page 236)

1. Pour the water into a pan, add the shallots, garlic, lemon grass,
   strip of magrut, lime or grapefruit rind, fish sauce, black pepper,
   salt and coriander stems. Bring to the boil, then reduce to a
   simmer.
2. Poach the whole piece of pork in the liquid for 20 minutes. Add
   the squid and prawns, if using, and poach for another 5 minutes.
   Draw from the heat and remove the pork, squid and prawns.
   Leave to cool. (The stock can be strained and used for a sauce or
   a soup.)
3. Slice the cucumber as finely as you can and sprinkle with salt.
   Set aside for 10 minutes. Meanwhile slice the squid into rings,
   then slice the pork, including the rind, into matchstick pieces.
4. Squeeze the cucumber slices to remove as much liquid as
   possible, then toss with the pork, squid, prawns if using, chillies,
   and some of the ground peanuts, mint and coriander leaves. Add
   fish sauce to taste.
5. Pile into a lettuce-lined bowl and scatter the remaining peanuts,

mint and coriander leaves on top. Serve the nuoc cham sauce separately. The prawn crackers can be used to scoop up some of the salad as you would use a spoon, or tiny morsels of salad can be placed on each prawn cracker and served as a snack, or simply eaten alongside a helping of the salad with a little nuoc cham sauce drizzled on top.

Serves 6 or more as part of a buffet

GA XAO SA
Chicken with lemon grass

1 small chicken, about 1.4 kg/3 lb
2 teaspoons sugar
4 stems lemon grass, lower part finely sliced and the top part bruised
4 spring onions, shredded
salt and freshly ground black pepper

4 tablespoons oil
2 red or green chillies, deseeded and sliced
50 g/2 oz peanuts, coarsely crushed
2–3 tablespoons fish sauce to taste (see page 234)

1. Cut the chicken into 8 or 16 pieces, as shown on page 59. Sprinkle with the sugar, then mix well with the hands to release the juices.
2. Reserve a few lemon grass slices for garnish and pound the remaining slices, then scatter over the chicken with most of the spring onions, season and set aside for at least 30 minutes before cooking.
3. Heat the oil and fry the chicken pieces, stirring all the time until they change colour and are sealed on all sides. This will take about 5 minutes.
4. Add the chillies and the lemon grass tops and toss all together. Continue to cook gently with cover for about 20–25 minutes, adding a little water to the wok to keep the chicken moist. Cook till the juices in the chicken run clear when tested with a skewer.
5. Finally add the peanuts and the fish sauce. Taste for seasoning and serve garnished with the remaining spring onions and lemon grass slices on a hot platter with freshly boiled rice or noodles.

Serves 4

THIT BO KHO
Beef stew

1 kg/2¼ lb lean beef, such as brisket or stewing steak, in a piece

1 tablespoon dark brown sugar

3 tablespoons black beans in salted sauce (from a can)

4–6 tablespoons oil

6 shallots, peeled and sliced

2 stems lemon grass, lower part sliced and pounded, top part bruised

25 g/1 oz fresh ginger, peeled and finely sliced

8 whole black peppercorns

1 stick cinnamon

75 ml/3 fl oz rice wine

approx 300 ml/½ pint water, or use half a 300 g/10 oz can concentrated consommé and make up to 300 ml/½ pint with water

2 tablespoons fish sauce (see page 234)

2 tablespoons tomato purée

1. Cut the beef into long strips and then into even-sized pieces. Place in a bowl and sprinkle with the sugar. Pound the black beans lightly in a pestle and mortar (this quantity is too small to put in the food processor) and mix with the meat. Set aside for 30 minutes.
2. Heat the oil and add the meat, stirring all the time so that the pieces of meat are sealed on all sides. Add the shallots and the pounded lemon grass, plus the top part of the stem which has just been bruised, the ginger, peppercorns and cinnamon.
3. Pour in the rice wine and the stock plus the fish sauce. Bring to the boil, cover and simmer gently for 1–1½ hours or till the meat is tender.
4. Stir in the tomato purée and cook for a further 10 minutes without cover. Remove the cinnamon stick and lemon grass stems before serving if liked. Serve with rice or freshly cooked noodles.

Serves 6–8

NUOC CHAM SAUCE

2 red chillies, deseeded and sliced
2 cloves garlic, peeled
1 tablespoon sugar
juice of ½ lemon or lime

3–4 tablespoons fish sauce (see page 234)
a little water if necessary

1. Pound the chillies, garlic and sugar together in a pestle and mortar till smooth.
2. Add the lemon or lime juice then the fish sauce and a little water to taste. Pour into a bowl and use as a dressing or dip.
3. If you have any sauce left over it can be stored in a glass jar. Cover top with clingfilm before screwing on lid. Keep in the refrigerator for several days.

GLUTINOUS RICE IN BANANA LEAVES

Eaten with great relish any time anywhere, this rice has a reputation for being sustaining food – akin to our steamed puddings but more so!

450 g/1 lb white glutinous rice
225 g/8 oz black glutinous rice
6–8 tablespoons groundnut oil
banana leaves

cooked pork and chicken meat, diced (optional)
a little soy sauce

1. Soak the white and black rice overnight in separate bowls, covered with cold water. Drain and rinse thoroughly. Heat the oil and toss the rice together in the oil until the grains are well coated.
2. Line a steamer with banana leaves which have been scalded with boiling water to make them pliable, or use a wetted muslin cloth. Spoon in half the rice and the pieces of meat if using.
3. Top with the remaining rice and sprinkle with soy sauce, then fold up the banana leaves or muslin to cover the rice lightly. Steam over boiling water for about 40–50 minutes or until the

rice is cooked. It should be *al dente*, i.e. still with a slight
resistance when you bite on a grain.

4. Draw from the heat, lift the parcel onto a serving dish and serve
   hot.

Serves 8–10

Glossary

Abon. A dry-fried shredded meat or fish, which keeps well and can be bought in packets all over Indonesia. It can be used as an accompaniment to a whole range of rice dishes, and indeed in poorer communities would perhaps be the main source of protein and flavour when eaten with a bowl of plain rice. Abon keeps well if stored in an airtight container. See page 162 for a full description of how abon is made.

Asam. See tamarind.

Aubergine. Known as eggplant or *brinjal*, a name of Indian origin. There are many different types, from the long purple variety we are familiar with in the UK to the white/green type about the size of a pingpong ball which can be either eaten raw with a *nam prik* sauce or, indeed, pounded with the ingredients for the sauce (see page 143). It can also be added to curries. The tiny, garden pea type can be used in the same way both in the *nam prik* sauce or as an addition to a green curry, giving a slightly bitter taste which is rather appealing.

Babaco. Related to the papaya, it is now being grown in the Channel Islands and can be served in the same way as papaya when ripe, i.e. in a wedge, seeds removed and with lemon or lime juice squeezed on to it. For the market salad (see page 140) sliced unripe papaya is normally used so I was delighted to find this alternative is now grown in the UK.

Bamboo shoot. Along with the coconut tree bamboo is one of the most useful. It has a host of uses; not only are its young, tender shoots served as a vegetable, but the stout, pliable stems are employed in the building of houses and the making of rattan furniture, and the slimmer stems are used to make ornaments, bowls, baskets, hats and a host of pieces of equipment for the home. It is rare in the UK to be able to buy the fresh shoot, which has to be peeled to the heart and then boiled before using. The canned winter variety is usually very good quality, creamy in colour and spear-shaped when whole. Bamboo slices are also available in cans. Once the can is opened pour the contents into a container with a lid, cover with fresh water daily, and use within a week.

Banana leaves. Used as the South-East Asian answer to kitchen foil, and available from some oriental supermarkets in the UK. The leaves are first either plunged in boiling water or held over a flame to make them more supple before placing the ingredients for cooking inside and folding over into a neat parcel. Often a thin satay stick will be used to secure the parcel. Food wrapped in this way is sometimes steamed and frequently grilled, the resulting food having added flavour from the banana leaf itself. No foil can match that but otherwise foil is an acceptable alternative. Banana leaves can be used as plates, and in markets banana leaves are cut into shape and used to line baskets to show off fruit and vegetables to advantage. The banana is a plant not a tree. We had at least seven varieties in our garden in Malaysia, the best being the tiniest and sweetest known as *pisang mas* there and in Indonesia.

Bangkuang. Also known as Chinese turnip or yambean. Well named as a Chinese turnip with its smooth, light, golden skin and turnip shape. Peel and cut into julienne strips to use in a stir fry, spring rolls, or any salad which would benefit from its crunchy crisp texture, a cross between an apple and a hard pear. Use a firm pear or moolie as a substitute if not available.

Basil leaves. Used all over Thailand and sold in the UK throughout the year, if you have a supplier who has an airfreighted weekly supply. Three varieties are available in Thailand and you can grow your own from seed in the summer months, either in a sunny window or in a sheltered spot in open ground, but beware of the slugs. They love it.

Bean curd. Fragile-looking 7.5 cm/3 in squares of fresh bean curd are sold in oriental stores from an open box covered with fresh water in the refrigerator. This bean curd is made from soya bean milk set with gypsum. In spite of its bland flavour it is full of protein and used throughout the whole region. It will keep in the refrigerator for three or four days if covered with fresh water daily. A long-life version is available. Check the best before date when buying; once opened use and store as directed.

FRIED BEAN CURD is used in many dishes from *laksa* to *gado gado* to *gudeg*. Cubes of bean curd deep fried till golden and packaged for the freezer are available in 100 g/4 oz bags. To use from the freezer, pour boiling water over them, then after one minute drain, cool slightly and squeeze to get rid of any excess oil. The cubes can then be used whole or cut into slices.

TEMPE is made from whole soya beans which have been fermented, resulting in a cake which is full of protein (much more than the bean curd), plus a valuable iron and vitamin B content. See page 163 for a description of the process. It is highly prized by vegetarians not only for its nutritional value but for its nutty flavour. Cut into cubes or slices to add to dishes or marinate first as directed on the packet, dry, then shallow fry and use as stated in the recipe.

Beansprouts. Readily available from greengrocers and supermarkets almost everywhere in 225 g/8 oz boxes. Choose only those which look fresh and white and have been kept in a cool place. I turn them out of the box and place in a container with cold water, changing this each day. Use before the date stamped on the pack. Most beansprouts come from sprouting mung beans, though soy beansprouts are also available. Used throughout the East for their appearance and texture. Removal of the brown root and sometimes the head makes them look more attractive but can be time-consuming and unnecessary, for instance if the sprouts are to be added to stir fry or spring rolls.

Mung and soy beans can both be sprouted at home. Wash mung beans well and soak overnight, then drain and rinse again. Line a deep plastic tray with a few layers of wetted kitchen paper, sprinkle with the mung beans and set in a warm, dark place such as the airing cupboard, covering with some clingfilm and maybe even a newspaper to make sure that the light is excluded. Sprinkle with water every day till the sprouts are fully developed. Allow six to nine days and use as soon as possible or store in the refrigerator as above. Don't try and grow too many at once. From 50 g/2 oz mung beans you should get 225 g/8 oz of sprouts. For soy beans follow the directions on the pack.

Besan (chickpea flour or gram flour). Used as the thickening agent in Burmese *mohinga*, this is the yellow flour from ground chickpeas and is available from Oriental and Indian stores.

Blachan (terasi or trasi, kapi or ngapi). An essential ingredient in the cooking of South-East Asia. It is made from shrimps or prawns and salt which are allowed to ferment and then pounded into a fine paste. Dull pink to dark brown, fermented shrimp paste is generally sold in 225 g/8 oz blocks, although the Thai variety is available in 50 g/2 oz see-through plastic containers. It keeps very well once opened if you rewrap it closely and store in an airtight jar in a cool place. It has an unforgettable smell on first acquaintance and strangely enough does not dominate other flavours but rather adds depth and pungency, which is so much a part of the foods of the region. Where a recipe indicates 1 cm/½ in blachan interpret this as a cube and prepare as follows: either mould the blachan on to the end of a skewer and rotate over a low-to-medium gas flame (or under the grill of an electric cooker) till the outside begins to look crusty but not burned, or to avoid such a strong smell, wrap the blachan in foil and place in a frying pan (no oil) over a low heat for five minutes turning from time to time. This process takes away the rawness from the blachan and is essential where the blachan is to be included in, say, a dressing. If the blachan is to be fried with other spices this preliminary cooking may be eliminated.

Buah keras. See macadamia nuts.

Cardamom. The green or white pods are readily available, the black variety are larger and coarser both in appearance and flavour. Clusters of the pods grow near ground level on a plant which is a member of the ginger family. The pods can be bruised and added whole to some dishes and can be removed before serving if liked. To capture the full exquisite flavour, which is warm and pungent with a hint of lemon, bruise the pods and prise them open then remove the tiny black seeds, which can be crushed and added to a range of dishes, particularly chicken.

Celery. The yellow leaves are used a great deal as a garnish in Indonesian dishes. The stems, which are miniature versions of the celery we know here, are used in salads and uncooked dishes.

Chayote. Also known as choko, these are gaining in popularity and are available in good-quality greengrocers and supermarkets. Shaped like a flat pear the chayote is a member of the squash family and its attractive green colour is a wonderful addition to stir fry and fish dishes. Peel thinly then remove the large flexible stone from the centre before slicing and using as directed. They can also be steamed but as they don't have a great deal of flavour of their own, fresh or dried shrimps and a squeeze of lemon juice are excellent additions. Can also be used raw in salads.

Chillies. Another indispensable ingredient. There are two main types, the finger-size chilli which comes in red or green and sometimes orange, and the tiny bird's-eye chilli which is even more powerful and is used extensively in Thai cooking. Chilli addicts can even be seen eating these whole. Whichever type you are using, treat with great respect as the oils from the chilli must not get near the mouth or eyes.

To prepare for cooking simply remove the cap from the stalk end then slit from top to bottom under running water and scoop out the seeds, unless you like your food fiercely hot. Use rubber gloves or wash your hands thoroughly with soap and water after preparation. Slice then pound in a pestle and mortar or use a food processor. Frozen red finger chillies can usually be bought from oriental stores when fresh are unavailable. These are fine for using in curries but cannot be used to make chilli flowers for garnish. You can buy a good quality chilli paste sold under the name of *sambal oelek* or *sambal ulek*, or you can make your own when red chillies are plentiful (see page 197). Two fresh chillies are equivalent to one teaspoon of chilli paste. Dried chillies are sold widely. These are deseeded if liked and then can be ground to a powder in a pestle and mortar or soaked in warm water first for fifteen minutes before pounding. Chilli powder is easily obtainable when all the other alternatives cannot be found. Buy little and often, and store away from the light so that it retains flavour and colour.

To MAKE A CHILLI FLOWER. Choose a small, finger-length chilli and, using the same technique as for the spring onion tassel (see page 241), slit the top two-thirds of the chilli into fine strips. Leave in cold, or even iced water to speed up the curling operation.

Chinese mushrooms. Good-quality ones might seem expensive but they do add a distinctive flavour to a variety of dishes. They must be soaked for at least ten minutes before using. The stems are removed and discarded then the mushrooms used whole or in slices. The soaking liquid can be used as stock or added to soups.

Chinese plums. These add a sour, salty taste (see the soup on page 41). They are sold in jars, and any leftovers will keep in the refrigerator, but do not discard the clear liquid in the jar.

Chinese sausages. Rich, red, rather gnarled-looking sausages which have to be steamed for ten minutes then cooled before slicing and using in stir fry and fried rice recipes, where they contribute their own distinctive flavour.

Cinnamon. Buy whole in quills (cigar shapes) or ground, which is sold loose or in jars. Cinnamon is more widely associated with sweet dishes in the West but in the cooking of South-East Asia its warm, spicy fragrance is appreciated in curries. Cassia, which might be used in Malay, Indonesian and Burmese recipes, is similar but does not have such a fine flavour.

Citrus leaves. See lime leaves.

Cloves. Grown on a tree which is a member of the myrtle family. The cloves are the flower buds which turn from pink to brown when dried. Not only are cloves used in cooking in Indonesia but in a clove-flavoured cigarette which is very popular. They have a high oil content, the oil being a well-known antidote to toothache.

Coconut milk and cream. An indispensable ingredient which now comes in many forms, dried powder, canned or frozen, though I still make it from desiccated coconut, especially when I need a large quantity. The liquid inside the coconut when it is shaken is coconut juice NOT coconut milk and is a refreshing drink, especially from the young green coconut. It is also made into palm wine which can be quite potent.

FRESHLY GRATED COCONUT. In Malaysia I used to buy freshly grated coconut from the market in bags. When a little water was poured on to this Ah Moi would then squeeze out the rich coconut milk by hand and feed the spent flesh to her chickens.

INSTANT POWDERED COCONUT. Some of the large supermarkets are selling this product now and I must say that I am completely sold on making coconut milk in this way. It's simplicity itself even though it's a bit more expensive than making your own. Instructions on the back of the pack show how to make cream, rich milk or milk according to how much water you add. The great advantage is that you can make very small quantities at a time, and quickly at that.

DESICCATED COCONUT. This is a very successful way of making good-quality coconut milk and cream and is also inexpensive. Empty the contents of a 225 g/8 oz packet of desiccated coconut into a food processor and pour over 450 ml/¾ pint boiling water. Process for 20–30 seconds and allow to cool a little. If making several batches then empty each lot into a large bowl after processing and leave to cool. Now place a sieve over a large bowl and line with muslin cloth. Ladle some of the coconut into the muslin and fold the edges over the coconut, then twist the ends to squeeze out the maximum amount of milk. Repeat with the remaining coconut, discarding the spent coconut each time. You can use it to make a second batch but do remember that it will be of poorer quality and should only be used to extend a good-quality first squeezing. Like Ah Moi, I used to squeeze the coconut by hand but I have found that using the muslin is much more successful. Making coconut milk in this way is advantageous when a recipe calls for both coconut milk and cream. The coconut cream will float to the top of the milk as it does with cow's milk, so after ten minutes you can scoop off the cream to use in the recipe as directed. Any leftover milk or cream can be stored in the refrigerator for a day, or for longer in the freezer. Do remember to label the package, noting the quantity.

CANNED COCONUT. This is available in 400 ml/14 fl oz cans, most of which are exported from Thailand. More expensive, but very convenient.

COCONUT CREAM. Sold in 200 g/7 oz slabs which must be kept in the refrigerator. Small slices can be added at the end of cooking curries.

DRY FRY COCONUT. Used in Malay and Indonesian dishes it gives a special flavour as well as acting as a thickening agent when added to curries such as *rendang* or fish *moolie*. To make, turn desiccated coconut into a wok and stir constantly until it is golden brown and crisp. Do not use any oil in the pan. Put the coconut into a food processor till the mass starts to look glossy and the oil begins to show. Add at the very end of the cooking. Dry fry coconut is also used in the coconut *sambal* on page 63.

Coriander. My desert island herb, which is also known as Chinese parsley. Available widely in good greengrocers and supermarkets, though I like to buy a real bunch, roots and all, rather than those mean-looking few stems in a see-through package which cost almost as much. As soon as you can, plunge the stems and leaves into cold water to remove any soil, then shake well to remove excess water. Stand in a jug of water to cover the roots, and when the leaves are almost dry cover loosely with a plastic bag and secure with an elastic band low round the base of the jug. This covering keeps the leaves moist and fresh. Refresh the water daily. In this way the coriander will keep for more than a week. The leaves are used all over South-East Asia in salads and as a garnish, but the Thais have gone one step further by pounding the stems and root to give an extra dimension to their many fine curries, especially the renowned green variety. Coriander grows well in the garden or in window boxes in

sunny climes. I love its distinctive pungent smell which complements so many different foods, and I wouldn't like to be without it
in my kitchen.

Coriander seeds. Rather ordinary-looking, tiny ball-shaped seeds
which disguise their potential as one of the most highly regarded
spices. For the full impact, dry fry over a gentle heat without oil for
a few minutes, either shaking the pan or stirring the seeds until they
start giving off a spicy aroma. Grind to a fine powder and savour
the heady perfume. It's magic, and will probably discourage you
from buying ready-ground coriander ever again!

Cumin seeds. Frequently used in conjunction with coriander seeds
as a blend of spices. These two are used in a garam masala and in
many fish, chicken and meat curries. The seeds look rather like hay
seeds and should not be confused with fennel seeds, which are
larger and have an aniseed flavour. Dry fry and grind to a powder
for the best results.

Curry leaf. Available both fresh and dried. When fresh the leaves
are small and shiny and should have a potent curry smell. I buy a
small packet of leaves and store in the freezer for future use.

Curry pastes. There are many ready-made curry pastes on the
market, some of very good quality which will cut corners on
preparation, but of course you may have to try out several before
you find the one which suits you. They are available in small
sachets or in 100 g/4 oz cans, which you might prefer to buy once
you have decided that you like that particular blend of spices.
Homemade curry pastes are not difficult to make and of course you
can make up a larger quantity than required and store the remainder
in the refrigerator or freezer. Do remember to indicate on the
container how many tablespoons there are.

Dry frying spices. See coriander seeds.

Duan pandan (pandan leaf). This resembles a gladioli leaf, and is
a very popular addition to rice dishes and desserts where it imparts

a warm flavour. To obtain maximum flavour hold the leaf at one end and pull the prongs of a fork through it, then tie it in a knot and add to the recipe as directed. Available fresh from oriental stores. I usually keep any extra leaves in the freezer for future use. The juice from the pounded leaves used to be added to puddings and confectionery but green colouring is more commonly used now.

Durian. To smell one ripe durian at close quarters is an unforgettable experience, a whole stallful almost offensive. Hotels forbid the eating of durian in their rooms and airlines refuse passengers permission to carry them as handbaggage! Descriptions vary from overripe Roquefort to unsavoury drains yet the durian retains its reputation as the king of fruit with its aphrodisiac qualities. The oval-shaped fruit covered with a mass of spikes has sections of custard-textured flesh inside. Each section has a stone. Durian are so highly valued that as they ripen a huge bag is placed over the fruit and where there are many fruit you might even find a guard on duty!

Emping. These are made from the flattened nuts of the melingo tree (see page 160). These little discs have a slightly bitter flavour when cooked in hot oil, as for *krupuk*. Drain, cool and serve with a host of Indonesian dishes, especially *gado gado* for which they are an obligatory accompaniment. Sold loose and in packets from oriental stores specializing in Indonesian ingredients.

Fennel seeds. Similar to cumin seeds except that they are larger and have a distinctive aniseed flavour.

Fish sauce. Also known as *nam pla* in Thailand and *nuoc cham* in Vietnam. This thin sauce is used widely as a flavouring medium, each nationality claiming that its brand is best. Thailand exports the sauce in great quantities. It is made by packing fish into barrels with salt; the liquid which is eventually collected is the fish sauce. It is strong in flavour, fishy and salty as you would expect, and is used to accentuate and complement other flavours. It is easy to come by and keeps very well in a cool place. You will probably grow to love it so invest in a large rather than a small bottle when you can.

Garlic. Used all over the region in very substantial quantities. The whole garlic is a corm and each segment a clove. Choose the plump-looking corms and store in a cool place. Many recipes require crushed garlic and for this I use a garlic press. To avoid a messy cleaning job, simply trim away the root tip, put the unpeeled garlic clove into the press and squeeze. The skin can then be lifted out of an almost clean press.

DEEP FRIED GARLIC FLAKES can be purchased from oriental stores and I have found them invaluable in the preparation of *balachuang* (see page 100) as well as for adding to soups, salads and vegetable dishes.

Ginger. Young ginger with its pale creamy root, delicate pink nodules and green tips can be bought all over South-East Asia. It is used finely chopped in many stir fry and fish dishes, but does not impart the pungent, aromatic flavour of the older, silvery-brown-skinned type that we can buy readily in the UK. Young ginger forms the basis for the exquisitely carved fish, birds and flowers in Thai cuisine. The older type, known as a hand, must be either peeled or scraped then sliced and either chopped or pounded before using. Bruised ginger is suggested in some recipes. Peel or scrape then give a sharp blow with the end of a rolling pin or in a pestle and mortar. The piece will then release its juices during cooking and can be removed from the dish before serving. Wrap closely in newspaper and store in the vegetable box at the base of the refrigerator.

Hosein sauce. Sold in cans and jars and sometimes called barbecue sauce. It is rather sweet and is made from soy beans, garlic and spices. It is used as a dip for *popiah* (page 47) and spring rolls as well as serving as the basis for many barbecued pork and chicken dishes. Once opened it will keep in the refrigerator.

Ikan bilis. Literally translated this means 'little fish', which couldn't be more accurate. In Malaysia these are often served simply deep fried until crisp and crumbled over curry dishes, added to a spicy sambal as an accompaniment or added to a vegetable dish. They are readily available in the UK. Look for the cleaned variety, as the heads can give a rather bitter taste.

Jackfruit. A large, heavy fruit which somehow, in spite of its weight, manages to stay on the tree till it ripens, though you often see them enclosed in paper bags to ward off predatory birds. When unripe it is sold in wedges like a melon and cooked as a vegetable and in soups. It is part of the famous Indonesian *gudeg* (see page 184). Once ripe it is very juicy, and its many yellow segments are very pleasant to eat. Sometimes available in the UK from April to August. Because of its size it is usually sold in wedges. Canned jackfruit is always available.

Jaggery. This sugar is the sap from the palmyra palm (see page 78). The tree can be tapped for four to five months annually and in that time can yield fifty to eighty gallons of sap. Where palm sugar is not available then substitute soft dark brown muscovado or even molasses sugar.

Kecap. A byword in the Indonesian kitchen. See soy sauce.

Krupuk. Sold as prawn crackers these have become universally popular not only as an accompaniment to South-East Asian food but also as a cocktail snack. They are sold in 225 g/8 oz packets which should be stored in a cool dry place. To cook, drop a few at a time into hot oil where they will immediately puff up. Do not allow them to colour as this detracts from the delicate flavour. Stir with a slotted spoon the whole time that they are in the pan, then drain well on absorbent kitchen paper and serve as directed. Any leftovers can be stored in an airtight container, though in my experience this is rarely necessary as they are very moreish!

Large, Indonesian-style prawn crackers are also available from oriental stores. They measure 15 x 4 cm/6 x 1½ in before frying, so you can imagine that they will swell up enormously when fried and tend to curl as they do so. Cook only one or two at a time, and allow not more than one per person where several of the smaller variety would be necessary. See also *emping*.

Lemon grass. Fresh lemon grass stems are available in oriental stores, good-quality greengrocers' and some supermarkets. Sacks of it are flown into the UK from Thailand every week. Indeed I have a pot of lemon grass in my kitchen grown from three stems which, when I bought them, had little buds at the base. These I put into water and left on the window sill for a week. When they began to root I dipped them in some rooting powder and planted them quite successfully. Now that warmer days are on the way I will put the pot outside and soon I will have a healthy clump of lemon grass to show off to the curious. Huge clumps of this grass grow freely in warm climates. The long, slender leaves are used to make a tea infusion in some places but the tightly packed stem, which is sometimes likened to a rather flat spring onion, is used in every country of the region for its wondrous lemony aroma and flavour. Stems of lemon grass are sold in bundles of five or six pieces. To prepare, cut off the root end and discard then trim off the lower 6 cm/2½ piece. This is sliced and pounded according to the recipe. Even as you cut the stem just smell the marvellous lemon aroma. The top end of the stem can be either bruised and added to a curry for extra flavour (remove before serving if you like), or it can be bruised to make a brush with which to anoint the meats on the satay sticks with a little oil as they cook (see page 46). This is another illustration of the resourcefulness of South-East Asian cooks; nothing is discarded. Lemon grass will keep well for two to three weeks if closely wrapped in newspaper and placed in the bottom of the refrigerator. For longer-term storage where access to an oriental store is not easy I recommend the following: prepare as directed above then place the pounded fleshy part into a plastic box in the freezer, making a note of how many stems have been pounded. When firm, mark into sections of, say, two stems per portion for future use. The top part of the stems can be wrapped closely and frozen too. There is a dried powder on the market called sereh powder which can be used instead. Use one teaspoon for each stem. Some books suggest a strip of lemon rind but no substitute is a match for the real thing.

Lengkuas, laos, kha or Siamese ginger. This is a member of the ginger family which can sometimes be bought fresh from oriental stores. It is creamy coloured with rings on the skin and if you are lucky enough to buy young lengkuas it may even have pink buds. To prepare, trim off the size you require then peel and slice before pounding. The flesh is much more woody and fibrous than ginger, and has a pine-like smell. Store wrapped in newspaper in the base of the refrigerator where it will keep for two weeks or more. Dried lengkuas powder (laos) can be bought; use 1 teaspoon for each 1 cm/ ½ in used in the recipe. It's not nearly as good as the real thing.

Lime leaves. These leaves really catch the eye; they are dark green and glossy with a waist. They come from the kaffir lime tree, and are used widely in Thai cuisine. They are torn then added to an enormous range of dishes from soups to curries, contributing a unique lime/lemon flavour. For long-term storage wrap washed leaves and store in the freezer. No thawing required before use. The fruit, known as the kaffir lime or magrut, resembles a rather gnarled lemon and is about the same size. Only the rind is used, finely grated, though a dried variety is available. It must be soaked before use. If all else fails use shredded grapefruit rind.

Macadamia nut, buah keras, candlenut, kemiri. The tree can grow to a height of forty-five feet, the fruits growing in a cluster with each fruit containing a single nut. These nuts are usually bought ready shelled, which you would appreciate after trying to crack a whole nut! They are an important ingredient in Malay and Indonesian cooking, the crushed nuts being used to help thicken the sauces. Brazil nuts or almonds can be substituted but use 2–3 almonds per macadamia nut.

Magrut. See lime leaves.

Mango. Happily now available even at the local greengrocer's as supplies are airfreighted from all over the globe. Green mangoes are very popular for making pickles and chutneys but the ripe fruit is at its best when eaten fresh. Wash and dry the fruit then lay it on its flat side and work a sharp knife from the stem end to the other, keeping close to the flat stone all the time. Turn over and repeat, then mark the two fleshy parts with a knife three or four times in each direction so that the flesh looks like a chequerboard. At this stage, lift the fruit up with both hands and push gently from the skin side so that all the squares of fruit stand up ready to eat.

Moolie. Also known as daikon or lobak. A large white radish which has a crisp texture and is used either grated coarsely or sliced thinly. It is also an ideal candidate for vegetable carving.

Noodles. EGG NOODLES are referred to as *mee*. Sometimes available fresh, these rich, yellow noodles can generally be found in the refrigerator or freezer in oriental stores. If not frozen use within two days. From the freezer either allow to thaw at room temperature or plunge into boiling water briefly till soft, stirring often, then drain and use as directed. Dried egg noodles need soaking for ten minutes in water before cooking in salted, boiling water for two minutes till tender, or according to packet directions.

RICE NOODLES, or *kway teow*, can be bought fresh from some oriental stores. The wide strips, which are folded sometimes, contain flecks of dried prawn or spring onions. Thaw frozen rice noodles overnight in the refrigerator or by plunging into boiling water. Drain, then cut the still-folded noodles into narrow strips and use in stir fry. Keep covered before cooking so that they do not dry out.

Rice vermicelli, the round type of rice noodle, come both thick (*lai fan*) and thin (*beehoon* or *meehoon*). Just to add to the confusion, both types are sometimes called rice stick noodles. The thick type, which are about the thickness of spaghetti, can be deep fried in handfuls for the famous *mee krob* (see page 150) or cooked as an accompaniment to *mohinga* (see page 83). To cook, place the noodles (*lai fan*) into a pan of boiling water, allow to return to the boil then immediately draw from the heat and leave for eight minutes. Drain and serve. If required for soup or a stir fry, simply soak in boiled water for eight minutes then drain and rinse in cold water, drain again and use. The thin noodles can also be used in the same way but allow only two minutes' soaking.

BEAN-THREAD OR CELLOPHANE NOODLES are made from the mung bean and rather resemble nylon fishing line gathered up into a skein. These are soaked in boiling water for three minutes before draining and cutting into short lengths as in *sri kaya* (see page 201). Add to soups or use in spring rolls.

Nutmeg and mace. The fruit is like a smooth chestnut and splits open when ripe. Mace is the web-like casing to the nutmeg and can be bought either dried or ground. Having removed the mace from the nut this is then cracked open to reveal the nutmeg which can be bought whole or ground. In Malaysia the outer fleshy case of the nutmeg is crystallized or pickled and sold in little packets as a snack.

Onions. DEEP FRIED ONIONS for use as a garnish can be bought ready made in markets in Indonesia. You might like to deep fry the dried onion flakes which we can buy here which are really meant to be added to soups and similar. They are quick and easy and any leftovers can be stored in an airtight jar. Use an 80 g/2.8 oz packet of quick-dried, sliced onions fried in several batches in 200 ml/7 fl oz groundnut oil. This gives 100 g/4 oz fried onion flakes. For the homemade version see the recipe for Burmese vegetables on page 96.

SHALLOTS. Used everywhere, but if they are not available remember that 6–8 shallot segments are the equivalent of one medium red onion (which will give a much deeper colour to your finished dish), or a brown-skinned, Spanish-type onion if red are not available.

SPRING ONIONS are a vital ingredient in the cooking of each country not only for flavour but for garnishes, from simple shredded spring onion which is cut at a long diagonal angle, producing real shreds, to spring onion curls (A). Hold in the centre and use a sharp knife to cut the stem into strips from the centre to the end in each

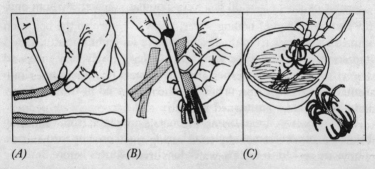

(A)   *(B)*   *(C)*

direction (B), then place in cold water where the ends will curl attractively (C).

Another interpretation on the theme is to thread a slice of chilli on to the finger-length piece of stem in the middle and repeat the cutting as above. A spring onion tassel is made using the white root part of a not-too-large spring onion which has a little green top to it. Again it should be finger length and the root discarded, of course. Hold at the base and using a sharp knife cut the top two-thirds through and up to the top several times then place again in cold water to curl. Makes a very attractive garnish for the centre of a dish.

Oyster sauce. Made from an extract of oysters, soy sauce, salt and starches. It gives a characteristic flavour to meat dishes and vegetables in particular. It keeps well but you may need to add a little boiling water if it thickens up as you get near to the end of the bottle.

Peanuts, groundnuts or kacang tanah. Aptly named, as they have to be dug from the ground at harvest time. In many countries this is done by hand. The nuts are highly nutritious with a thirty per cent protein content and a forty to fifty per cent oil content. They are used widely all over the region in *sambals* and sauces (to accompany *satays* and *gado gado* for instance) and for garnishing. If salted peanuts are used as a substitute, do remember to taste before adding extra salt. Crunchy peanut butter is a realistic alternative to crushed and pounded peanuts in the sauces in this book.

Peanut or groundnut oil is a very popular cooking medium and widely available.

Peppercorns. These grow on a vine which is trained up a tripod-shaped structure. The berries grow in clusters like tiny grapes and are harvested when ripe. They are then dried in the sun on large mats, where they are turned regularly and become black peppercorns. For white peppercorns the berries are soaked in running water for a week to rot the hard casing then rubbed by hand to remove this completely. They are then dried in the sun.

Pork crackling. Also known as *chicaron*, this is made from pork rind which has been deep fried, forming puffy, crisp crackers. It is sold in packs in oriental stores and is served as the crunchy element alongside curries or sliced in salads. Used in Thai and Vietnamese dishes.

Prawn and shrimp. The dried variety are sun dried and therefore have a long shelf life. They are usually sold in packets and need to be soaked in water and drained before using either whole or chopped in soups or with vegetables.

Powdered prawns can be bought in packets but I prefer to put dried prawns in the food processor for a few minutes, stopping from time to time so as not to overheat the motor. Powdered prawns are used a great deal in Burmese cooking.

Rice. Staple food for two-thirds of the world's population. Thai long grain rice is widely available and has a high reputation for quality and fragrance as it cooks. I prefer to cook it without salt. Many homes where rice is consumed in large quantities now have a rice cooker. If you do not have one, use the following method:

PLAIN BOILED RICE. Wash 225 g/8 oz rice thoroughly in several changes of water till the water looks clear. Place in a pan with 500 ml/18 fl oz water and bring to the boil. Reduce heat, stir, cover pan with a well-fitting lid and cook gently for twelve to fifteen minutes. Remove lid and stir with a chopstick or roasting fork so you do not break up the grains. Use at once or clamp on lid and enclose pan in a sleeping bag or blanket. In this way the rice will keep warm for at least 1 ½–2 hours.

Microwave-cooked rice is very successful. Wash as above but cook the rice in 450 ml/15 fl oz boiling water in a large bowl three-quarters covered with clingfilm for fourteen minutes in total i.e. nine minutes on full power and five minutes resting in the microwave. Take out and stir as above.

For easy-cook rice follow the packet directions.

GLUTINOUS RICE. Available in black and white, this is very starchy, hence its common name, 'sticky rice'. It can be gathered up into a ball with the fingers then dipped into curries etc., which was the usual way of eating before spoons came on to the scene. In

Northern Thailand, Cambodia and Burma glutinous rice is often served as the staple food, but all over the region the white variety is cooked with coconut milk as a dessert.

To cook 225 g/8 oz glutinous rice first soak overnight in water to cover, then drain and rinse. Turn into a muslin-lined colander or steamer and place over gently bubbling water for about twenty-five minutes then taste to check whether the rice is cooked. It should be just tender with a little resistance. The cooking time relates directly to the soaking period. The longer the soaking the shorter the cooking as a general rule.

Rice wine. If not available, substitute dry sherry.

Rice wine vinegar. A mild vinegar which I like to use in oriental cooking, but you could use white wine or cider vinegar if you prefer.

Sambal ulek. See chillies.

Satay skewers. Available in packets of fifty from oriental stores. Soak well before threading on the meat so that they do not char too easily. Scald with boiling water after use and dry well before storing for a future occasion.

Sesame seeds. After India and China, Burma is the third largest producer of sesame seeds. The whole plant is cut at harvest time and stacked upright till the seed pods begin to burst open, releasing all those tiny seeds which we can now buy easily in any health food store. The seeds are used a great deal in Burmese cooking either dry fried or toasted to extract their delicious nutty flavour.

Two other products come from the seeds. TAHINI, which is a crushed sesame paste and SESAME OIL. The seeds are rich in oil (forty-five to fifty per cent). The oil is not used for frying as it has a low burning temperature but it is often used to dress vegetables at the last minute, see Anita Wong's Vegi (page 61)

Soy sauce. An indispensable ingredient in the cooking of South-East Asia. Basically each country uses a thin and a thick soy sauce, with the Indonesian kitchen requiring an extra variety called *kecap manis*. The sauce is made from fermented soy beans, wheatgrain, salt and water. Light or thin soy sauce or *kecap asin* (Indonesian) is the most widely used.

Thick or black soy sauce is, as the name suggests, much darker in colour and treacle-like in consistency, so add with care. It also has a sugar content which is absent in the thin sauce. Just to add to the variety there is a *kecap sedang* of medium consistency with a sugar and salt content used in some Indonesian recipes.

Kecap manis is imported to the UK from Holland and is available from oriental stores in some areas. If there is a problem in obtaining this you can substitute a homemade version by boiling together eight tablespoons of thick soy sauce with two tablespoons black treacle and one tablespoon dark brown sugar. Cool and use as directed, storing any extra in a screwtop jar.

Straw mushrooms. Sold in cans, these are an attractive addition to many vegetable, fish and stir fry recipes. They are grown in straw, as the name suggests. If you cannot track them down, button mushrooms can be used instead.

Tamarind (asam jawa). Used to add tartness to recipes all over the region just as we might use vinegar or lemon juice. The tamarind tree is a magnificent specimen which produces large pods about the size of a broad bean pod. I have seen them sold loose in the UK but the more usual way is to buy the purée from the pod in a 225 g/8 oz block which looks rather like a block of dates. It keeps for a long time if closely wrapped in a cool place. In the recipes I have usually suggested, say, one teaspoon tamarind pulp mixed with a few tablespoons of warm water. This is then left to stand for ten minutes, mixed by hand to release the purée from the seeds, then the whole lot is strained through a sieve, the pulp and seeds discarded and the resulting juice used in the recipe. A readymade jar of juice is now available from some oriental stores which makes life easier.

Dried tamarind, or *asam keping*, looks rather like dried apple slices. Again it needs to be soaked but as it's dry, allow thirty minutes to extract the maximum flavour, then strain and use the juice. Use two slices in water just to cover.

Tempe. See bean curd.

Turmeric. Usually bought ground in sachets or jars this spice gives more colour than taste to curries and rice dishes. Very popular in Burmese and Indonesian dishes, it is a member of the ginger family but the tuber is a lot smaller. It can be scraped or peeled and pounded but beware, the juices can stain clothes and hands. Enjoy the warm aroma given off as you cut it.

Water chestnuts. Fresh water chestnuts must be kept covered with water once peeled, to prevent discoloration. Canned water chestnuts are easy to find and, like the fresh variety, are often added to dishes for their crisp, crunchy texture. Any leftovers can be added to a fruit salad.

White jelly fungus. A crinkly, almost coral-like fungus which when soaked in water or syrup swells up considerably yet retains a strange, crunchy texture. On the pack it says, 'This is a Chinese traditional food for nutrition. It is helpful for the strengthening of human body and spirit and especially for the maintaining of the youth and beauty.' With these promises guests never turn it down! I like to soak it in a cooled sugar syrup and then add it to fruit salad. It makes an unusual addition to clear soups, too.

Winged bean, goa, asparagus bean or kecipir. A very unusual-looking, light-green bean with a kind of frill down four sides. This attractive feature is shown to advantage when sliced diagonally before cooking.

Wrappers. SPRING ROLL WRAPPERS come in two shapes, square and round, and in different sizes. They are usually to be found in the freezer section of your oriental store. Allow to thaw and when ready for use open the pack and very carefully tease up one corner from the pile and peel away. Repeat this till all the wrappers have been placed in a separate pile. Cover with a slightly damp cloth to prevent drying out which can create a problem when rolling up.

WONTON WRAPPERS. Use the same procedure as above but when filling, arrange eight or ten ready to fill to speed up the process.

RICE PAPER WRAPPERS. These large, round wrappers come in dried form in packets. To use for spring rolls it is necessary to place on a cloth and brush with water to make them damp and easy to roll.

Suppliers

MATAHARI IMPEX
11–12 Hogarth Place, London SW 5. Tel: 01–370–1041

328 Balham High Road, London SW17. Tel: 01–767–3107

102 Westbourne Grove, London W2. Tel: 01–221–7468

Michael Wong is the owner of these shops, which stock food from Malaysia, Singapore, Indonesia, Burma, Thailand, the Philippines, and China. A mail order business is operated from the Hogarth Place Branch. Send an s.a.e. for the latest catalogue.

MONSOON
5 Hogarth Place, London SW5. Tel: 01–373–8305

Philip Tran and his family sell food from all over the Orient, including Vietnam. They also have a fresh fish counter.

NICHOLSON
4b Devonshire Road, Chiswick, London W4. Tel: 01–994–0809

A wet fish shop in the old tradition, which has customers far and wide and supplies my every order with the finest quality fish, large and small.

Index